TWAYNE'S WORLD AUTHORS SERIES
A Survey of the World's Literature

Sylvia E. Bowman, Indiana University
GENERAL EDITOR

DENMARK

Leif Sjöberg
State University of New York at Stony Brook
EDITOR

Martin A. Hansen

TWAS 419

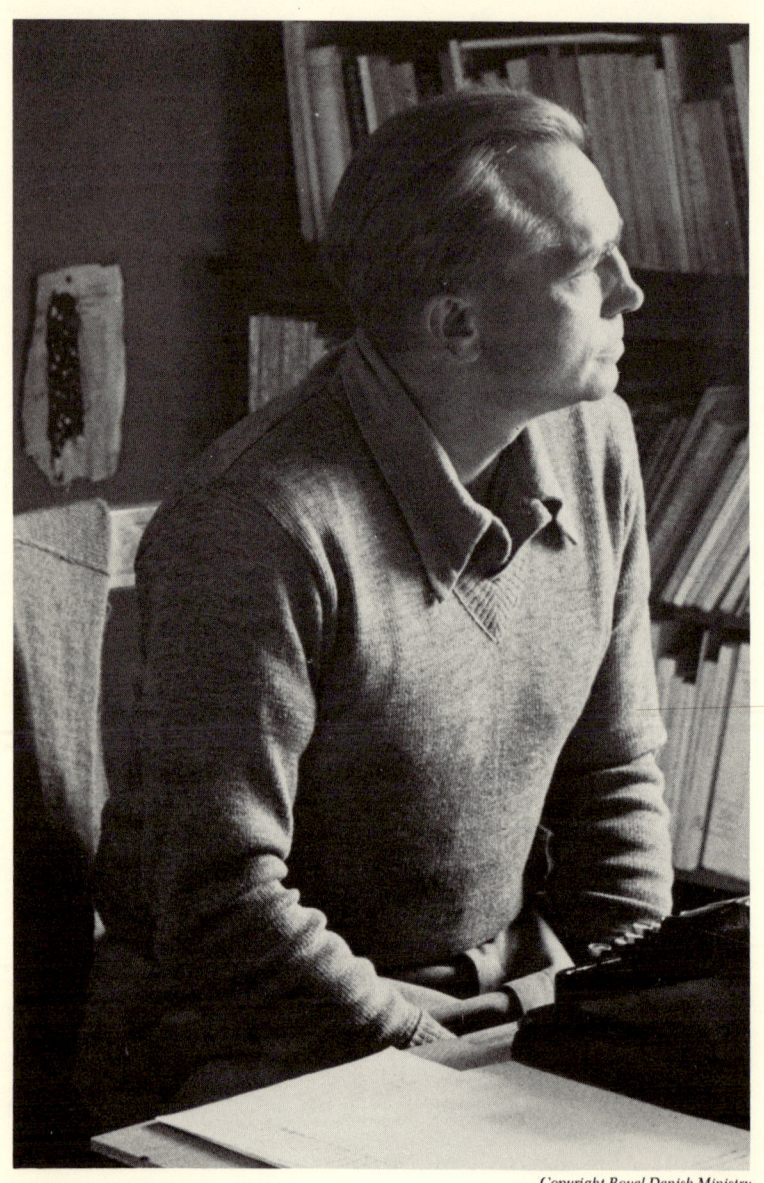

Copyright Royal Danish Ministry for Foreign Affairs

Martin A. Hansen

MARTIN A. HANSEN

By FAITH and NIELS INGWERSEN
University of Wisconsin — Madison

TWAYNE PUBLISHERS
A DIVISION OF G. K. HALL & CO., BOSTON

Copyright   1976 by G. K. Hall & Co.
All Rights Reserved
First Printing

Library of Congress Cataloging in Publication Data

Ingwersen, Faith.
  Martin A. Hansen.

  (Twayne's world authors series ; TWAS 419 : Denmark)
  Bibliography: p. 187 - 91.
  Includes index.
  1. Hansen, Martin Alfred, 1909 - 1955 — Criticism and interpretation.   I. Ingwersen, Niels, joint author.
PT8175.H33Z7   839.8'1'372   [B]   76-21278
ISBN 0-8057-6259-0

MANUFACTURED IN THE UNITED STATES OF AMERICA

Contents

About the Authors
Preface
Chronology

1. Background   11
2. *Now He Gives Up* and *The Colony*   37
3. *Jonatan's Journey*   45
4. *Lucky Kristoffer*   59
5. *The Thornbush*   73
6. *The Partridge*   99
7. *The Liar*   111
8. *Apples of Paradise*, *The Conch*, and *Aftermath*   130
9. Essays and *Leviathan*   140
10. *Serpent and Bull*   154
11. Chronicles of Travels   162
12. Conclusion   169
    Notes and References   173
    Selected Bibliography   187
    Index   193

About the Authors

Niels Ingwersen was born in Horsens, Denmark. He studied at the Universities of Stockholm, Oslo, Chicago, and Copenhagen where he received his *cand. mag.* degree in 1963. His thesis was a study of the Norwegian novelist Sigurd Hoel's works. He is presently professor of Scandinavian Studies at the University of Wisconsin, Madison, where he has taught since 1965. He has published a number of articles on nineteenth- and twentieth-century Danish literature and on literary criticism.

Faith Ingwersen is from Sheridan, Wyoming. She attended the University of Wyoming (from which she received a B.A. and M.A.), the Universities of Oslo, Copenhagen, and Chicago, from which she received a Ph.D. in Comparative Literature in 1974. Her dissertation was a comparative study of Knut Hamsun's *Mysteries* and Hansen's *The Liar*. She has translated short stories from Danish and Norwegian and is presently a guest lecturer on Scandinavian literature for the University of Wisconsin-Extension.

Preface

The primary intention of this book is to give English-speaking readers a comprehensive, but brief, introduction to the writings of Martin A. Hansen. The complexity of Hansen's works and the abundance of criticism focused on them make it difficult to do both; therefore, a rather lengthy first chapter, on the coherence and ambiguity inherent in Hansen's art, was furnished in order that the individual works could be treated in a fairly limited space. Although, in many cases, this study owes a debt to the views of other critics and, in other instances, takes issue with their views, direct debate is avoided, for it would go beyond the scope of this book. The authors of the present volume hope of course that some new insights into Hansen's authorship will be provided by their study.

The authors would like to thank Ole Wivel, the literary executor of Hansen's estate, for permission to quote from Hansen's works, as well as from Wivel's own monograph on Hansen. The authors' gratitude is also extended to the patient editors of Twayne Publishers and to those people who in various ways have contributed to the completion of this study, particularly to Carol and Dean Schroeder who carefully read the manuscript and suggested many valuable stylistic revisions.

FAITH and NIELS INGWERSEN

Chronology

1909	Jens Alfred Martin Hansen born August 20 in the region of Stevns.
1918	Moves to a small farm bought by his family in the same area. Attends school until age fourteen, then works on nearby farms.
1926 - 1930	Attends Haslev Teachers' College.
1931 - 1945	Employed at Blaagaard Teachers' College training school.
1935	Marries Vera Louise Marie Jensen. Serves five months in the Danish military. Publishes first novel, *Now He Gives Up*.
1937	Publishes *The Colony*.
1940	April 9, German troops occupy Denmark.
1941	*Jonatan's Journey*.
1944	Writes articles — advocating action against the Nazis and their Danish collaborators — for the underground magazine *People and Freedom*. Lives in hiding from September.
1945	*Lucky Kristoffer*. May 5, the German occupation of Denmark ends.
1946	*The Thornbush*.
1947	*The Partridge*, a collection of short stories. Thorkild Björnvig publishes the first book-length study on Hansen.
1948	*Thoughts in a Chimney*, a collection of essays.
1950	Publishes *The Liar*, a novel commissioned for, and read over, the Danish Radio. Publishes *Leviathan*, a cultural essay. Co-edits, with Ole Wivel, the journal *Heretica* until 1952.
1952	*Serpent and Bull*, a cultural history. Tours Iceland with Sven Havsteen-Mikkelsen, his friend and illustrator.
1953	Publishes *Kringen* and *Danish Weather*, impressions from travels in Norway and Denmark; and *Apples of Paradise*, a collection of earlier short stories.
1954	*Travel on Iceland*.
1955	June 27, death of Hansen.

CHAPTER 1

Background

I *Introduction*

MARTIN A. Hansen's writings show that he perceived of the human being as a traveler. That had been his own experience: he had left an age-old agrarian culture and arrived in the complex and confusing world of twentieth-century issues. Although the way of life he had put behind him was dying, he came to feel that it harbored a harmony unknown to the contemporary world; thus, the cultural tradition of his childhood milieu became his supreme frame of reference. It would hardly be unfair to suggest that he almost became obsessed with his own heritage and gave it mythical stature, but that fact by no means made of him a regional writer or a bucolic romanticist. Through his works, Hansen definitely intended to bring the existential problems of his age to the fore, and if he often looked backward, it was with the purpose of recapturing the values or the sense of direction that modern man had lost.

These general comments should suggest that Hansen never claimed residence in that notorious ivory tower in which poets supposedly dream themselves away from this world. He was intricately caught up in, and agonizingly inspired by, the issues of his day; consequently, an introduction to his life and his times seems warranted. Part two of this chapter serves this purpose and gives the reader an impression of the general development of the authorship.

In spite of the variances in, and complexities of, Hansen's works, they seem to reflect striking similarities and a unity of vision that make it tempting to speak of a universe unique to his writings. Part three of this chapter views his works as a whole and attempts to delineate the main features of Hansen's fictional universe: the major themes, overriding values, and inner tension that are to be found there.

The present analysis relies heavily upon the many studies on Hansen, particularly upon those by his personal friends Thorkild Björnvig and

Ole Wivel. Anyone who seeks more information about Hansen, especially about his development as a man and writer, must consult these two critics, who have been more helpful to the writing of this book than its footnotes indicate. It was in fact Björnvig who, with his doctoral dissertation *Kains Alter* (1964), caused the critics to pay serious attention to Hansen.[1] This immensely thorough and inspiring study called forth numerous opponents, one of whom was Ole Wivel, who later wrote an impressive and sensitive two-volume biography of Hansen.[2] These two critics disagree about a good deal, and thus they have created a dialectical view of Hansen's writings that cannot help influencing those who follow them. Anyone who concerns himself with Hansen must take a position on Björnvig's and Wivel's very authoritative works.

During the decades since Hansen's death, his works have been more widely read and debated than any of his Danish contemporaries'. Aage Henriksen and Torben Kragh Grodal have recently suggested that Hansen himself seems to have become a myth to the reading public.[3] Grodal points out that Hansen's early death made him the object of a cult that mourned the loss of an artist in the midst of his creativity, and Henriksen comments that the abundance of critical attention paid to Hansen's works and the exquisite editions made of them have fortified this myth.[4] One factor contributing to the mythical stature that Hansen has achieved may also be his projected image of himself as a man who devoted his life to the cultural mission of combatting the spiritual crisis of his age. To many readers, Hansen seems to be the epitome of the man of healthy mind who, with his deep insight into his crisis-ridden age and with his strong roots in the harmonious past, could not only depict both worlds brilliantly but also offer hope for the future. As a writer with a cultural mission and an artist whose career was prematurely cut short, Hansen's image has those appealing traits from which myths are created.

The problem with such an image is that it produces a narrow understanding of the texts, which therefore may eventually seem dated. Although Aage Henriksen belongs among those critics who voice this opinion, he also offers an alternative view, corrective of the myth of Hansen's authorship.[5] He finds not only that both Björnvig and Wivel supported the myth with their monumental studies of Hansen and his thinking, but also that the two critics questioned the myth of that harmonious man by probing into the severe personal crises he suffered. Björnvig and Wivel may disagree vehemently as to the nature of these crises, but they concur in the fact that Hansen's art became a haunting problem to him. Thus, although the myth of Hansen as a sage may lose — or have lost — its attraction and validity, his works can be perused as studies in the anguish of inner conflict and, as such, be of significance for the present day reader.

II *The Man and His Times*

Martin A. Hansen was born August 20, 1909, in Ströby Parish on Stevns, a fertile peninsula in the southeastern part of the island of Sealand. His parents were of old peasant stock native to the region, and in their youth they had had to work hard to keep the ever threatening specter of poverty at bay. In 1918 they took over a modest place of their own, which they managed to cling to even during the difficult years after World War I. This little farm and the surrounding land, with its dusty roads, small villages, meadows, and woods, are the scarcely disguised setting of numerous stories from Hansen's hand.

Not only the landscape but also the way of life emerges from these stories. The economic hardships of the age and of his own family figure prominently, and although, as a child, he was keenly aware of his parents' fear of what the next day might bring, he grew up in a world that seemed relatively secure, and even tantalizing. It was undoubtedly those qualities, for which he gave credit to his family and their culture, that later caused the Stevns of his childhood to assume a mythical stature in his thinking.

The texts that recall life in Stevns may convey a mood of harmony, but they do not make the childhood milieu contrivedly or simplistically idyllic. In fact, Hansen is often painstakingly realistic in his portrayal of the past, but it is equally obvious to the reader both that Hansen is conjuring up childhood's lost paradise and that he now views that world in a mythical perspective. It is this dual quality of the texts, the fusion of the very real with the mythical, that gives them their special, easily recognizable tone.

At times these texts strike harsher notes that shatter their basic harmony. In childhood Hansen sometimes seemed to be possessed by wild impulses, through which he not only was spurred to do what was forbidden but also was made to feel a sudden indifference to his life and his world. According to Hansen's biographer, Ole Wivel, those moments are important to recognize, for they became indicative to Hansen of a fundamental, inner conflict. Wivel explains that Hansen saw the origin of that tension in the antithetical character of his parental heritage, an opposition of forces that, in turn, could be geographically understood.[6]

His father, who — in contrast to his mother — often figures in Hansen's stories, came from the agricultural region near the sea, whereas his mother's family had its home in the wooded areas farther inland.

Whether or not one can accept this theory of the antagonistic traits in Hansen's heritage hardly matters, for he himself believed in them, and they became a part of his myth of Stevns. It should be noted, however, that Hansen found evidence in his area's tradition for the theory. In "Pilgrimage" ("Valfart")[7] he describes a certain day of the year on which the boys from his father's and his mother's home territories would gather by a creek that marked the regional border and there, as if in observance of a ritual, would fight out the age-old conflict between the two inimical mentalities.

To Hansen, his father stood for a strong sense of both individual and social responsibility and of allegiance to the land, whereas the inheritance bequeathed him from his mother's side of the family tended toward the demonic, pensive, and visionary — those qualities that are associated with the mind of the poet. Hansen's writings reflect a tension between those ethical instincts that serve culture and those individualistic and aesthetic impulses that may counteract social responsibility.

When Hansen had been confirmed at the age of fourteen, he was sent out, in keeping with the customs of his milieu, to live and work on nearby farms. The stories that depict the lives of young farmhands render both the sheer delight that such youths may feel in mastering the strenuous work in the fields and the confusion that they may experience in awakening to the sexual facts of life. Although a youth can easily control plow and horse, his secret, persistent thoughts of fair female bodies tempt him into a realm that is beyond his control. In "Midsummer Wreath"[8] ("Midsommerkrans") Hansen recalls that, when nervously attending the beery and noisy Saturday dances at the inns, he and his young friends were both shy and overwhelmed. They would stalk out into the night, as if in contempt of such raw pleasures; but as the boys hid in the darkness of summer, everything around them seemed to whisper with enticing voices. It was as if everything in nature had transformed itself into something provocatively sensual.

When Hansen was seventeen years old, he left his native region to enroll in Haslev Teachers' College. Although the distance to Stevns was perhaps infinitesimal and Hansen was to spend many summers at home helping in the fields, he had become in fact a mere vacationer who no longer belonged to the old, waning culture. He himself felt estranged from much in the old culture and reacted against its Christian heritage and its conservatism. His meeting with the intellectual milieu of the late 1920s radicalized him and led him to admire the robust, materialistic outlook in Johannes V. Jensen's Darwinistic writings.[9] It was also during those years at college that Hansen, ever an avid reader, became acquainted with the writings of Sören Kierkegaard, whose thoughts were to exert a lifelong influence on him.

In 1930 Hansen graduated. Although the effects of the Depression were being fully felt, he found employment, just one year later, in a school connected with a teachers' college in the heart of a poor district of Copenhagen. His pedagogic talent quickly asserted itself, and he held that position until 1945, when he could finally afford to devote himself completely to his artistic career. Several articles, gathered in the volume *Martin A. Hansen and the School (Martin A. Hansen og Skolen* [1968]), reveal that he was a committed and critical teacher, who was deeply concerned with making the hours spent in the classroom consist of more than pointless memorizing.[10]

It was during those first years in Copenhagen that Hansen, who had started to write in a modest way during his years at the teachers' college, began to take his authorship seriously and embarked on that strenuous program of writing which was to last the rest of his life.[11] In this painful endeavor, in which he was often forced to function to the point of exhaustion, he was sympathetically supported by his wife, Vera. They had known each other since 1931 and had married in 1935.

Hansen thus attempted to combine a demanding artistic vocation with family life and a steady job. For a man with Hansen's ingrained sense of responsibility, the situation was tantamount to a dilemma, as it would be for any artist who could not accept the legitimacy of the creative process's overshadowing other human duties. Hansen's job suffered, and he quite clearly came to feel that his compulsion to write also resulted in a neglect of his family. Ole Wivel, who, with a sensitive mixture of discretion and openness, deals with this aspect of Hansen's life, makes it clear that Hansen, at times, regarded his vocation with guilt-ridden suspicion.[12] This suspicion was to become one of the major themes in his works.

In 1935 he made a competent, though hardly striking, debut with the collective novel *Now He Gives Up (Nu Opgiver Han)*, which was followed two years later by its sequel, *The Colony (Kolonien)*. With these two "studies" of the farming milieu during the Depression of the 1930s, Hansen joined a literary tradition with which he should have felt quite at home; the tradition was that of Social Realism, which, during this decade, flourished in Denmark as it did elsewhere. He clearly felt a kinship with such writers as Hans Kirk, Knuth Becker, Jörgen Nielsen, and Erling Kristensen, who realistically — and often indignantly — wrote of the bleak lives of ordinary people in the grip of economic hardship. Hansen wrote of what he knew from experience: the stifling and uncertain atmosphere of the small farming communities, as their old way of life was slowly being eroded by the flagging economy and modern technology. Although Hansen seemed to advocate a radical solution to the agricultural crisis, that of communal farming based on Marxist principles, these two novels show that the author's main interest lay in the psychology of the individual.

Through a stinging portrayal of a semi-Fascist farmers' movement, both novels testify to Hansen's apprehension with regard to political developments in Europe. Watching the rise of Hitler with anxiety, Hansen anticipated that he might be called upon to defend his country against barbaric invaders.[13]

This growing feeling of disquiet coincided with Hansen's disillusionment with political ideologies and the kind of literary criticism that demands a strict social message in any and all works of literature. After his years as a radical and a realist, he had found Realism to be too dominating and mechanistic, and his subsequent reading, which included such authors as Hamsun, Dostoyevsky, and Kivi, suggests that he was searching for a new outlook and a new way of writing that would go beyond the polar opposition of radicalism-conservatism.[14] The result of this reorientation was *Jonatan's Journey* (*Jonatans Rejse* [1941]), on which he had first started working in 1937.

Jonatan's Journey is clearly a turning point in the authorship. The grey, sober realism of the first two books is replaced by a whimsical, imaginative, and humorous narrative style, for which Hansen happily gives credit to Miguel Cervantes and other such old storytellers. Following their example, Hansen has his hero travel through many milieus and endure all kinds of fantastic experiences. Hansen does not, however, give up satirically prodding his contemporaries; political ideologies, severe rationalism, as well as a romantic adulation of the past are all made subjects of ridicule. The form of the book is that of a quest, and through its exciting train of events it asks many perturbing, existential questions. Jonatan's wandering takes him from the time-honored farming culture into the complex modern world with its moral ambiguity. Good and evil become indistinguishable, and the good man, out of the simplicity of his motives, may well end by serving evil. This theme was to last throughout Martin A. Hansen's authorship and to be formulated more solemnly than in this exuberantly told story; but in

Jonatan's Journey the reader can still vest hope in the hero who, in spite of his confusion and many errors, stubbornly persists in fighting evil.

That the power of evil was an issue which had to be dealt with was made explicit on April 9, 1940. On that day the German forces invaded and occupied Denmark. For Hansen this was an ignominious moment; he felt ashamed that he was not one of those who had vainly fought against the Nazi juggernaut, and he was bitterly disappointed in his country for having resisted so briefly. In the following years he was to deplore the docile mood with which the Danes accepted the Occupation and the way in which Danish politicians collaborated with the enemy; but at the same time, he had to question himself accusingly: how should he, as a writer, deal with the situation?

His calling had become both more demanding and more problematic to him. This challenge may account for the burst of inspiration he experienced, which resulted not only in a number of salient articles but also in a splendid novel, *Lucky Kristoffer (Lykkelige Kristoffer* [1945]). The articles were largely of a historical nature, but as always, when Hansen wrote of the past, he intended to make it relevant to the present. Hansen revalued the so-called Dark Ages in order to show that there exist telling parallels between the Middle Ages and the contemporary situation. In "The Dark Ages" ("Den Mörke Middelalder")[15] he implicitly equates the spirit of the imperialistic Vikings with that of the Nazis, and he points out that the often maligned Catholic Church, in replacing the Viking Spirit, brought about a much needed change, for the church instituted a democratic society. That society was based upon a sense of justice, which gave all its members the feeling that their lives were secure and meaningful. This essay, which foreshadows the author's grand cultural theory in *Serpent and Bull (Orm og Tyr* [1952]), casts an excellent light on what can be called Hansen's individualism. In an interview given in 1944, he explained the new direction in his thinking and authorship that *Jonatan's Journey* had signaled, by stating that, when "one has lost his belief in both the old and the radical ideologies, he realizes — something one might have known beforehand — that he must turn to that which is primary and essential, to man and his personality, . . ."[16] This realization by no means indicated that Hansen turned his back on society's plight, for he definitely considered the individual to be an integral part of society, and if the individual was to come to terms with his own existential problems, he could do so by recognizing that he was a part of a social totality. In fact, Hansen's self-confessed individualism seemed to strengthen his sense of the single individual's responsibility toward others.

The war years formed Hansen's understanding of his age's existential problem. The old systems, whether they were of a philosophical or political nature, could no longer map man's existence, for they confused the issue of good and evil and thus left man in a meaningless moral limbo. The Occupation amply demonstrated this point, and in *Lucky Kristoffer* Hansen indirectly charted this modern confusion through the depiction of a journey during the turbulent, strife-ridden years of the Lutheran Reformation in the early sixteenth century. The parallel between the past and the present becomes quite clear, for in *Lucky Kristoffer* evil is ever present, whether it is in the outward forms of brutal war, exploitation, and manipulation, or the inward forms of a hunger for political power and a coldness of heart. The cause for this confusion, the moral ambiguity that is one of the distinguishing features of the modern mind, Hansen attributes to the secularization of the Renaissance. The spiritual harmony of the Catholic Middle Ages was shattered by the rise of science, which made moral choices seem absurd.

Lucky Kristoffer was Hansen's first solid success, and although it is less satirical or fanciful than *Jonatan's Journey*, it shares many features with the earlier work. Both depict a wandering into the modern world, and both suggest a distinction between a past that was relatively simple because its values were clear-cut and the modern age that has grown complex because of a crisis of values. This may be indicative of Hansen's idealization of the past, but it should be noted that he did not close his eyes to the misery and poverty of the past and that he lashed out at those reactionaries who turned the past into a false, saccharine dream. Still, he mythified the past, for in it he found spiritual qualities that no material or scientific gains could ever outweigh.[17] He discovered there a sense of personal and societal responsibility that governed and protected the individual and granted him a meaningful life in a just society. Hansen, who in this myth discovered his thinking and authorship's sustaining values, was to turn this mythical world into a reserve for qualities relevant to the individual who is lost in the modern world's confusion.

At times during the Occupation, especially after the Danes had risen against the escalating oppression, it seemed to Hansen that his people were again reasserting the moral values of the past. The nagging doubts and the shame of these years were as if swept away, and the issues of the day seemed clear-cut. In his well-known article "July '44" ("Juli 44"),[18] which conveys a quietly jubilant mood, he describes a general strike called to protest the forces of Occupation and the fortifying effect of that strike upon the inhabitants of Copenhagen. He tells of various incidents from those rumor-ridden and turbulent days; and although his eyewitness report is an interesting historical document, the actual events are overshadowed by the author's barely restrained euphoria. He saw the Danish people's ancient instinct for justice finally reawaken and assert itself through a unified and courageous resistance against which the Nazi rulers, in all their power, could do little. Whether Hansen's impressions from those days are reality or myth can be debated, but not his feeling that, in spite of the terror in the streets, life once again was blessed with direction and purpose.

Shortly before the strike, Hansen had been urged by some members of the resistance movement to write for their underground publications. As could be expected, Hansen agreed, and he wrote a large number of articles for the illegal magazine *People and Freedom (Folk og Frihed)*,[19] in which he reproached those who despised Nazi repression but hesitated to be involved in active resistance. As a consequence of those articles, in September 1944, Hansen had to go into hiding.

One essay, in particular, was to assume fateful significance in Hansen's later life. In a fictional dialogue between Socrates and one of his disciples, Hansen argued the necessity of slaying informers who betrayed other Danes to the occupation forces.[20] Shortly after May 5, 1945, the date of liberation, Hansen was given undeniable proof of the might of the written word: he was told that young men who were persuaded by his article had joined the resistance movement and that two of them were later killed. Ole Wivel points out that this knowledge lay like a dark shadow over Hansen for the remainder of his life. In Hansen's works this shadow is made manifest by his brooding and unremitting preoccupation with death, and if in his earlier writings, he can be said to have engaged in a search for a meaning in life, that search was now expanded into a quest for a meaning in death.

For a man with Hansen's deep-seated sense of ethics, it was extremely difficult to advocate the killing of other human beings, but he was convinced that it had to be done and that, when freedom had been regained, the nation would legally assume full responsibility for the slayings and exonerate those people who had been forced to suspend culture's ethical laws.[21] No such public exoneration took place, and although, in the revealingly subdued and somber postscripts to "July '44," Hansen reaffirmed his belief in the necessity of those acts, he felt deeply hurt; it was as if he had been outlawed from his country's system of justice.

The feeling of loneliness and abandonment was one that Hansen shared with many people who had participated in the struggle against the Nazis. A return to depressing normalcy, with its political bickering, its rhetoric, and its depreciation of the achievement of the resistance movement, turned to ashes the hopes of those who had expected a national rejuvenation. It was a period of bitterness, but in spite of Hansen's own disillusionment he fervently argued, in a number of articles, that the spiritual resistance against limiting ideologies and crippling skepticism had to continue in each individual's life, no matter how bleak the situation seemed.

In spite of his persistent call for spiritual resistance, Hansen undoubtedly went through a severe crisis during this period of his life. The question of whether the many sacrifices during the Occupation had been worthwhile inevitably came to plague him, and he began to look at the artist as a manipulator who isolates himself from those people for whom he bears responsibility and who engages in a destructive spiritual seduction of others through the demonic power of his language. The nature and intensity of this crisis were brought out in the brief draft for "Cain's Altar" ("Kains Alter"), written in December 1945 and January 1946.[22] In this outline for a proposed trilogy Hansen perceives the artist to be a sinful person, a Cain, who sacrifices others for the sake of his art. One passage, which both Björnvig and Wivel quote, is illuminating in its harsh, rancorous diction:

What most honest, useful caretakers of poetry do not know is this: the greedy cripple, the poet, is a sinner against life; he creates in sin, and sin inspires his talent. The spirit who is close to God does not create poetry, and what the angels sing has not been composed by them, but by a filthy, lousy shepherd. And in the hymnist you see the same thing: a heathenish, thirsting field calling for sacred rain. This crippled sorcerer is a Cain among his brothers; he is homicidal.[23]

In this work Hansen intended to utilize his own family's history and his own memories of the past; thus, the project signified a "return" to Stevns, but the return of a ravager who would not merely utilize but exploit and exhaust all that he knew best. It would be a work of destructive force, a work with a nocturnal vision of the human condition. It would voice many accusations and would direct one especially against the artist, the spiritual criminal.

In a key chapter of Ole Wivel's biography he advances the theory that the conception of such a grandiose and desperate plan enabled Hansen to cope with his sense of guilt.[24] His "return" to Stevns made him finally see the old culture in a new, unsentimental light, and he discovered its *tradition*. This discovery redeemed him, for he came to

Background

realize that guilt does not separate one from, but rather binds one to, humanity; all guilt is the negative expression of responsibility.[25] The old culture vouched for his understanding: there, the living felt responsible for the cultural heritage of the dead and made their own lives meaningful by fulfilling the duty of upholding the values of the past. Wivel maintains that, through a sudden flash of insight, Hansen understood that tradition, and in it, he found his life's motif. Stevns, the lost land of childhood, now spiritually regained, gave Hansen a new sense of purpose in life.[26] It was at this point that the myth behind Hansen's writings assumed its final form, with Stevns and all that Stevns came to represent as its core. In "At the Crossroads" ("Ved Korsvejen"),[27] a series of articles that treat cultural crises and their literature, Hansen voices his newly won belief in tradition: "It is in such poverty-stricken generations that the evangelical will can be reborn. When traditions collapse like moldering walls around these generations, they come close to the core of tradition, the evangelical, the eternally revolutionary."[28]

Wivel points out that the writing of "Cain's Altar" became superfluous. Hansen could now view his vocation in an ethical perspective and even express the thought that "to be a poet is a moral, religious destiny."[29]

During the last part of the war Hansen worked on a number of short stories that were eventually published in *The Thornbush (Tornebusken* [1946]) and *The Partridge (Agerhönen* [1947]). Neither of these works was given final form until he had discarded his "Cain's Altar" plan, and both of them seem to mirror his crisis, as well as its resolution. In both collections — which, in terms of technique, range from realism to daring experiments in form (especially evidenced by *The Thornbush)* — the texts contain a movement from despair to spiritual rebirth, and this transformation is usually caused by the individual's recognition of his responsibility for others. In both works, but without being intrusive, the values of the mythical past, of tradition, function as a residue from which the despairing nihilists may gain the understanding and strength to live on in the modern, morally confusing world.

The works thus testify to a crisis overcome or, more precisely, to a "will" to overcome the crisis; but before this positive moment of final transformation is reached, they have painstakingly given a detailed, many-faceted, and disturbing picture of the inner hell of the nihilistic state of mind. What makes this nihilistic state seem particularly demonic, however, is not only its destructive abandonment of all values but also its allure in all its devastating negativity. To the modern disillusioned mind, wallowing in nihilism and even in self-destruction seems a temptation, and Hansen, who had almost given in to that temptation in "Cain's Altar," knew how to depict the dangerous depths of that state of mind. In some texts it even seems questionable whether the final moment connotes a spiritual rebirth or an extinction of the mind, and this ominous ambiguity may suggest that Hansen only precariously maintained his newly won standpoint.

In 1948 Hansen published *Thoughts in a Chimney (Tanker i en Skorsten)*, a collection of essays that, in part, date back to the early years of the Occupation. Although these essays treat a variety of topics, ranging from childhood memories to literary criticism, they form a commentary on Hansen's work and its dominant thoughts. As could be expected, the past — the immediate as well as the distant past — is juxtaposed with modern times, and thus not only the desolation of the modern age but also the sustaining values from the past are brought out.

At this phase of his career Hansen was acknowledged as one of the major writers of his nation; thus, when a small group of young critics and poets — notably, Ole Wivel, Thorkild Björnvig, and Björn Poulsen — decided to start a new literary journal, it was natural that they ask for his collaboration. *Heretica* first appeared in 1948, and for two years, 1950 - 1952, Hansen served as its coeditor. The Heretica-circle was a dominant force on the Danish literary scene until the middle of the 1950s, and during the journal's short life span of six years, it was a forum for an amazingly talented number of young writers.[30]

The contributors to *Heretica* may have differed a good deal tempermentally and philosophically, but during the first years of the journal's publication, they were quite conscious of the necessity of forming a united front culturally and aesthetically. Together, they brought European Modernism into Danish literature.[31] In their attempt to deal with their age's cultural crisis, they utilized highly symbolic and experimental forms, which brought upon them the criticism of being cryptic. Hansen, who had contributed substantially to the Modernistic tradition with his radical experiments in *The Thornbush*, felt at home among those serious young poets, who shared his profound skepticism toward political solutions to the postwar existential crisis. In *Heretica* one met what Hansen called "ethical pessimism": the recognition that the current crisis had to be acknowledged in all its painful aspects, for only through a thorough and honest analysis of the ailing culture could eventual values be rediscovered.[32]

Heretica, of course, was not alone in representing new trends in the postwar period; and by the political left, the journal was accused of being socially indifferent. Hansen took up the gauntlet; and from this challenge springs his long, philosophical essay *Leviathan* (1950), in which he takes a strong stance against those systems of thought that offer only partial explanations of existence but dangerously proclaim that they are the means for solving mankind's problems. Marxism, in particular, and science, in general, are exposed for their incapacity to cope with moral questions. The alternative that Hansen offers is, not surprisingly, the tradition whose values had saved him from paralyzing pessimism. The attack upon the Heretica-circle may nevertheless have struck a sensitive cord within him, for from the beginning, notes Ole Wivel,[33] Hansen was apprehensive of certain tendencies within the Modernistic trend. He foresaw that the urge to experiment with symbols and form could lead to a further dissolution of values.

Although, for the time being, Hansen had reconciled himself to his calling and shared in his contemporaries' view that the artist's primary responsibility is to art itself,[34] it is not surprising that he, who also wanted his works to be ethically significant, could hardly be comfortable with the doctrine of the autonomy of art. In about 1948 his suspicion of his calling seemed to be awakened once more, and it is in light of this fact that his dwindling fictional production and his devotion to cultural history must be seen. Ole Wivel points out that the relative peace of mind that Hansen had gained after the "Cain's Alter" crisis was fairly short-lived and, in the long run, was stifling to his creative powers.[35] With his rediscovery of tradition his inspiration waned; this put an incredible strain on him, and in his journal he noted, "The ability to feel joy is paralyzed. Hope has committed suicide."[36] Some of his short stories and an intensely woeful poem, "Man" ("Menneske"),[37] testify once more to the artist's tormented conscience over his pursuit of a vocation that caused him to neglect the people closest to him. These texts suggest that his creation of a myth as a positive alternative to a permeating sense of crisis may well be judged as a construct that could not permanently quiet the painful questions that haunted his mind.

This discomforting surmise seems to be born out by *The Liar* (*Lögneren* [1950]), which records a melancholy schoolmaster's spiritual and erotic crises during a few spring days. This brilliant *tour de force* in diary form, a novel that has been reissued in numerous printings, was commissioned by the Danish radio. It was thus a work that could scarcely be said to have sprung spontaneously from the artist's imagination. *The Liar* may depict the familiar fictional development toward spiritual transformation, but in the protagonist's case, it would be simplistic to speak of rebirth. In fact, his narrative is more about conflict than resolution and more about desolation than rebirth. Although he is a manipulative artist who abandons his destructive ways, he gains little that can make his own life meaningful.

Since the protagonist of *The Liar* does nevertheless find some solace and purpose in engaging in educational and cultural pursuits, he plans to write an account of his island's nature and culture. Such an endeavor, he hopes, will be honest. It is illuminating that Hansen followed in his protagonist's footsteps and turned to more factual genres with his works on nature and culture in the Nordic past and present. This new direction in authorship, which seems to have eased Hansen's sense of crisis, does not actually signify any renunciation of fiction but only signals new uses for it. In these works, Hansen consciously employs narrative to conjure up the life of the past, and many such passages equal the best in his earlier writing.

Storytelling as an evocative means served Hansen particularly well in his monumental *Serpent and Bull (Orm og Tyr* [1953]). This work of love was inspired by his fascination with the medieval churches that so plentifully dot the Danish landscape. The very fact that they still had a cultural function seemed to prove that the beliefs of the past were, even in the modern age, existentially significant. To Hansen these churches attested to the vitality of his concept of tradition.

Serpent and Bull delineates the changes in the religious beliefs in Denmark from the Stone Age to about 1250, when a major transition took place in Christianity, a change reflected by the replacement of Romanesque with Gothic art. This book gave Hansen a magnificent opportunity to express what he meant by tradition and, in addition, to demonstrate how this concept was relevant to modern times. With masterly, epic strokes, he draws the contours of an ever-repeated existential drama: when man finds himself in a purposeless and fearful world, he can be rescued by beliefs that restore harmony to his existence.

A healthy cultural tradition, like that established by early Christianity, imbues the individual with the knowledge that both life and death are meaningful, and this knowledge is the focal point of Hansen's book. The emphasis, however, is upon death, for Hansen's distinction between harmonious and discordant eras rested upon whether the living existed in a peaceful or fearful relationship with the dead. If a culture degenerates, it is evidenced by the fact that the dead begin to haunt the minds of the living. In such a world, in which the dead are perceived as a hostile force, their spiritual presence permeates and poisons all life.

Hansen's searching preoccupation with history and its relevance to modern culture was to last for the remainder of his life. In 1950 he and his family left Copenhagen and moved to the Sealand countryside, to a region that was filled with memorials from the distant past.[38] In this area, where grave mounds abundantly testified to man's age-old presence, Hansen was to spend the last five years of his life.

During those years Hansen wrote very little fiction. The slim volume *Apples of Paradise (Paradisæblerne* [1953]) contained mostly older stories, and his attempt to get together a more significant collection was cut short by his illness and untimely death. In 1952 he had, however, undertaken a commission to write a book about Iceland, and in the early summer of that year, he and his friend and illustrator, Sven Havsteen-Mikkelsen, traveled by jeep across the rugged island. Upon Hansen's return he completed two other "travel books": one about the Gudbrand Valley in Norway, *Kringen* (1953), and one about his impressions of Danish landscape and climate, *Danish Weather (Dansk Vejr* [1953]). In both books as well as in *Travel on Iceland (Rejse paa Island* [1954]), one meets a keen observer who rejoices in the ways in which history, the living spirit of past tradition, has changed nature into landscape, but who reacts with discomfort when faced by the wilderness.

In the last years of his life Hansen frequently felt tired and ill. He tried to keep up his exhausting activity as a lecturer, but in April 1955 he was hospitalized. He was diagnosed to be suffering from fatal uremia. He endured some often excruciatingly painful months and died on June 27, 1955, at forty-four years of age.

Hansen's friends report that, during the last phase of his life, he continued to write whenever his condition allowed it. The many unfinished drafts he left behind show that he had become engrossed once more in fiction.[39] Whether or not this indicated that he stood on the threshold of another creative period is a question that the stark fact of death leaves unanswered.

Several of his works, mostly short stories and essays that had not come out in book form, were published after his death. The *Conch (Konkylien* [1955]) contains short stories; *Midsummer Wreath (Midsommerkrans* [1956]), essays; and *Aftermath (Efterslæt* [1959]) reaps the final remnants of both genres. There have appeared several anthologies of both short stories and essays — some hitherto unpublished — as well as several paperback editions of his most popular works.[40] In 1961 a ten-volume memorial edition was issued.

III Thematic Overview

In "Legends in September" (1947), as so often in Martin A. Hansen's writings, he celebrates a homecoming to Stevns. He imaginatively travels back not only to the natural scenes of his childhood but also to its preindustrial culture, which had taken on mythical qualities for him and had provided his thinking and his artistic universe with a vital sense of values.

This essay contains a passage that sheds light on what Hansen perceived the storyteller's function to be. Legend and storytelling serve to consecrate the land:

There is one who knows that scenery, landscape, land have not come "from Nature's hand" but are the fruits of culture, are spirit, something that the beliefs and gods of many generations have eventually given final form. The one who knows this is the Genius of Art. What man has experienced, believed, and thought — including the legend and the localized story — have not merely animated the landscape but have created it.[41]

Art transforms nature into culture. This short and simple formula contains an important aspect of Hansen's view of the function of his own work. Although he may have often suspicioned his own vocation and regretted the price it exacted, he nevertheless considered his job as a writer to have a definite purpose. Like those who once plowed the land and like those who once told tales, he too was to serve culture, but by his pen. The obvious question that he inevitably had to ask himself — and one that his readers may repeat — was whether or not his authorship actually fulfilled its mission.

In order to consider this question and to ascertain more precisely the distinct character of Hansen's writing, one must delineate its major themes and value system — which make up a complex universe that is more generally suggested in the preceding biographical sketch. The passage quoted from "Legends in September" offers a fitting focal point for this consideration, since the opposition expressed between nature and culture is one that is made with telling frequency and consistency throughout his works. This opposition surfaces clearly in *Jonatan's Journey* and *Lucky Kristoffer* and asserts itself again in the desperate fervor of Hansen's very last writings. It thus seems valid to suggest that a thematic birds-eye view of his work can aptly be given from the vantage point of this opposition.[42]

If one reads the body of Hansen's works consecutively and, preferably, chronologically, it becomes evident that what Hansen prizes is not nature as such, but the fields and meadows that have been formed by the peasants' age-old and work-worn tools. When Hansen is confronted with unspoiled nature, he may praise its beauty, but he will often hasten to add that it is foreign, and even threatening, to the spirit. Nature — whether it is the forest, the swamp, the stream, the mountains of Norway, the vast panoramas of Iceland, or even the ordinary landscape obscured by fog — gives him the feeling that he is in a region inimical to man, a region that suggests extinction.

The positive counterpart to nature, however, is not just civilization, for the modern technological world cannot furnish the meaning in life that the individual needs. This world may seem as indifferent to man's existential need for meaning as does unfeeling nature itself. The relativism of modern civilization provides no basis for making those moral choices that constitute a human being's identity. Hansen thus distinguishes between culture and civilization.

Culture, as has been previously suggested, must be broadly understood to be a mode of existence that, no matter how difficult may be the lot of the individual in any age, will grant him and his fellow human beings the assurance that they are leading purposeful lives. This definition may indeed seem vague and bordering on the cliché-ridden, but it reveals nevertheless the essential, positive credo to be found in Hansen's writings. Fairly early in his career (evidence is to be found even in *Now He Gives Up*), he felt that the old agrarian tradition offered the individual the sort of guidance through which he could cope with inevitably arising existential questions and by which he could thus live in close contact with nature without being overcome by its demonic aspects.

Hansen's concept of tradition, which was partially formed before he underwent his so-called "Cain's Altar" crisis, is at the core of what he calls culture.[43] Tradition gives man the needed feeling of being a part of a whole and of working for that whole. The man who walked behind the plow and toiled for culture knew this intuitively, and it was Hansen's wistful hope that he who wielded a pen might also share in this spontaneous knowledge.

Perhaps the ultimate reward of a culture based upon a benevolent tradition is that life and, equally significantly, death seem meaningful to the human being who is firmly rooted in that culture. The cultural worker serves to uphold values, not only for the present day and his own sake but also for future generations. For such a man, the thought of extinction — a lot that is implied by both indifferent nature and nihilistic civilization — is nonexistent, for although he will die, his cultural effort endures. It would be a mistake to judge such a life to be idyllic, for the human lot is not easy and may entail much suffering; but such a life must still be called harmonious, for even if the individual were to make great sacrifices, he would find these sacrifices to be justified. He would live and die in accordance with the values of his tradition; thus, in spite of his personal fate, he would not be vulnerable to that nihilistic despair to which modern civilization would subject him.

One question is inevitable: how could Hansen be assured that his view of the old culture was correct? It was bound to be doubted by skeptics, who would find it to be a poetic fabrication. The answer lies less in the fact that Hansen conducted much painstaking historical research than in his conviction that, during his childhood on Stevns, he had experienced an essential harmony that had its origins far back in time. He came to believe that he could transcend both personal and familial memory and grasp the essence of that age-old tradition. Memory became *remembrance*,[44] the supranatural recollection of times long past. Late in his life, in *Serpent and Bull*, he exercised with artistic mastery what he thought to be the faculty of remembrance and created his most concrete and comprehensive picture of the cultural tradition that had inspired him in his works.

It should be obvious that Hansen's view of the old culture deserves to be termed mythical. He allots to the past a sense of values that he elevates into guardian principles for his own age; in fact, he invokes the past to assume an existential function in the modern individual's life. The cultural tradition of the past becomes a state of consciousness that is promoted through art. Myth in this context shall be understood as a means by which the individual can confront and attempt to cope with his own and his age's spiritually crippling problems.[45] Myths, which have put man in touch with the sustaining values of the past, have been expressed through tales told from generation to generation; and Hansen's narratives — as well as his contributions to cultural history — are written to serve the same mythical, therapeutic function. Skeptics, as mentioned, may balk at the *oeuvre's* myth about a meaningful life in the past, but it is important to grasp the fact that this very myth of a redeeming culture operates with a compelling power in Hansen's writing and constitutes the core of its value system. It was this myth that gave Hansen the spiritual strength to rise up against his age's moral confusion and to attempt to defy its destructive tendencies. The strength of the myth, as *Serpent and Bull* demonstrates, lies in its power to transform nature into culture and, thus, to exorcise nihilistic demons from the individual's life.

Although Hansen appears to be a guardian of the past, his work mainly depicts either the modern situation or a transition between the past and the present. Not unsurprisingly, the journey from the old into the new culture is deemed to be problematic: many of Hansen's travelers find themselves lost in an uncharted land. Whether this journey-motif is presented realistically or symbolically, the basic experience is the same: the travelers have left a world of order and now find themselves in an uncontrollable and chaotic world. Although the travelers may have once been cognizant of cultural values that could guide them, all their present knowledge is dissipated into a nothingness that leaves them without identity and in a limbo. Many facets of nihilism are presented in Hansen's writings, and it is revealing that he frequently chooses nature imagery to convey the destructiveness of this state of mind. He refers to the slimy depths of a swamp, to the bottom of a forest where plants rot away, to unfathomable waters into which one may sink and forget all human responsibility, or to dungheaps swarming with insects that follow only mindless instinct. Nihilism is clearly equated with nature or, rather, with all in nature that defies cultural endeavor.

This identification between nature and nihilistic culture may seem curious; but, as mentioned, they both are indifferent to cultural striving and to all human values, and ultimately they both offer man nothing but extinction. They also seem to signify a sense of man's beginning and ending and, thus, to form an ominous, fatalistic circle: culture originates in man's resistance to nature, but his emancipation and victory may be only temporary, for culture can degenerate into forms that deprive man of any sense of purpose. Hansen uses one particular setting, that of the dumping ground filled with civilization's debris and slowly being transformed into a jungle of tall weeds, strongly and symbolically to suggest this forbidding knowledge.[46] The mind that has lost all cultural values finds itself once more in a demonic wilderness.

It is against such fatalism, which mocks all human striving, that Hansen posits his myth of the old cultural tradition. Culture and nature — which, with regard to the human being, are understood to be both external and internal phenomena — were posed as the positive and negative poles in works in which the author insisted on asserting the possibility of exorcising the demon of nihilism and establishing — or, rather, reestablishing — meaning.

The myth of the old culture served Hansen well. It gave him alternatives to what he viewed as being insufficient or dangerous solutions to the modern world's futility and, thus, provided him with the reassuring knowledge of his serving culture through writing. The typical structure of numerous of his narratives leads the bewildered protagonist through spiritual confusion and darkness, toward a resolution that promises rebirth, in the sense that the protagonist rediscovers an ethos and chooses to accept responsibility for himself and others. This may sound a bit didactic, not to say pat, and sometimes Hansen does approach sentimentality in his rendering of the past or postulates in his assertion of the rebirth theme; but often, within the given contexts, he convincingly depicts both the image of the old world and the spiritual transformations of his characters.

In part, the reason for Hansen's brilliant aesthetic accomplishment may be that, in spite of his sometimes quite didactic advocacy of fixed values, he refused to offer idyllic, simplistic solutions to the modern dilemma. In his works, rebirth does not denote the attainment of "happiness ever after," but merely a rejection of the temptation of nihilism in a determination to face an ambiguous and taxing world through repeated moral choices.[47]

The above delineation of the value system inherent in Hansen's writings is — so to speak — the "official" one directly stated in many of Hansen's fictional and nonfictional works. The given characterization is however neither exhaustive nor sufficient, for it has hinted only very vaguely at the unrelieved tension that the authorship harbors. At times, a dark foreboding that nature or its spiritual twin, relativistic culture, will eventually negate all man's cultural striving seems to gain the upper hand.

It has been mentioned that the motif of a wandering or journey figures prominently in Hansen's *oeuvre;* and his writings may well be seen as stages in an unending quest for the sense of meaning that the past supposedly possessed. Like the author himself, the fictional wanderer who enters the modern world may be armed with the myth of the old culture, but numerous texts reveal that the strength of the myth is limited in the here and now. The myth casts a shining light over a culture that has disappeared, and although such a wanderer may hope that this sunken world will be spiritually resurrected, the rebirth theme is sometimes questioned through an undeniable ambiguity.

Hansen's use of symbolism underscores this tension in his work. He utilizes a symbolist technique that reinforces a mythical — or mythifying — perspective even in those works that on the surface seem realistic. Positive symbols are mainly taken from the cultural realm (the well-used tool, the tamed animal, the cultivated land, the instructively written page, the well-told tale, and the cultic site — such as mound or church), whereas those that are patently negative belong to nature (the fog, the swamp, the bottomless water, the barren land, the monstrous animal) or to the wasteland of culture (the dumping ground, the marl pit, the ravaged land). Such a clear-cut listing is nonetheless hazardous, for a great number of symbols are presented in an ambiguous light, and this ambiguity projects the confusion and mixed motives of the modern mind. Whether a symbolic element shall be judged to connote rebirth or spiritual extinction, or whether that element presents a fusion or — more precisely — even a confusion of these two concepts is an exasperating problem for any reader who penetrates into Hansen's complex, mythical universe.[48]

For an author who was possessed by the idea of spiritual rebirth, Christianity was an obvious cultural source of symbols. Although the protagonist's situations and hopes are often conveyed through religious references, his alienation from Christian dogma is also felt. The use of the Christian frame of reference, which can be seen as an invocation of a waning tradition that once granted man harmony, shows an estrangement from, rather than a nearness to, God. It is as if Hansen's sufferers, born as they are into a world where old myths lose their strength, can well understand their plight in terms of Job's misery and lament, but rarely in terms of his vindication and restitution.[49] Although Hansen wished to project a genesis through a spiritual renewal, the apocalyptic mood of his narratives is often so permeating that it actually subverts the theme of rebirth.

One feature, in particular, seems devastating to the hope vested in rebirth. At times, the nihilistic state becomes strangely and beautifully alluring and tempts the mind to forsake its cultural striving. Some characters trapped in this state either may voice a demonic delight in the destructive strength of the nihilistic mind or may yearn for release from the struggle for meaning and seek extinction. The seductive power of these nihilistic moments tends to overshadow any ensuing transformation that might vouch for their repudiation.

This fascination with what was destructive both to others and to the self was of course not in keeping with Hansen's values and, in fact, posed a threat to the therapeutic power of the myth of the old culture. The myth forced Hansen to write in a subtly didactic manner in order to advance his cultural mission, but in some texts Hansen seemed to be undertaking forays into regions — states of mind — over which the myth held no sway. These curious texts are filled with ambivalence, for they bear witness simultaneously to a revulsion from, and an attraction to, all that was forbidden by the myth.[50] This peculiar feature implies that the myth restricted Hansen's *vision du monde* and left him vulnerable to perplexities or paradoxes to which he could find no resolution.

In order to clarify what is meant with the restrictiveness of the myth, one concrete example, that of sexuality, should briefly be examined. It suggests that the ideological restriction in Hansen's thinking prohibits the realization of his ideal: the gap between the old and the new could not be bridged — at least not for an individual striving to be a bridge-builder through artistic means.

The relationship between the two sexes is at the core of many of Hansen's works, and the reader often encounters the existence of a polarity between an indulgence in "loose" sexual desire and the assumption of an ethical stance. Sexuality is judged according to what Hansen viewed the standards of the old culture to be; these standards were epitomized in the stories that the old "epic women" told.[51] When they related tales of romance, they never indulged in teary, modern notions of the right of passion but cooly made it clear that unfettered sexual desires went against the unwritten social rules of the old culture. Inevitably, it seemed that such individualistic excesses in the name of love led to pitiful fates for those involved.[52] Throughout Hansen's writings passion is suspect, and although a deeply felt passion may be described, it is usually shown to pose a threat to the culturally constructive. Quite significantly, passion is depicted in terms of destructive nature (as the lurid swamp, the dangerously fragrant flower, the swarming of insects, or the sabbat of soulless demons). The presence of a certain sexual ideology becomes particularly clear, since it is the woman who is associated with nature and, thus, with temptation and destruction. Although the male desires sexual pleasure, he is often ambivalent toward passion and may feel that he is being drawn down to his ruin by a temptress and by his own lust. The sexually attractive woman may thus be reluctantly rejected by a male who is himself in the grips of passion; in Hansen's work the male's rejection of the female would be interpreted as a cultural inclination.

The above characterization is admittedly a simplification, and one may argue that the woman often serves as an agent of culture and that she may warn the male that mere sensuality leads to alienation and meaninglessness. Often, however, such ethical women have left, or will leave, sexuality behind, a fact that, in itself, questions the value to be placed on sexuality.[53] It is quite evident that, in the view of the male protagonist, woman assumes a place that is either above or below him in spiritual awareness. This inequality of the sexes excludes any actual communication between them and ensures a loneliness for both. It seems as if the spiritual transformation or rebirth that is valued so highly in Hansen's works entails a renunciation of intimacy between the sexes.

The way in which the value system inherent in Hansen's fictional universe affects sexuality should indicate the restrictiveness of the myth: sexuality is viewed to be one of nature's alluring traps, one that is detrimental to the individual's search for meaning and that, consequently, must be renounced. It should be obvious that Hansen's mythical approach to the cultural crisis of his age led him to judge the spiritual to be superior to the physical or material: the individual must choose the spiritual, for only by so doing does he ally himself with culture, and only then can he feel that he transcends death.[54] Through this choice he becomes, so to speak, culture's protector, and, thereby, an integral part of mankind's cultural striving. Although his name may be forgotten, he will have generated a cultural significance that will ensure his being a spiritually constructive part of the future. It is in this frantic wish to reach an areligious concept of eternal life that the innermost drive of Hansen's creative quest as well as the core of the myth he consecrated are to be found. This concept is one that spiritualizes or "mythicizes" life to the point that the human being is forced to denounce much in his own nature.

Against this background, it is highly understandable that the protagonists who seem most surely to be made of flesh and blood find it extremely difficult to make the "right" choices and often make them only grudgingly and bitterly. They sense their loss of this life's possibilities, and their ethical resolutions to refrain from "natural" desires do not lead to any kind of spiritual bliss or religious joy, but rather to a gnashing of teeth and a loneliness of the soul. Hansen's dualism, which demanded a rigid choice of the spiritual over the material, could not help giving associations of death to life. This is not a judgment pronounced by the dissenting reader, but one that is voiced in various ways by many of the fictional characters, as well as by the narrator of their fates.

A cruel irony is obviously at play here, for the individual who, through difficult choices, wills his reintegration into a meaningful culture can achieve it only through an alienation both from other human beings and from a part of himself. This outcome is of course a far cry from that spontaneous existence posited by Hansen to have existed in the past. It seems consequently that, when Hansen used the myth — a static image of lost harmony — as a dynamic tool to recapture past harmony, the myth revealed its severe limitations. The myth of the past projected the ideal of a human being who was not haunted by an inner dichotomy, but the man who now attempts to realize the values of that very myth is made the victim of precisely such a dichotomy. The ironic paradox is that, whereas fulfillment in life supposedly was granted the human being of the past, fulfillment is now denied to modern man as if by a metaphysical law. This paradox is naturally of damning consequences, for the choice of the spiritual over the material signifies a disintegration within both the culture and the self, a disintegration that is thoroughly detrimental to the individual's sense of purpose in life and that, in fact, removes him further from his cultural ideal.

The tragic dilemma found in Hansen's writings arises, to put it simply, from the myth's failure to deliver what it promised. If the texts are studied carefully, they acknowledge the myth's inadequacy, but they do not do so in such a way that it seems possible to transcend it. The myth, which promised — and in some measure granted — spiritual liberation from the cultural crisis, became an ideological trap.

This characterization of Hansen's work may seem extreme, since it offers a number of examples of less tormented human destinies. It is however necessary to operate with a distinction between *the individual* and *the others*. The latter may be oblivious to, or victorious over, the inner tension that haunts the individual. He, in turn, must view his life as being dominated by that tension. He may cry out in anguish, but he persists nevertheless in deeming his sacrifices to be meaningful, for he knows — or frantically hopes — that others will benefit from them. Through these sacrifices, he realizes — or wants to realize — his dream of serving culture. Sadly enough, his situation is such that, although he may be the medium through whom harmony is granted to others, he cannot share in their spiritual renewal. Like a Moses, he may look into the promised land, but he himself cannot take part in the last phase of the exodus, the actual entry into that land; thus, he is brutally set apart from others.[55]

Hansen's writings consistently reveal that the artist feels particularly caught in this trap. The tragic irony is that this cultural servant, who exerts himself to formulate and possibly resolve his age's existential problems, becomes an unwilling prisoner in the notorious ivory tower.[56]

As he works for his cause, he realizes that his very vocation estranges him from the kind of life he thinks ideal, and this desperate realization makes him prone both to an immense fatigue and to a feeling of having wasted his life. In such a moment he may want to throw all cultural aspirations overboard and may wish for the finality of death, but at the next moment he may shudder over his alienation, grope for new chances, and mourn life's pitiful brevity; thus, he fluctuates between an intense yearning for peace through death and an equally intense fear of death.

At last, in order to probe into the unresolved, paradoxical tension in Hansen's works, it is pertinent to return to the opposition between nature and culture and to arrive at a final modification of that opposition. The artist, Hansen, who produced a consummate, if mythical, picture of the old culture, sometimes admits that the absolute opposition between culture and nature is a fabrication. He knows that culture is not totally separate from nature, for when man emancipated himself from his so-called natural state, he did not reject nature, as such, but allied himself with its beneficial aspects and thus attempted to tame those sides of it that were inimical to his cultural striving. Although man had a healthy suspicion of nature and repudiated all notions of oneness with nature, he remained close to it and could see it for what it was. Man could then lead a meaningful life and perpetuate a harmonious culture. In such a world, as exemplified by the old agrarian tradition, the spiritual and the material, the reflective and the spontaneous were integrated; and much to the benefit of the human being, that detrimental opposition between culture and nature was neutralized. The man of that culture knew that nature bears a Janus head whose one face is benevolent and the other malevolent, whereas modern man sees only the latter, demonic countenance of nature and becomes utterly alienated from it. Nature discloses to him only the fact that he stands apart from nature's cyclic promise of rebirth.[57]

Driven by fear, modern man vehemently rejects nature and all that he feels it stands for, and he seeks refuge in what he views to be culture; thus, he makes a false opposition between the two absolute. He thereby demonizes nature and, in effect, transforms culture into nihilistic civilization. The result is that death and life become equally meaningless.

Although fear of nature is expressed with gloomy eloquence in Hansen's works, that fear did not eliminate his attraction to nature's eternal and disturbing beauty. Hansen's ambivalence testifies to his entrapment in an insuperable emotional paradox.

Hansen's writing gradually became less abundantly humorous and more somber and searching. In spite of its constructive message, its explicit cultural mission, and the convincing ring with which its sense of values was offered, his work came to reveal an acknowledgement of its own profound and tortuous problem. This central feature of Hansen's *oeuvre* constitutes its complexity and limitation: its scope is determined by the fact that it contains its own contradiction and, intermittently, an authorial awareness of this contradiction.

If, finally, the question of whether Hansen's writing fulfilled its intended cultural mission is to be answered, the response must be a "both/and," for his work questions all the answers it gives. This may be why Hansen's works are so perplexing, so successful, and so compellingly fascinating and why they call forth so many readers and interpreters.

CHAPTER 2

Now He Gives Up *and* The Colony

I Now He Gives Up

MARTIN A. Hansen's first two novels, *Now He Gives Up (Nu Opgiver Han* [1935]) and *The Colony (Kolonien* [1937]), are both firmly planted in the tradition of social realism and are intended to be volume one and two in a chronicle treating a narrow farm community during the agricultural crisis of the 1930s. Both novels broadly depict a milieu made up not only of a village with its farm houses, general store, and inn but also of the outlying farms with their cottages for poor day laborers and open fields in which the daily toil takes place. A solid cross section of the inhabitants of the area is presented. There is much to cause these people to worry, for the market is falling and the crops may fail. In Hansen's portrayal of this milieu and its problems, he has given his social indignation and satirical bent free rein. Deceit and pettiness are shown at play: old grudges are nourished, and gleeful gossip is rife. The atmosphere can be quite poisonous.

At the story's center is a family which, for years, has been split by a dispute between two brothers, Kristen and Lars Jörn. The former is a mild-mannered and clever manipulator, who has made himself into something of a leading figure in the community. He understands how to cope with the times and seems to represent those who are shedding the old culture for a new and more vapid life-style. In contrast, aging and arthritis-ridden Lars Jörn bitterly keeps to the old ways, and only in forlorn, lonely moments does he admit that he is fighting a losing battle. The strife between the two brothers, which dates back to their youth, has intensified because Lars Jörn feels that Kristen has conspired to estrange his two sons from him.[1] The older, Henrik, left for South America when Lars forbade him to continue his education. The younger, Niels, has also left home, but he intends to return, take over the farm, and convert it into a collective project run according to Marxist principles. The title of the book refers to Niels's attempt to get his father to give up his farm.

Two other characters important to the action, which takes place during one spring and summer, are Hilde, Kristen's daughter, a somewhat spoiled young woman who has adopted city manners and thoughts, and Thorkild, Lars Jörn's farm foreman, who has fallen in love with Hilde in spite of the social distance between them. Around these primary characters cluster a large number of figures, notably, Kristen's utterly incompetent son, Jörgen, who plays the part of local leader of a Fascist farm movement; his erotically frustrated wife, Marie; and the young boy Knud who — like his friend and ideal of manhood, Thorvald — works for Lars Jörn.

For some of these people, this is a time of bitter disappointment. Lars Jörn feels that his strength is failing him, and his struggles against Niels's onslaughts become gradually weaker. Lars Jörn must also suffer the fate of seeing Henrik, drained of energy and ambition, return home and take up residence with the hated Kristen. Just as Lars Jörn's way of life deteriorates, so does that of the old farm culture. Kristen, foreseeing the severity of the agricultural crisis, acts accordingly and sells the old family farm, an act for which the older members of the community find it hard to forgive him. Kristen must endure the shame of seeing his son cuckolded by Thorvald and of seeing the relationship between that young man and Hilde severed.

The bitterest fate is suffered by Thorvald. He is a competent young man who has tried to rise above his peers. He has studied, put money away to assure his future independence, and on the whole has conducted himself in a manner quite different from that of his fellow farm workers. The rough tone of the barnyard and bunkhouse is beneath him, and once, upon discovering that young Knud has been reading a pornographic magazine, Thorvald even beats the boy. Thorvald's motives in this scene are, however, not all that pure, for he acts in frustration over his relationship with Hilde. When he meets Hilde in the evenings, he attempts to seduce her, only to be fended off by the young girl, who firmly believes that wedding bells must first chime. In theory, he always agrees with Hilde. Their romance has indeed proceeded on her terms, but his sexual desperation causes him to turn to Jörgen's willing wife, Marie. Thorvald and Hilde break their engagement.

Thorvald's problem is, in part, that he alone is of a contemplative nature. In spite of his obvious ability and intelligence, Thorvald is not a man who can cope with personal crisis. He is reflective, but his perennial mulling over of his problems leads only to a feeling of being mentally split and emotionally exhausted. His passion for Marie saps his spiritual strength. As he takes an evening swim with Knud, Thorvald toys with the idea of giving up and allowing himself to sink to the bottom of the dark water:

> Maybe it is the times; the type that he belongs to is doomed; it is inclined to luxury, not in clothes and outer habits, but in spirit! Harder heads own the future, people like Niels: simple, strong minds without superfluous afterthoughts, without any romantic wrappings. Maybe that is the way it is!
> Shouldn't one then give up?
> For instance, drown oneself? . . .[2]

A few minutes later Thorvald drowns, and although this is an accident and not a suicide, the passage is so structured that his death seems to be the consequence of his self-defeating thoughts. Through Thorvald, the reader is introduced, for the first time in Hansen's writings, to the reflective individual who seems doomed by his inability to act in accordance with his imagined values and who is thus dangerously drawn toward the solution that will give him peace: death.

Although Thorvald may be one who finds himself to be bankrupt in the balancing of his emotional and philosophical accounts, other figures counterbalance this portrayal. Thorvald's friend Knud, after vainly having tried to save Thorvald, walks sleeplessly about in the summer night until he finds shelter and consolation in the servant-girl Kaja's bed. This scene is clearly one of initiation for both the young people, and the boy achieves the assurance of his own manhood. While this transformation may seem a bit pat, Hansen gives a sensitive impression of the young Knud's growing pains, his sexual curiosity, and his adulation both of the spiritual Hilde and of the seemingly perfect Thorvald. Knud is shown slowly learning to detect the motives of others and the weaknesses in those he admires. He finally demonstrates his insight by telling Niels that some of his so-called reforms on the farm may actually be products of his jealousy of his older brother, Henrik. When Niels rails at him, Knud firmly gives notice that he is leaving. By the end of the summer he is engaged to Kaja and has become a very competent truck driver and mechanic. It seems clear that he is a man cut out to manage his own life.

To an even greater degree than Knud, Niels emerges as a contrast to the reflective Thorvald. The highly pragmatic Niels may be termed an idealist because of his strong belief in Marxist thought, but certainly not because of any belief in romantic ideas about the difference between spiritual love and animalistic sex. It is in fact doubtful that Niels would ever use the word love. He identifies with the proletariat and is wholeheartedly materialistic in his outlook. Niels plans to marry a girl of lower social standing and, as soon as Lars Jörn "gives up," to move her and a couple of poor families from Copenhagen out to the farm. Niels brusquely demands that his father retire, and although Niels meets resistance, he still manages to modernize the farming. As has been indicated, his motives may not all be pure, but his striving — which, at least, is indicative of his attempt to find a possible solution to the crisis — is seen in a positive light. Niels stands as a refreshing contrast not only to Thorvald and Hilde but also to the Fascist movement; to the incompetent, confused farmers; to the mealymouthed Kristen; and in short, to the decadence of the old farm culture. It is quite telling that Thorvald does not like to be around Niels and that the latter does not include Thorvald in his plans for the commune. The outspoken, capable, and boundlessly energetic Niels is suggestive of the not very amenable, but necessary, man of tomorrow. At the end of the book, when a farmhand, who is something of a juvenile delinquent, sets fire to Lars Jörn's farm, the reader may interpret Niel's cry, "Now he will give up," as the promise of a perhaps regrettable, but needed, change.

It should be pointed out, however, that *Now He Gives Up* does not read at all like a Marxist tract, for at no point does the author explicitly laud the new as the ideal. In fact, the most sympathetic character in the story may well be Jacob, a small-holder, who — unlike his fellow farmers — resists the lure of the Fascists and who feels a deep respect for the land. In comparison with this upholder of the old ways, Lars Jörn appears to be almost a parasite. In one very telling scene, while Jacob points out some age-old graves that he has discovered in his field, he tells Lars Jörn that such graves are to be found on his own land as well. Lars Jörn immediately starts figuring out how he can sell the stone, but to his amazement, Jacob indicates that he intends to leave undisturbed the graves he has found. This deep respect for one's forefathers who have tilled the land is also revealed when Jacob stubbornly declares, to some farmers who are advocating striking, that it is a sin not to work the fields. A farmer is responsible for the soil.

There is quite a distance in outlook between Jacob and Niels, but one must realize that, in the book, the attitudes of both men are valued highly. It is however necessary to add that, whereas Niels stands for a future possibility that grim economic realities force one to test, Jacob represents those attitudes of the past — a sense of history and a feeling of responsibility toward the land and one's fellowmen — that have not been corrupted by the degeneration of the farm culture.

II The Colony

The Colony begins shortly after the final major event, the burning of the farm, in *Now He Gives Up*. Silhouetted against a heavy grey sky, four shabby huts now stand among the rusty and sooty rubble of Lars Jörn's old farm. Here Niels lives with his wife, Klara, and the people from Copenhagen whom he has brought with him in order to realize his dream of a collective farm. The winter has been severe; not all members of the experimental community work as hard or as willingly as Niels could wish; and he has gradually been forced to modify his ideals and to impose some not very egalitarian discipline to ensure that which is absolutely necessary: the success of the colony. The rest of the farming community look at the experiment with both skepticism and hostility, but cunning Kristen Jörn, who now lives as a kind of rentier and who is still very much the unobtrusive leader of the community, has put money into the experiment. This act gives him a say in its management and the possibility of directly taking over its leadership. Niels is fully cognizant of these dangers, but he desperately needs money in order to carry out his plan on a productive scale.

Life in the colony is very much at the center of the narrative, whereas the rest of the community is more in the periphery than it was in the former novel. The voice of the community is still to be heard, and it is as petty and venomous as before; but the book's main emphasis is on the experiment, the struggle to make it successful, and its eventual failure. Niels and his father, old Lars Jörn, who has remained in the colony, are the principal characters; and although they are as strongly opposed as ever, during the spring and summer they experience a feeling of kinship through their work on the land. Niels is definitely *primus motor* of the project. Through his frantic work and brusque manner, he rules the other members, and he refuses to condone any grumbling whatsoever. Niels, however, is himself no longer quite the same, for he has become more introspective than before.

During the summer Niels has an affair with a woman from Copenhagen, who is a dilettante at her painting and who may be a hypocrite in her views, but who addresses some rather stinging comments to Niels about his radicalism. She calls him a fantast. Niels's personal crisis becomes full-blown after a devastating thunderstorm destroys the crops. He still admonishes his supposedly worthy fellow members of the colony in the old tones, but he now doubts that these people are capable of living up to their task. "They can't," he declares of them; but the point is that, this time, it is really Niels who "can't," and it is he who *gives up*.

Shortly after the rainstorm Niels is invited to a party given by his mistress for a number of young leftist intellectuals. On this occasion, when the value of the colony is questioned by an avid espouser of the party line, Niels gives a very revealing answer: "Politics do not interest me," and he adds, "I want to get the colony on its legs."[3] It could be suggested that what has happened to Niels is that, without knowing it, he has followed the natural inclination of his family, particularly that of his father: what matters, first and foremost, is to see the land bear crops.

Soon after the party Niels decides that he must leave the colony. He explains that he wants to go back to Copenhagen to read, study, and find out why the colony failed. Niels maintains that he must investigate the whole matter "from the bottom."[4] This quest for understanding, which entails one's grasping his own motives, is an endeavor that was to become the pursuit of many of Hansen's future characters. Niels's departure is interpreted, of course, as the ultimate form of treason by old Lars Jörn, who, after all, has enjoyed a grudging feeling of kinship with his struggling son and who now bitterly promises Niels that one day *his* own son will also betray him. The reaction on the part of the gardener and his wife, the only two who have wholeheartedly participated in the daily toil of the colony, shows that they, too, brand Niels as a traitor. She slaps him hard across the face, and her husband hits him with blow after blow; but the most telling reaction is Niels's own, for by his lack of resistance he seems to accept the thrashing as a deserved punishment.

The book, as many critics have pointed out, may mirror Hansen's growing distrust in the ideological solution that he had presented two years before in *Now He Gives Up*.[5] If one disregards the gardener and his wife, one must admit that none of Niels's helpers (including his own wife) have any real ability at, or much interest in, carrying out such an experiment in the spirit in which it was planned. His helpers are either dilettantes or self-centered people caught up in their own private concerns, petty squabbles, and ambitions. One can see why Niels becomes exhausted. In facing the perennial dilemma of the idealist who sees that his followers are not worthy of the ideal and who, therefore, lets people become subordinate to the ideal, Niels allows the ideal of equality itself to become corrupted. Although Hansen thus demonstrates a possible weakness in the leftist solution to the agricultural and spiritual crises, it would be incorrect to judge the idea of the colony to be completely worthless. One must note not only that the hostile community surrounding the colony comes to admit that Niels and his people are apparently doing quite well, but also that the clever Kristen would not have put money into the project if he had no belief in its chances of success. Of course, he may simply have been waiting to take over the fertile land on easy terms, but there may also be some truth in his parting words to the fleeing Niels: "I trusted that you would have stuck it out until we had investigated this form of farming."[6] In the last chapter, Jacob, whose words one must heed, points out that people who are ahead of their times often lose their property and the esteem of others, but that their ideas may well be successfully adopted by their detractors in the future. With Jacob's words in mind, one might suggest that the book ends not necessarily with the failure of Niels's idea, but with Niels's betrayal of that idea.

The Colony follows up the fates of other characters from *Now He Gives Up*. Knud marries the pregnant Kaja and completely takes charge of his pathetic father-in-law's newly started trucking firm, but the strictures of his society, which he — like Niels — despises, give him the uncomfortable feeling of having forsaken his ideals and of having lost his youth. Hilde, who, after Thorvald's death, lived through a pietistic phase and a feeble attempt at serving suffering mankind as a nurse, feels drawn to the quiet, diffident Henrik, and for his sake she is finally willing to sacrifice her virginity. They marry and move to Lars Jörn's old farm — where Hilde happily establishes herself as matriarch, while Henrik, as indifferent to his life as ever, putters about on the land. Lars Jörn's dream of seeing Henrik succeed him has thus come true, but in a bitingly ironic manner, for it is Kristen, the actual owner of the land, who has installed the two young people on the farm.

Now He Gives Up and *The Colony* have much in common. They both show the effect of the times upon a culture in transition and voice the author's social concern and indignation, but the novels differ in their sense of crisis. It is striking that the trait of introspection, which Thorvald was alone in harboring in the first novel, has now been extended to Knud and Niels and that these two, who in the former work served as specimens of the sturdy men of the future, are not counterbalanced by more robust types in the latter work. Consequently, the sense of crisis is much more pervasive in *The Colony* than in *Now He Gives Up* and, in fact, grows into a sense of defeat.

In both works this sense of defeat is often linked to the relationship between the sexes. Sexuality, which promises so much pleasure and fellowship but entails so much misery, comes to determine the lives of several characters. Desire may draw man and woman together (like Knud and Kaja), but the distance between the sexes soon reasserts itself. The books do not exclude the possibility of sexual unions with some mutual love but include numerous relationships of hostility, disloyalty, betrayal, and torment.

Sexuality seems to be viewed in a dualistic light, and this dualism is suggested to be a male convention (as it is for Thorvald).[7] For the female to demonstrate a division between flesh and spirit is a perversion (Hilde), but the male tends paradoxically to uphold this sexual ideology: the male desires the uncompromising, unreflective — the natural — female yet feels that she represents a danger to him and that she robs him of his youthful strength. To Thorvald, Marie seems nearly vampiric, and to Knud, Kaja spells the end of his youth.

Consequently, the two novels make sexuality suspect. Men and women seem engaged in a battle that can be halted only by the depleting wear of years. In the next two novels this issue remains in the background, but in *The Thornbush* it again emerges and assumes a major significance.

CHAPTER 3

Jonatan's Journey

THE book *Jonatan's Journey (Jonatans Rejse)* was published in 1941 and republished in 1950 after the author had extensively revised it. This analysis treats the revised text.[8] It is perhaps Martin A. Hansen's most satirical work: within the assumably innocent framework of the fairy tale, men and society are depicted with gallows' humor. As the story progresses, it becomes less of a fairy tale in nature and assumes more the characteristics of a picaresque novel with apocalyptic overtones. Its language bemuses and charms the reader with its mixture of contradictory wisdom about diverse experiences. There are many bits of wisdom drawn from sources that have become a part of cultural tradition: biblical proverbs are mixed with folksy saws and literary maxims. The language may consist of either a misplaced understatement or exaggeration, and its charm is often in this description of an expected attitude with an unexpected emphasis expressed in slightly incongruous terms. The spirit of the first half of the book — like that of its protagonist — is that of a sly innocence, optimism, and levelheadedness. It is a spirit that seems basically light-hearted, swift-footed, and deaf to those prophets of doom who appear in its pages.

Jonatan, the book's protagonist, is a village smith. He is a large, good-natured man who has a number of seemingly minor weaknesses: he brags, shows off, talks too much, and drinks too much. These are not constant sins, but ones that take on significance because of his impulsiveness. Jonatan stresses that he thinks slowly, but this is perhaps more an excuse for his lack of action or pursuit of wrong action. He is shrewd and naive and, above all, readily involved in the woes of others, for he is not only helpful and understanding, but really rather curious. He is actually vain and too eager to help others, a combination which makes him something of a busybody. Although he chides, cajoles, flatters, questions, and preaches, he is too slow in opposing wrongdoing. Jonatan's negative characteristics are glimpsed, but initially ignored, for the reader is swept along by Jonatan's charm and his journey, with its ever-changing cast of eccentrics.

The book is introduced, as well as bidden farewell to, by its author, the so-called editor who has supposedly compiled this collection of stories from oral tradition. The tale itself is divided into four parts: a glance at Jonatan's life in the village and at the events that are the background for his journey; his journey through the countryside, during which he meets those who are to be active, either in thought or deed, in the resolution of his moral fate; his sojourn in the city itself, where the perversions of his ideals and deeds become innumerable sins, which pursue him like the multitude he arouses; and finally, his punishment and his resumption of life in the village. The light-heartedness of the first half of the tale gives way to a more and more somber, ominous, and chaotic picture of dishonesty and suffering during Jonatan's stay in the city. Although the tale — filled with the irrational, magical, traitorous, and evil — is humoristic, it bares, on the whole, a quite pessimistic view of man and society. Jonatan's journey is one through life and through a changing culture; it is a pilgrimage for the sake of the realm, and it is an adventure that will now be carefully paraphrased.

In the little village where Jonatan lives, he is viewed as a man who enthusiastically goes to church, to work, and to the tavern at the proper and accepted times. Although he drinks a bit too much and brags of his moral rectitude — he claims to have preached from "Luther" to the devil himself — the smith seems to have but one problem: the keeping of a proper apprentice at the smithy, for Jonatan's wife, Laura, is thought to have cuckolded him many times.

The smith employs a new apprentice who soon proves himself to be a master at his trade. He quickly becomes the master of the smithy and Laura as well, and when Jonatan decides to teach the apprentice a lesson through a show of strength, the apprentice demonstrates supernatural powers. By introducing modern frivolities that make him popular with Jonatan's eager neighbors, the stranger soon extends his influence over the whole village.

The smith, resolving to put a stop to the moral decline of his village, forms a bottle from an old, cracked church bell, Gabriel, and places fragments of the skull of an unbaptized child within the bottle. Jonatan lures the devil into the bottle and sets out, bottle-in-hand, on his journey. The reader eventually learns that Jonatan intends to present the bottle to the king.

The journey gets off to a slow start, for after stopping at a tavern and causing panic on a train, Jonatan continues on foot. In the dark he literally stumbles into the instrument of his ultimate fate, a body hanging in his path. Jonatan cuts down the nearly dead man, who tells Jonatan a sorrowful tale. The man has been a soft-hearted idealist, one easily destroyed by the good intentions of friendly people. They have given him money (which he has squandered), have supported him through his studies to be a doctor, and have paid the heavy debts he has accrued. He has now stolen money to pay a new debt and hanged himself. Jonatan uses his bottle to produce the required money and takes it upon himself to return it.

Jonatan is arrested for the theft and put in jail. The police chief is a man who believes in punishment and who feels a strange kinship with the criminal, whom he feels Jonatan so aptly represents. The chief hopes for the imposition of a long sentence. The jailer, who harbors his own affinity for the criminal, believes himself fit to be an excellent judge, for he does not concern himself with truth, but rather with law, which is a matter of evidence. Both chief and jailer are disappointed that the accusation is for theft and not for murder, a far more interesting crime. Ultimately, both men's hopes are partially realized.

Jonatan slips out of jail to join the town's celebration in honor of its long history. Since that history is not as long as it could be, nor the town so famous as it should be, the town has saved its money to build a ruin. Its unveiling and the subsequent banquet are the high points of the festival. Jonatan, mistaken as a famous professor, takes part in the banquet with the town's finest citizens, such as the doctor and the police chief. The chief drunkenly agrees to let Jonatan continue his journey on the promise that he return to take his punishment. Jonatan returns to jail to gather his things and finds that his bottle has been stolen. Both the jailer and the doctor have been there and have fled for the capital, but Jonatan is slowed in his pursuit of them by the jailer's flirtatious wife.

In pursuit of the bottle thieves, Jonatan comes to a region where the land is poor, but the farms are large and well kept. He meets a man on the road and asks him to explain this paradox. The man is a stern believer in the "truth": all men shall reap as they sow, in this life and the next. He proclaims that sorrow and difficulty are needed to break down man's arrogance so that he may find the way of truth. Although Jonatan battles against this hard man's philosophy with other biblical quotations and sayings, Jonatan leaves feeling that it is impossible to hold his own with this righteous man.

Jonatan attends the funeral of a man who, in his youth, was a robber and a murderer by arson. He is now being buried as a suspected suicide.

The minister speaks of the man's many trials, of his understanding help to others, and especially of his setting a good and God-fearing example. After the burial Jonatan agrees to harvest the widow's fields. This he does in an afternoon, and through his help he sets an example for her neighbors. This is one of the few times that Jonatan helps another through his own strength and good will. It is done without the help of his bottle and has no evil consequences.

The minister warns Jonatan against ever using the bottle, for from evil comes evil; and even though one were to use the bottle from a sense of compassion or in the service of one's country, its use might still be viewed by God as a sin.

Upon parting with the minister, Jonatan meets Anna, a woman for whom he once cared and who is now the wife of a wealthy old farmer. For the second time Jonatan delays his journey to spend the night with someone's dissatisfied wife.

The next day Jonatan comes upon two women who are fighting over the ownership of a can of milk. Someone has already stolen one can, and Jonatan stops the fight by stealing the remaining can. He overtakes the thief, a young man called Askelad.[2] Askelad is too proud to beg, and he takes what he wants, unrepentantly, for he knows he is a genius who will do great things in the world. He maintains that he is not afraid of anything, for evil is only stupid superstition. During the night Askelad's views undergo a change: he is afraid of the dark, and darkness seems to imply both stupidity and death. Askelad explains his fear as that of being "too late"; it is a fear of others' making "his" scientific discoveries before him; it is a fear of the end of the world and a fear of his own death. Time and accident are the enemies of the fanatic rationalist Askelad.

Between their meeting and nightfall Askelad and Jonatan find themselves involved in the problems of a miller and his wife. The miller believes in duty and insists upon grinding a friend's corn for the next day, even though a storm is coming that could and does destroy his mill. Urged by the miller's wife, Jonatan goes into the mill to try to dissuade the old man. Accusing Jonatan of the devil's work, the miller maintains that the more his wife humbles him, the more stubbornly he must stand by his honor. Impressed by these words about honor and duty and encouraged by aquavit, Jonatan helps the old man mill his corn. When the mill bursts into flame, Jonatan saves the corn from burning and, thereby, the old man's honor, an honor born of a fanaticism that leaves the miller and his wife without a livelihood, but with the fame of having dared God.[3] Jonatan leaves the countryside and the old culture behind and bears the tired Askelad through the dark night to the modern city, Askelad's great laboratory. There they part.

The city presents the smith with old and new acquaintances. The first person he meets is the bragging jailer, who brazenly pretends to have been looking for the smith to arrest him. Jonatan beats him until he admits not only that he has long believed himself to be a zero who ought to commit suicide, but also that he had stolen the smith's bottle, which was then stolen from him by the doctor. The smith and the jailer try to find the doctor, but after a couple of unsuccessful attempts, they fall asleep on a bench.

Jonatan awakes to see two men in hot pursuit of an agile old man. Jonatan interferes and saves the man, only to find that "he" is a young woman. "Individual Likka" is a "Kasparist," one who seemingly believes in anarchy, in which all individuals will be respected, equal, and free to fulfill their wishes. She has been pursued by political opponents.

The next morning Jonatan reaches the doctor's house, which is in a state of chaos over the loss of the bottle. A maid has sold it, for a few cents, to a junk dealer. The doctor again faces ruin. In disgust, Jonatan addresses himself to one without deceit, the human skeleton in the doctor's office. The skeleton seems to represent the only thing one can count on with men: they will die.

The smith next meets a man whose self-ordained ministry is the watering of weeds. It is his belief that nature would be better off without man, for it would again be clean and innocent. While admiring this fanatical conservationist's plants, Jonatan espies his bottle in a secondhand store window. In an attempt to find someone from whom to borrow money, Jonatan finds Askelad washing windows. The man who owns the window-washing equipment gets the bottle for Jonatan, while Askelad describes his vain attempts either to come into the university, where one must have a degree to get one, or to study at the library, where one must be established enough to afford books to borrow them. Askelad is feverish and weak, and Jonatan realizes that he must be put to bed immediately.

The smith finds lodging for the two of them at an evangelical hostel. Their room proves to have already been rented by a secret society of seven men: a handsome and wealthy misanthrope, a tongue-tied musician, an ailing poet named Vilhelm, a former scientist named Sallust, a naive young man named Christian, a cynical fat man named Kaliban, and their thin, idealistic leader called the Freeborn, a man who believes in original sin. Since it is agreed among them that Askelad needs a proper bed, Jonatan asks the bottle for the landlady's. It comes with her young assistant still in it, and a few days later, this shamed young man kills himself.

The seven men agree to help look after Askelad, and they give Jonatan their advice as to what to do with his bottle. It is decided, upon Christian's suggestion, to help the neighborhood poor.

This aid to the poor causes a great stir among the leading citizens, who would have the reputedly wealthy smith enlisted in their various causes. He is first approached by a prominent religious dignitary; then by editor Kvik, who represents those who govern public opinion for reform; and finally, by the industrialist Aleksander Aleksander, whose businesses are changing the country's way of life, while he himself advocates the past and its simple virtues.[4] Jonatan becomes suspect in the eyes of all these power groups, for he has given money to all the needy who have approached him, and some have been the secret representatives of political causes.

When visiting Aleksander Aleksander's home for boys, Jonatan had met his old acquaintance the doctor. He not only works at the home but also has begun a practice among the poor. Soon afterward, at the harbor, Jonatan meets a second acquaintance, the jailer, who feels that the smith has betrayed his trust.[5] Looking like a scarecrow, the jailer drunkenly sits in judgment over Jonatan, who has disrupted and destroyed people in his blind and eager desire to do the right thing. His good intentions are of no avail as a defense, and the judge's verdict is that Jonatan must accept his responsibility and guilt by remembering his jailer and judge. The jailer feels that he represents a supernatural right and that he has momentarily gained honor, but that he must commit suicide before he loses it. He drowns himself in the harbor.

Jonatan and the Freeborn stop their philanthropic work, for the public has become suspicious and aroused. One stubbornly proud old man, who would save his daughter Margaret's honor, will not be denied, and finally Jonatan agrees to help if he can do so without actually committing some misdeed. The misdeed he has indirectly agreed to turns out to be the temptation of the woman s husband, who, for a large sum of money, agrees to leave her.

The smith tries to give his bottle to the king, who declines to accept it. The king has in his possession a similar secret weapon once developed by Sallust. It is a machine with all the attributes of a magic mirror, a "bugging device" through which the king can follow the activities of his subjects. Realizing its inherent potential for harm if it should fall into the wrong hands and realizing that God's are the only hands into which such power should fall, the king destroys his own machine and indirectly advises Jonatan to do the same with his bottle and to leave the town for his safety's sake.

Jonatan does not leave the city at once, for he feels he must first visit the woman forsaken by her husband. Margaret is distraught, and leaving her child in the smith's care, rushes out to seek her husband. Despairing of finding him, she drowns herself.

While caring for the child, Jonatan remembers that the ailing poet of the secret society lives on the top floor of the same building. He goes to visit him and finds that a stranger — death — has also come to call. Since the poet still has a vision to express, death is denied for a little while. The poet's vision resembles that of the weed-waterer, for the poet sees the city as the embodiment of a gigantic, growing force: death, which wishes to be eternal. The city is a force that destroys nature; the city is both the poetry and garbage can of human existence and a dump that must at last poison itself and return to grass.

The next day Jonatan is arrested by the police and put in jail to await trial. There he finds the Freeborn. At the smith's trial many testify falsely against him, but some testify for him. The bottle has been opened and studied, and Jonatan discovers to his chagrin that the best witness in his defense is the devil himself. Jonatan points this out to the court and is sent to a mental hospital.

Part of Jonatan's sentence is served in this hospital, where another of his acquaintances, Margaret's father, now resides, violently mad. Jonatan receives two visitors who wish help from him. Askelad and a stranger, whom Jonatan recognizes as being the devil, have made a pact in which the stranger will support Askelad's studies if Askelad, in turn, will do those experiments required of him. Without realizing it, Askelad has accepted the devil as his spiritual guardian and now needs Jonatan to be his guardian and sponsor here on earth. If Jonatan agrees, he will receive his freedom.

During the discussion Jonatan finds that the three of them are flying through the air. In vain, the smith advises Askelad against his arrangement with the devil, and the devil mocks Jonatan's newly acquired stubbornness. The devil implies that Jonatan's motives in using the bottle were never really pure. The devil declares that there is no one with whom he would rather travel than Jonatan, but that there is no need to stay longer with either Askelad or Jonatan, since they each have one of the devil's brothers within them.

For his own entertainment the devil shows Jonatan and Askelad two wonderful sights. The first is a cavern in which the devil's own commander, an ancient dwarf, works at forging the tiny silver bell of eternity, a work that is constantly being interrupted by the necessity of feeding a baby bird of gigantic dimensions, the bird of judgment.

On a barren field the devil then lets the imagination of each create what he most desires. Jonatan creates his own village, slightly improved, and Askelad destroys it to create a city. Jonatan now seems to take the devil fully seriously for the first time. By doing so, Jonatan finds the strength to force the devil to show what he himself would do, and all is destroyed.

Askelad refuses to believe what he has seen and determines to continue with his plans. It is his call to create something new, and that can be done only if one ignores the fact that it may be misused. If one were always to fear destruction, one would not dare to create anything.

The smith returns to the hospital, from which he is later transferred to the jail in the town where he was accused of stealing money. Jonatan refuses to reveal the doctor's guilt and takes the punishment for theft upon himself with "old-fashioned" dignity. He has accepted the judgment of the jailer, and he imagines that God has nothing against this arrangement for Jonatan's punishment, which seemingly allows him to expiate crimes of which he was not directly convicted. Jonatan is however advised that, if he is not guilty, to accept a sentence is to mock justice and that not to name the real culprit is to commit a crime.

After a year in the small town jail, Jonatan is freed. He returns to the city for Margaret's child and, at last, arrives back at his smithy to resume his work and to raise the child. His wife has left him, and most people are hostile toward him, until pastor Tadæussen shows a marked preference for his company. Then others again begin to visit the smithy. After the deathbed confession of a doctor for the city's poor, Jonatan is once more accepted by the villagers, but his name is never cleared of rumor. The only office of trust he ever receives is that of churchwarden, but at his death everyone, at last, understands that few better men are ever born.

Such is the story of Jonatan the smith. It is a somewhat disjointed story, but it is held together by certain themes. One of these is the moral ambiguity of supposedly virtuous characters. Each of them has strengths and weaknesses that are usually one and the same. Each character seems to represent an ideal and, in so doing, also represents its opposite (for example, the police chief who feels his duty to prosecute is more important than justice and who feels a disdain for others, but who also feels a close kinship to, and understanding of, the criminal). Each character thus seems to be typified by a fixed idea — such as duty, punishment, the law, nature, knowledge, judgment, indulgence, honor, or death.

Jonatan the smith's fixed idea is that evil is separate and apart from man, who can somehow control it and use it for beneficial purposes.[6] Jonatan seems to believe that man, given the opportunity, will repulse evil in all its many forms. In some instances Jonatan's belief is born out, but it is done so at the cost of the individual. The jailer, for example, does see himself for what he is and has a moment of honor before he commits suicide. He realizes his dream, for he is, at last, a judge who pronounces sentence not only on Jonatan but on himself as well. He is crushed by the weight of his own conviction.

As the devil has once assured Jonatan, evil works through man. It would seem that the more self-righteous and unreflective man is, the more the devil enjoys his company and the more jolly is the journey. This was the lesson Jonatan had to learn. Jonatan set out on his journey with a grand conviction of its importance, but the concept of evil was something he had not pondered.[7] Evil seems to be brought about by this very lack of reflection whereby virtue becomes vice. This is perhaps expressed most aptly in the visions of the poet Vilhelm. His tales are parables of man's need for appreciation and a feeling of self-importance, without which there is only decline and death, and of man's need of an ideal, in which he will believe to the point of ignoring unpleasant truths about the unworthiness of that ideal. These are the reasons that one embraces a loved one, a fixed idea in the form of a virtue, or an ideological cause.[8] The final parable reveals that the wisest words about life in this ever-changing world will cause those who believe in them to suffer. Such suffering is adequately attested to in the figures of the jailer who believed in "proofs" and the old man who believed in "honor," but the parable leads to a vision of unavoidable evil: the world is ever-changing; thus, men's ideals are distorted and doomed by time. They become false.

The poet's final vision of the city is closely connected to the basic problem of evil itself. For the poet, a city is a living being that seeks to become eternal at the expense of all else. While the city grows, it destroys; and finally, although it carries man's dreams on its spires, it carries the seeds of destruction within it, and it rots from the bottom up: it destroys itself.

The living organism of the city is like man himself, for just as man strives to accomplish something by which to be remembered, whether it is to build a village or a city or to embody an ideal, he bears the seeds of his own destruction within him in the form of the devil's ilk. Man's lack of knowledge and his blind striving will finally cause his own self-destruction.

Just as the devil loves to travel with a man like Jonatan, the devil loves a city, a place where things are going on, where there is life and movement, action and new accomplishments. In contrast with the old culture, such a quickly changing world rushes toward its destruction. Evil would seem to be in the nature of things, for it is allied to that which is conceived of as life — striving and growing — and to that which is shown to be death — the self-destructive.

It is startling at the book's end to meet the devil's master in the form of a wizened dwarf busy at work in his smithy. Although a smith may call to mind an artisan who was the foundation of a past generation's simple culture, he may also call to mind those mythic representatives of more questionable powers, such as general troublemaking, vengeful judgment, and even death.[9] The dwarf is not only hammering out the bell of eternity, while fearful shadows await the outcome, but feeding the voracious and thriving bird of judgment as well. The dwarf is in fact a pessimistic picture of God, an ancient being subservient to a symbol of an all-devouring and ever-growing force of nature that will probably bring about judgment and death before the bell of eternity can be finished.

The human skeleton is said to be without deceit, for the skeleton is a true reminder of man's fate and makes no promises that will not be kept. The skeleton is truth; it is the judgment that no man can escape, and the devil and the dwarf are in charge of the bird of judgment. If (as the jailer pointed out to Jonatan and as the devil has assured both Jonatan and Askelad) to live is to sin, and yet the devil stands for the destruction of all things, evil not only becomes a part of the natural order of things in its workings through man but also becomes the very nature of things.

Evil becomes paradoxical: it is to build and to destroy; it is nature and it is culture; it is to live and it is to die; it is in charge of the bird of judgment and the bell of eternity. It is at odds with itself, but it is also the truth of man's condition. It cannot be overcome, for it seems to be the indistinguishable twin of goodness.

In the dwarf's creation of the bell of eternity one might suppose there to be a corrective parallel intended with regard to Jonatan's destruction of the church bell Gabriel in order to imprison evil. Jonatan had perhaps interrupted the larger process whereby judgment and eternity are served. In other words, the devil may be the "necessary evil" that gives the concepts of judgment and eternity meaning. Since, however, each man carries one of the devil's ilk within him, he aptly becomes the forger of his own fate. The amazing part of this parable must be the idea that evil is once more pictured as the bond servant of that operation whereby evil means may produce good results.

The scene of the tiny smith, shown by the devil to Jonatan and Askelad, may be a seductive illusion similar to those subsequent ones of the village and city that the devil would help them build. Jonatan forces the devil to show his destructiveness, and the vision turns to war, pestilence, and ruin; yet, Askelad's assertion — that, if one were always to fear a thing's misuse and eventual destruction, he could create nothing new — rings true. The book leaves the reader with the question of whether evil may serve some useful purpose or whether this idea is merely evil's ploy. Evil willingly seems to serve man's desires, but it is man's own weaknesses, in the form of self-righteousness or ambition, that make possible the consequences that lead to destructiveness.

While in jail awaiting trial, the smith has read the Old Testament. Although he is declared to be no Job, the passage has caused him much thought. If one is to draw any conclusions from the foregoing, brief examples of the acceptance of suffering (the Freeborn and the murderer by arson), he may have to see them in relationship to the suffering of Job. Evil serves no earthly purpose at all in the book of Job except that of suffering, for Job was ever faithful to his God; but in the case of lesser men, the suffering that evil inflicts may be the fire in which the steel of their faith is forged.[10] It seems that some are able to bear suffering better than prosperity and worldly joys. In the former situation it would appear that evil serves a good end, but this is perhaps owing purely to the mettle of the persons concerned, since others are destroyed by suffering (Margaret), and others, still, are nearly destroyed by a lack of it (the doctor). Evil surely serves the exaggeration of man's desires. If that desire is toward doing penance for wrongs and seeking God, evil must also serve that end. Its function is, perhaps, to bring down judgment on those desires.

Jonatan is transformed in the course of the story from a good-natured man, to a sorcerer's apprentice, to the sorcerer himself. Jonatan resembles those two nearly indistinguishable strangers, death and the devil. The breakdown in the moral climate of the village, which the stranger, the devil, accelerates by making available his wonderous goods that everyone comes to desire, is paralleled by Jonatan's activities for the welfare of others in the city. Although the smith accomplishes a number of good deeds along the way, it is also important to note that he has, directly or indirectly, caused three deaths, one case of raving madness, an unjust imprisonment, two cases of adultery, one case of abandonment, several thefts, innumerable acts of dishonesty on the part of others, and much civil strife. By the time Jonatan has accomplished his pilgrimage to the king's palace in behalf of temporal power, he has admirably carried on the devil's work. The smith has done so in an unintentional way, but at the devil's release to take charge once more, much has already been destroyed and the seeds of future destruction implanted. Askelad, who was unofficially under Jonatan's physical guardianship, now comes unredeemably under the spiritual sponsorship of the devil. Jonatan and the devil have coexisted as alter egos, but by the book's end Jonatan has lost his control over the devil, which was the same as the devil's control over him, and appears to be a man chastened and sobered. He has turned his back on sponsoring Askelad, who, for all his intelligence, has not been able to learn any lesson from the evil he has witnessed. Jonatan now becomes a guardian for the child left in his care by its mother before her suicide. Because of Jonatan's responsibility for the final tragedy that has befallen the child's parents, the care of the child has become his obligation. The child is a victim not only of Jonatan's interference in the lives of its parents, but also of the city, that representative of the modern age from which Jonatan rescues him.

There is one more force that has victimized the child, and that, indirectly, is the element of art. As the baby boy's sternly proud and artist-scorning grandfather and his painter father have both explained, art is an illness that sacrifices others on the altar of its own misprised genius, and art is without honor, for it will prostitute itself.[11] The soul of the artist is the sick, the weak, and the derelict.[12] As the poet Vilhelm has expressed it, he — like death — suffers from an illness from which the child must be protected. The poet explains his gift as that of having something great within him, which is perhaps not even his own. The rest of him amounts to nothing, but that "something" within him, which he also describes as his beloved city, as the wonderful and the terrible, as reckless aberration and blind will, is death. The book's author has earlier pointed out that poetry's muse takes wing in nature or in a concern with the passing of time and generations. Poetry is thus not only equated with the city but also seen as having its impetus in nature and in man's sense of transitoriness, death. Poetry partakes of the evil of all man's strivings. This evil becomes so paradoxical that it seems to be merely another name for the amoral.

Vilhelm admits that he has sold his knowledge about Jonatan to his enemies for the price of a poem. He foreshadows Askelad's contract with the devil, since Vilhelm has not attempted to find out to what use his knowledge would be put. He had not dared to spend the money on a gift for the child's mother, as he had planned, but he now gives the gift of his insight to the child's guardian. At sight of the child, the poet gains the strength to pronounce a judgment on the city with the only words that seem true there, poetry's words of destruction. Vilhelm admonishes Jonatan to take good care of the child, and to do so, Jonatan must turn his back on the kind of striving typified by modern man and the city. Jonatan brings the child back to the village. The village represents a simple age in which man may survive on simple virtues and with simple vices, even though life's dangers may be inherent there as well as in the city.

Thus ends "the unfortunate journey" to which the book's "editor" — and author — refers in his introduction. Life's riddles were not solved on that journey, but Jonatan was taught something about existence. He has realized that moral ambiguity rules it and that one often serves evil when he tries to serve goodness. This knowledge has not stopped him from operating with moral categories, and Jonatan's unfortunate journey can be seen as his *felix culpa* (his "fortunate fall" from innocence into a state of sin that makes redemption possible). In spite of all the dark insights he has gained, he remains morally committed.

The editor implies that it is this simple wisdom that exists in the old tales and the great works of past cultural tradition and that makes them wiser than modern reason.[13] It would seem that cultural tradition, not the sciences (whether political, sociological, economic, or mechanistic), must be modern man's refuge and support. The sciences seem unable to help man endure what he must, whereas that vital, if somewhat embellished, history in the fairy tale gives a magical and moral dimension to the journey of life. If one accepts the journey of life and the share of blame and punishment he has accrued upon it, he acquires a "fate" that is worth relating and, thus, immortality within the cultural tradition.

By allying himself with an age-old literary tradition, Hansen may have tried to escape modern art's amoral character, but he admits in the "Farewell to the Book" that the work has grave flaws. He declares that these flaws are the same as his own as its editor, and they cannot be concealed by striving, dreaming, or pretending. The book's worst fault is that, besides being just a story, it was supposed to treat something that was barely revealed to him and whose "severe shock waves" and "inexplicable hope" were not quite understood by him.[14]

If the subject to be treated was man's eternal struggle against evil, then surely the editor has represented the diversity of traditional responses as to the weapons with which to face it, as well as to the ambivalent nature of the evil that is being faced. Tradition — whose diversity is represented in the many tales about the smith — neither gives clear advice nor supports any one premise that might be found to be false. That is only an error that the individual author may commit by his editing. The editor of *Jonatan's Journey* has declared his premise in his choice of hero and that hero's fate: Jonatan belongs to, and is most at home in, the cultural tradition of a tiny village, where he is able to make his contribution through his good nature, his skill and hard work, his faith in God, and his hope for men.

It should be remembered that the editor has warned the readers that the book has the same flaws as he does. The author may be like the wise man in one of the poet Vilhelm's stories: when a mote got in his eye, he kept writing and, therefore, made a mistake in his book about life, a mistake that caused much suffering to those who believed it. It would be the perpetration of an illusion worthy of the devil himself.

With *Jonatan's Journey* Hansen's authorship was put on a course that was to be earnestly pursued ever afterward. Since the book contains a number of themes that are recurrent in Hansen's works, it seems pertinent to point them out.

In Hansen's choice of hero and that hero's ultimate fate in *Jonatan's Journey*, he seems to foreshadow his own conclusions in *Serpent and Bull* as to what constitutes an ideally rewarding life. The similarity of good and evil is explicitly handled in Hansen's most artistically experimental novel, *The Thornbush*. There, as in most of the works, sexual involvement becomes both the means to power and the frustration of its goals. Often Hansen's protagonists are — like Askelad — amoral. They are involved — like the devil — in the exercise of a personal control over others. The possession of some "magical power" (whether oratorical, pedagogic, or poetic) that enables one man to lead others and to mislead them; the assumption of guilt and penance for the way in which one has, or has not, carried out his responsibility for his neighbors; and the recognition of ambiguous motives for one's good actions — all are themes that recur in the "manuscript" of *Lucky Kristoffer* and the "diary" of *The Liar*. The portrayal of companions on a journey, the object of which is ostensibly to combat evil and to serve the good, changes from a partial fairy tale setting in *Jonatan's Journey* to that of the historic legend in *Lucky Kristoffer*.

CHAPTER 4

Lucky Kristoffer

IT is common to pair *Lucky Kristoffer (Lykkelige Kristoffer* [1945]) with *Jonatan's Journey,* and they do share similar features. Both depict a journey, and both give the author abundant opportunity to let his imagination roam about in the whimsical and the humorous. Although it is a hapless task to locate *Jonatan's Journey* in time and place, *Lucky Kristoffer* is firmly placed within a historical context, that of the Lutheran Reformation in Scandinavia early in the sixteenth century. In both works ideological discussions are interwoven with action-filled, colorful events, but at times the balance of these two elements is disturbed in *Jonatan's Journey,* whereas it is masterfully maintained in *Lucky Kristoffer.*

As the main characters travel through the strife-ridden countryside of what is now southern Sweden, they gradually become involved in the bloody and bewildering civil war of the Reformation years. The political situation is sorely confusing to them, and since the reader may share their confusion, a brief historical outline is warranted.

The union between the Scandinavian countries had been in shambles for decades. In the early 1520s a number of events occurred that were permanently to rend it asunder. The Danish king, Kristian II, with the help of pro-union forces among the Swedish nobility, seized Stockholm. He was proclaimed the hereditary king of the Swedish nation. The aftermath of this victory was one of the most notorious and blood-curdling events in the history of either country, for eighty-two of Kristian's leading opponents were tried, condemned to death, and beheaded.

Shortly after the so-called Stockholm Bloodbath, an insurrection took place in the province of Dalecarlia *(Dalarna)* under the leadership of young Gustav Eriksson Vasa. Aided by the wealthy merchants of the powerful German Hanseatic city of Lübeck, Gustav Vasa managed to beat back the Danish troops. In 1523 he was elected king of Sweden. At the same time the Danish nobility rebelled against Kristian II and offered the crown to his uncle, Duke Frederik, whose troops, under the command of Johan Rantzau, crushed the opposition. The last bastion to fall was, as it was to be again a decade later, stubborn Copenhagen, which now saw its king, Kristian II, flee into exile. Mediated by Lübeck, a peace agreement between Sweden and Denmark was finally reached in 1524. The Danes recognized Gustav Vasa's right to the Swedish throne, but in return Sweden had to allow the southern provinces of Skåne, Halland, and Blekinge to be subjected to Denmark's rule; thus, throughout the action of *Lucky Kristoffer*, the travelers are on Danish territory.

The forces of the Lutheran Reformation were making strong inroads into Scandinavia. Gustav Vasa and his more cautious Danish counterpart, Frederik I, both of whom wanted to see the wealth of the Catholic Church transferred to the Crown, helped undermine Rome's considerable power. Neither of the two monarchs officially denounced the Roman Church, but they allowed the Lutherans to gain much influence in both countries, and this caused a good deal of unrest. In 1531 Kristian II returned to reclaim Denmark and Norway. He was captured through deceit and imprisoned for the rest of his life. Many of his countrymen, notably the burghers and the farmers, still harbored the dream of seeing him as the ruler of the realm. The death of Frederik I in 1533 signaled the outbreak of new strife, since Frederik's son, Duke Kristian, was a declared Lutheran and *Rigsraadet* — a council consisting of a number of Catholic bishops and influential noblemen — would not agree to accept him as his father's successor. The election of the king was postponed by *Rigsraadet*, which ruled in his place. This was understandably unacceptable to the burghers, a class whose influence had been on the rise earlier in the century and especially under the reign of Kristian II.

Denmark was not allowed to settle matters internally, for both Lübeck and Sweden, in turn, decided to have their say as to the future of Denmark. At this time Lübeck was fearful of growing Dutch competition in waters it hitherto had dominated, and Lübeck's mayor, Jürgen Wullenwever, appealed to *Rigsraadet* to take action. He was however rebuffed. He then turned to the leading burghers in Copenhagen. A deal was made: *Rigsraadet* should be deposed; Lübeck should be assured control of the trade in the Baltic Sea; and Kristian II should once more be made the king of Denmark. The plan called for revolution, and although Lübeck felt no great love for Kristian II, it was understood that civil war would be possible only if the burghers and the farmers felt that they could restore their beloved, imprisoned monarch to the throne.

In June 1534 the Lübeckian army landed north of Copenhagen. Both Sealand and Skåne were taken by this invading army. In Jutland, however, the nobility finally agreed upon electing Frederik's son, Duke Kristian, to be king of Denmark as Kristian III. The war then became more violent. Various farmers' uprisings undertaken in the name of Kristian II were crushed through the aid of Johan Rantzau of Holstein, who moved northward with an army of German mercenaries. At this point the Swedes, too, decided to interfere in behalf of Kristian III. By 1535 the Lübeckian troops were pushed back on all fronts, and they were finally forced to make peace. Copenhagen kept up its resistance and endured a severe siege, until starvation finally forced its gates open to the forces of Kristian III. It is in this confusing war that the travelers of *Lucky Kristoffer* are caught and in which most of them lose their lives. The senselessness of war speaks from the novel's pages, and many scattered comments reveal that the struggle had taken on forms that rendered its many sacrifices meaningless.

Some thirty years later, as the chronicle *Lucky Kristoffer* was being written by cleric Martin, Denmark and Sweden were again at war. Kristian III's son, Frederik II, had entertained high hopes of reasserting the Danish claim to the Swedish throne, and in 1563 he declared war. Violence again ravaged the border regions. It proved however to be impossible to conquer Sweden, and in 1570 peace was once more attained.

One does not read much of *Lucky Kristoffer* before discovering that, as in *Jonatan's Journey*, some of the masterpieces of Western literary tradition loom behind it. The hero, young Kristoffer, bears a strong resemblance to Don Quixote. Kristoffer, like his literary predecessor, is accompanied by a more worldly-wise, but less gangly and less heroic, figure who has no trouble in recognizing the folly in the idealist's behavior. Kristoffer's Sancho Panza is a former cleric, the thirtyish Martin, who, three decades later, assigns himself the onerous task of putting their journey on paper. It is thus through Martin that the events are transmitted to posterity. This Martin is quite learned. He is a man with a taste for literature, and although — for the obvious reasons of his temporal precedence — he cannot compare Kristoffer to the Knight of the Sorrowful Countenance, Martin does occasionally equate their journey, from Skrokhult in Halland to Copenhagen, with those long, fateful voyages in Homer's epics. At one point, when death seems to be imminent, Martin reminds young Kristoffer, who longs to prove himself in battle, that the most beloved character of *The Illiad* is Hector, who died so prematurely for Troy. Later, when death finally comes to Kristoffer in Copenhagen, a deeply moved Martin likens besieged Copenhagen to that ancient, tragic city which heroically — and absurdly — met its destruction for a cause whose worthiness was questionable.

Martin himself is once likened to a Homeric character: he is called a sly Ulysses. There is much truth in this characterization, for on various, convenient occasions, the cleric seems to be a cunning manipulator who sees to it that the world turns his way. Literature is one of the means he employs, for it is he who has filled Kristoffer's head with stories of great heroes who valiantly fight and die for grand causes. Martin is employed as the tutor of the young Kristoffer, the hereditary master of the pitiful estate Skrokhult, deep in Halland's rain-drenched forests. When the story opens, Kristoffer feels "called" to become "a hero." He believes that St. George has appeared to him as a sign that he should journey forth to fight for justice. The cleric then declares that he will follow Kristoffer as his historiographer and later subtly averts the possibility of Kristoffer's changing his mind. By the beginning of summer Kristoffer has procured the proper equipment for a knight, and the two men finally set off toward the south, whence all the confusing rumors of war stem. They are accompanied by Mr. Paal, a crusty old warrior, the actual master of Skrokhult, and the young man's guardian. There is little love lost between Kristoffer and Paal. Paal cannot see the heroic in the awkward youth, and Kristoffer has declared his enmity to Paal, who once gravely insulted his father. In spite of their continuing feud, it is the rambunctious and coarse old-timer who oversees Kristoffer's training in swordsmanship.

The members of this unlikely group leave Skrokhult behind and ride out to meet their fourth companion, Father Mattias. This devout, but dauntless and practical, old Catholic has established a humble cloister for persecuted monks, a refuge far from the Protestant-traversed highways. The Lutherans, however, are suspicious of him, and he must now go south in order to respond to a complaint leveled against him.

As the men make their way southward, they ride mostly through lonely woods, for whenever they venture into inhabited areas, they run into trouble. After a skirmish with some jittery soldiers, the travelers are forced to stay at the manor of Vaabenhöj. This measure is supposedly taken for their own protection. They soon realize however that their protector, Mr. Ditmar, and the mistress of Vaabenhöj, Lady Lucia, are genuinely untrustworthy. When, in Ditmar's absence, they manage to flee, Lucia desires them to take her along. They are pursued and forced to fight for their lives, whereas Lucia quickly changes sides and rides away with her lover, Ditmar. Wounded, the travelers spend an uncomfortable night in the forest. The next day they seek refuge at a lonely farm, whose owner shamelessly empties their pockets for his minuscule services. When the men again set out, all but Paal are soon captured by a band of rabble that prefers robbery to the less gilded life of soldiery.

In the robbers' camp the travelers are made to endure a good deal of hardship, but their lot is eased a bit by a beautiful young girl who briefly speaks to them and by a scientist, Thygonius, with whom Mattias engages in discussions on the nature of existence. Egged on by the idealistic Kristoffer, Father Mattias one day disastrously decides to celebrate the mass, and the enraged mob tortures and hangs him. That very same night the sheriff's men attack the camp and carry the travelers away to Hälsingborg, where they are kept in a state of semicaptivity by the garrison's suspicious old warlord, Tyge Krabbe.

The travelers find that Anna, the young girl from the robbers' den, is languishing in a prison cell. They manage to free her, and she soon occupies all of Kristoffer's heart and a bit of the cleric's. Outside the walls of the city the war rages. Martin helps one of the contending parties to exert some influence on Krabbe, but Martin, Paal, and Kristoffer all still end in the stinking dungeon of the prison.

The three men finally escape and set out to cross the sound to Sealand. At this point Kristoffer and Paal settle their quarrel, and the young man joylessly reaps his revenge by killing Paal. Kristoffer proceeds alone, while Martin, who again prefers the lazy, idyllic life, stays with his old mentors in the cloister at Elsinore. They finally urge him to go to Copenhagen in order to warn their spiritual leader, Paulus Heliæ, that his life is in danger. Reluctantly, Martin enters Copenhagen, where he again meets both Anna, who has finally been reunited with her parents, and Kristoffer, who has become one of Copenhagen's defenders. Martin tries to mediate between the lovesick, awkward warrior and the rather experienced young girl, but time for such things is running out. Copenhagen is being slowly starved into submission by King Kristian's besieging troops. Kristoffer has fought valiantly, but without really finding the cause for which he has been searching. His meeting with Paulus Heliæ is decisive, for Kristoffer determines that, for this man, he would be willing to sacrifice his life. This he does: the enemy storms the city, and Kristoffer dies bravely in battle in front of the old Catholic's lodging. Here the narrative abruptly ends.

The chronicle of the journey is framed by the comments of the now aged Martin. Some thirty years after the events described, he sits in the besieged town of Varberg, which he has foolishly refused to leave. Since the town will fall, death is inevitable, but Martin's only fear is that he will not have time to complete his chronicle. He muses over the problems he has with his story, comments on the present war, and offers a few glimpses of the intervening years. Although he had married Anna, who has since cuckolded him, he has otherwise managed his affairs well and has established himself as a wealthy and influential merchant. In light of all this, it is curious that he has chosen to remain in Varberg and to devote his last days to chronicling the lives and deaths of people who have been long forgotten.

All the book's characters are indeed trapped by history in a situation so confusing that they can scarcely grasp it. Their plight is of course one that many later generations were also to experience, and it would be naive to read the book as a novel solely about the civil war that ravaged Denmark during the Reformation. The book treats a universal situation: the painful transition that occurs when old values are being threatened and new ideas, new ways of understanding existence, are becoming ascendant.

The loss of harmony caused by the destruction of old values is very much at the heart of *Lucky Kristoffer*. As the travelers approach their destiny, the reader experiences the turbulent transition from the ordered, medieval outlook to modern scientific thought, which seems ultimately to promise moral chaos. The dialogue in the robbers' camp between the captive Father Mattias and Master Thygonius is a clash between the old and the new outlook. Thygonius (a chillingly cold version of the likeable rationalist Askelad in *Jonatan's Journey*) advocates the Copernican view, which reduces God's heaven to a mere emptiness and man to a well-functioning machine, for whom all questions of good and evil are futile. The old monk, who is intrigued by debating and by the scientist's reasoning, never for a moment allows reason to bring doubt into his mind. He has lived and eventually dies for the old belief, which grants the human being meaning, even though his lot may be that of suffering. The strength of Father Mattias's belief may give him the semblance of a saint, but the old monk would clearly disavow such an appellation. He is no mystic who has been blessed with sacred moments of insight but, rather, a steadfast believer who has achieved serenity by being a practical servant of the Lord and by being a teacher and competent consoler of weaker souls. He shakes his head at Thygonius's teachings, for he knows what their dire effects will be: if Christianity is condemned as a lie, man will learn that he is a destitute, superfluous being on earth. Chaos will rule.[1]

The portrait of Father Mattias is lovingly drawn by the narrator, Martin, who may well realize that Thygonius makes sense and that the monk is the loser in their philosophical debate. Another figure whom the passing of time makes superfluous is Kristoffer, who in this bewildering age, when shining white knights are being relegated to tales, confusedly searches for a cause for which he may sacrifice himself. As Björnvig has astutely pointed out, the passing of the Middle Ages with its sense of order is represented in the fates of *the monk* and *the knight*, the two figures associated with the days before modern knowledge shattered the belief that earth was the center of a divinely ruled universe.[2] Both figures meet their deaths, and those who assume power over man's thinking are, in a sense, of lesser stature. Thinkers of Thygonius's ilk — the scientists, the materialists, as well as the politicians who deal in ideals without believing in them — may offer guidelines in life, but they cannot cope with moral issues and, thus, cannot ultimately offer man meaning in life.[3]

Although a sense of irretrievable loss permeates Martin's account, the waning of the Middle Ages is not rendered in an idyllic light. Scenes may be idyllic, but brutality, filth, and corruption are not underplayed. The dying figures of the religious and chivalric past are portrayed with much sympathy, but also with wry irony. Father Mattias may end his life as a martyr, but up to that point — much to his own regret and the readers' pleasure — he displays a good deal of human weakness; and Kristoffer, as idealistic and valiant as he is, may seem both humorless and intolerant. The spirit of romance, which Martin knowingly undercuts in his narrative, is also given a solid antidote in the figure of Mr. Paal, the superstitious, swearing, utterly obnoxious old warrior who has no use for either the religious or chivalric ideals of his traveling companions. He seems, rather, to harken back to older times, when man lived in a fearful, demonic universe that always had to be kept in check by magic. With the possible exception of Kristoffer's magnificent and colossal horse, Rufulus, Mr. Paal is the book's supreme comic creation.

Mattias, Kristoffer, and Paal all die by violence. Although Martin pays homage to the attitude with which they meet death, he does not idealize their final moments. They themselves would undoubtedly deem their deaths to be meaningful, but in Martin's eyes their demises are somewhat grandiose. Men like Mattias and Kristoffer do not merely die; they sacrifice themselves for a higher cause. It is nevertheless doubtful that their deaths are of any consequence. The victorious Lutheran Church will falsify the legend of Father Mattias and will ignore Kristoffer's death for Paulus Heliæ, which seems to be more a last desperate choice of a cause than the actual finding of one that would render Kristoffer's life and death meaningful. The usefulness of sacrifices is severely questioned, even though the spirit in which they are performed is not.[4]

In order to understand *Lucky Kristoffer*, it must be remembered that Hansen chose to let the story be narrated by the ironic, self-depreciatory Martin. Through this excellent choice of narrator, seriousness and humor are made to coexist in the work in such a delicate balance that neither cancels out the other. This choice makes it necessary however to probe into Martin's mind and motives, for it would be naive to believe that this manipulative, but pleasant, man is either entirely reliable in his recollections or straightforward in his recounting of the whole story. First and foremost, one may wonder why old Martin writes about his former traveling companions. It is only in answering this complex question that one gains a full comprehension of the novel.

Martin has always been a rational fellow, one who would not allow himself to be caught in difficult situations and who, if cornered, knew how to save his skin through small compromises and clever stratagems. He often became infuriated with his traveling companions' lack of common sense, and his very survival proved that reason rewarded its patron. Although he married the girl and secured wealth, he has nevertheless repeatedly admitted that he harbored a deeply irrational weakness for those "fools" who lived and died without reason. This sympathy may indeed have inspired him to write.

In order to pay reverence to those long dead, the old merchant objectifies himself as Martin, the cleric, and makes Kristoffer the hero of the account. The writing is not easy for Martin. His difficulty in coming to grips with the story may be indicative of his motives for chronicling the journey. As he writes, he confronts himself as he once was, and this may be a disturbing experience for him. In spite of the novel's title, Martin is unmistakably its protagonist. His writing of himself in the third person may also indicate that he sees himself as a man changed by the journey. He implies this by pointing out that he started the journey as *the cleric* but ended it as *the merchant*.

When the book opens, Martin is presented as a man who has flirted seriously with serving Christianity. He has been a novice in the cloister at Elsinore, has studied under Paulus Heliæ in Copenhagen, and has received a lowly degree. Although his superiors found him promising, this circumspect man cut his clerical career short and moved to the miserable Skrokhult. Here he lives a fairly easy, although monetarily unrewarding, life, which seems to suit him excellently. He undertakes

Kristoffer's education, occasionally beds one of the young man's aunts, does some sampling of plants for the medical book he is preparing, and idles about a good deal.

One may ask why this rather lazy man manipulates Kristoffer into embarking on a quest that is bound to cause severe inconveniences and dangerous situations. One answer lies of course in Martin's weakness for high, irrational idealism; but one must question the nature of this weakness. To his former superior, Abbot Mads, Martin admits that he has little taste for experiencing exciting events but takes great delight in recollecting them, and he adds that he envies those who can live life spontaneously.[5] Martin seems to be an observer who experiments with the lives of others. The fact that he now writes of the past intimates that, in Martin, one may glimpse the artist and the darker aspects of the artist's vocation.[6]

Martin is quite aware of his own shortcomings, and his narrative brings them out in several incidents. The night following the fight with Mr. Ditmar and his men is particularly revealing. As Kristoffer keeps watch, his companions lie under a tall spruce in the middle of the dark forest, and Martin allows his mind to roam about and to become one with the minds of others. He identifies with an animal of the forest, with literary characters, with Mr. Paal, and with Kristoffer, but Martin hurries to cut the last visit short, for he finds it altogether too chilling to be one with the young knight's pure, uncompromising, and vulnerable mind. This reaction alone is telling, but the fact that he does not even try to enter Father Mattias's mind is even more significant. This pure spirit of indubitable integrity is not Martin's ground; Mattias belongs in another realm, to which mixed and mixed-up minds have no access. The cleric and the old monk are subtly posed as opposites.

Although it would be unjust to make of Martin the devilish opposite of saintliness, he is nevertheless a man allied with that perverse instinct in man which wreaks havoc. Father Mattias is no manipulator; he is a leader who gives others the spiritual strength to endure hardships and to find consolation in them. He is overt in his influence on others, whereas Martin is exactly the opposite. Those who are to die and Martin who survives are thus juxtaposed, and through this implicit comparison, the survivor — the modern skeptical man — is judged. Martin and the coolly detached scientist Thygonius may not be all that dissimilar, but before one indicts Martin as a wholly cold-hearted manipulator, it is necessary to speak in his defense. At times he proves that he can rise to the occasion and, albeit grudgingly, act compassionately and unselfishly. He also sees much more in his traveling companions than mere objects to be coolly observed. He is not only fascinated by, but nearly in love with, the kind of idealism they embody. He cannot act as an uncompromising idealist would, but Martin can appreciate the attitude that governs such action. In his judgment calculating individuals like Thygonius fall far short of the grand fools. Behind Martin's well-preserved mask of rationality one finds a halfhearted and secretly stubborn idealist who displays his idealism in a rather backhanded way. At one point he declares that he might have functioned quite well within the Protestant Church,[7] but that, although he was willing to forsake much, he could not forsake everything and, accordingly, hid out at Skrokhult. Now, as death draws near, the old man decides, for the first time, that he shall not hide but shall act against his better judgment. Belatedly and perhaps futilely, he finally gives his hidden idealism free rein and allies himself with those fools who died so many years ago.

Martin never suspects Kristoffer or Mattias of duplicity, but he detects his own mixed motives and circumventions in many others. His suspicions seem to be particularly justified by the women whom the travelers encounter, and although he by no means scorns either the company or favors of these women, he does not trust them. As he wryly admits, both his unfaithful wife, Anna, and Lucia of Vaabenhöj amply prove their unreliability; nonetheless, he understands Kristoffer's adoration of the two women as elevated, pure beings. In recounting a dream, Martin reveals his own sexual idealism. He sees a beautiful young girl whose foot is caught and who vainly strives to free herself. She shyly looks away and cries as he comes up to her. He, too, sheds tears as he tenderly helps to free her. Although he is very aware of her physical beauty, she seems sacred to him. He has an urge to fall on his knees and to promise to protect her against brutish males — against himself. He looks down at himself and realizes that he is young and dressed as a novice. The girl smiles at him and gives him a piece of grass, which, at her touch, is transformed into a rose. As he is left standing there alone, he is filled with both happiness and longing.[8] Deep within him the older, experienced Martin still harbors that youthful dream of the pure woman, but she is only a dream, for all the women in Martin's narrative appear to be sensual, dangerous creatures of whom men ought to beware.

Such examples illustrate Martin's own strong touch of idealism, but being a man of common sense, he does not believe that one can understand or cope with the world in terms of idealism. Consequently, his perception of the world differs from that of Mattias and Kristoffer. They believe in, or search for, a moral order behind life's apparent confusion and emptiness, but Martin does not share their confidence and sometimes seems to have an attitude that is precariously close to the nihilistic. After the travelers have been captured by the robbers, Martin admits to Father Mattias that he is a pessimist, an avowal that brings a strong reproach from the old monk. Pessimists are the worst species of mankind, the old monk snaps back, for they poison the lives of others and ruin the joy of life. The idealist, hereby, indicts Martin for negating the idealistic side of his own nature.

As old Martin carefully composes his chronicle, he faithfully records not only this indictment but several others as well. It gradually becomes clear that, through this subtle and ironic confrontation, Martin indirectly passes judgment on himself. He does not wallow in self-accusations, but one realizes that this complicated man, who is ruled by inner tension, now strongly disapproves of his decision to leave the cleric behind for the merchant.

The reason for this change in Martin's vocation is stated very specifically. During the battle with Mr. Ditmar's men, the cleric's horse galloped away with the cherished notes for his medical book. This loss caused him to give up his spiritual pursuits for material ones. Later, with vehemence, he told Kristoffer that those notes were "honest," a description that indicated their unusual significance for Martin.[9] In order fully to understand the man, it is necessary to recognize what those notes meant to him.

While Martin lived at Skrokhult he wandered about in nature, picked various herbs, and experimented with them. Martin took this job seriously. If one listens carefully to his discourses, one realizes that he was deeply fascinated with nature and was intent on luring its secrets from it. What he found there was an inherent duality, which was at odds with the Christian view of nature. To the pious, God's nature encompassed no evil; to Martin, nature bore a Janus head: on the one hand, it produced insanity, filth, and contamination; and on the other, it effected cures.[10] Martin effectively used that knowledge not only to heal, but also to concoct poisonous brews. It is tempting to suggest that the cleric found his own duality mirrored in nature; he, indeed, seems to be a man with the dual outlook of a Janus.

Martin has always known that an identification of the self with nature is dangerous and that the distance between nature and man must be maintained. He emphatically stresses that a human being's becoming one with the wilderness reduces him to an animal. This animal does not possess the noble qualities that ancient mythology ascribed to the spirits of nature. "The closer man gets to nature, the more unnatural he becomes,"[11] Martin states bluntly. On other occasions he gives nature the epithets of evil and of female; thus, it is clear that a good share of Martin's fascination with nature is apprehension. His fascination with nature nevertheless makes him sensitive to its beauty, and he, the ironicist, never becomes more lyrical, nor less deliberative, than when he describes his sensuously intoxicating rambles in nature. At times he expresses a deep sadness over man's necessary separation from nature.[12] Man is a cultural being, and like Father Mattias who was trying to build his little cloister in the midst of the wilderness, man must tame nature. Martin's contribution to this cultural activity was to be his medical project, for with such knowledge as it would contain, nature could be somewhat controlled and be made to serve mankind.

It was that work which gave Martin's seemingly erratic life some sense of direction. It saved him from feeling the world to be total chaos, but he would hardly have been himself if he had not doubted the validity of his endeavor. That nagging doubt, that even "for . . . Wisdom nature dissolves into chaos,"[13] explains his halfheartedness where his project was concerned.

When the notes were irretrievably lost, Martin gave up his cultural striving for good. Ironically, from this time on, things went very well for him, and he became a successful merchant. The consequences, however, were that he experienced the feeling of emptiness and superfluousness that Father Mattias had predicted would be humanity's lot if the thinking of the Thygoniuses of this world were to conquer the old beliefs. It is evident that Martin did not become a man lost in despair. As usual, he managed his life quite well, but his materialism, one of nihilism's many facets, made a lesser man of the former backhanded idealist.

Martin's choosing to become a merchant changed his relationship to nature, for at that moment, he gave up his attempt to control it and allowed its darker aspect to gain the upper hand. He who had confronted the Janus head of nature has eventually hidden in fear from it. He himself has admitted this; he states that, after being saved from the robbers, "never again did [the cleric] dare to go into the forests."[14] One result of his choice is that he has inherited fear, a fear that his nihilism naturally cannot overcome.

When Martin gave up his cultural "mission," he entered the modern world. Culture, which must be understood as a form of existence that grants meaning to the individual, was left behind for a civilization that, as Father Mattias had predicted, was destitute and purposeless. Martin may have feared that nature had become totally demonic, but he has found himself in a civilization that, in its nihilism, is similarly demonic. In view of this one understands why Martin so feverishly writes about a past in which such nihilism was kept in check, not only by his traveling companions but also — to some small degree — by himself. His chronicle of their journey becomes an attempt to achieve a form of personal redemption.

Although nature and culture seem to be posed as opposites, both seem to bear a Janus head. Nature is simultaneously hostile and benevolent to man, and so is culture, since man's striving for insight can either give or deny meaning to the individual. To be precise, the man who excludes either nature or culture from his life is bound to be lost in a world that is without values; he is an unnatural man in an unnatural world. It is this lesson that old Martin has learned from his life. It is thus understandable that Martin reaches back in time toward those people who were guided by a set of fixed values and were therefore capable of striking a balance between nature and culture and of making their lives and deaths meaningful. Nature and culture may be posed as opposites, but it would be more correct to make culture, which is exemplified by those who try to control nature, the ideal middle ground between the wilderness and nihilistic civilization.

This balance is one that Martin once precariously maintained but then lost. His having faltered is not surprising, for his tightrope act was never very safe. Skeptics are always in danger of stumbling, for they seem to be either too fascinated with the dangerous aspects of nature or too engrossed with the nihilistic sides of culture. Since both attractions cancel a sense of values, Martin has doomed himself to stare into chaos. It is this sense of chaos — which takes on a very concrete form as Varberg is being besieged — that old Martin is trying to combat through his narrative. In fact, through recalling the past, old Martin has made a choice by which he again becomes the cleric and by which his fear of nature once more becomes a fascination with its duality. By following Paulus Heliæ's dictum, that the man who cannot put a plow in the ground must serve culture by setting a pen to paper, Martin once again engages in a cultural activity.

Martin's narrative of the journey has many motivations: a sheer enjoyment in recalling the past, a paying of homage to friends and their ideals, a self-confrontation of a confessional nature, and a desperate, personal quest for redemption. As he writes, his sense of loss grows; insistently, he tries to bridge the lapse in time between the then and now, so that his death may bear at least some resemblance to those of his traveling companions. They themselves felt they died meaningfully, and only by Martin's gaining the same feeling may he hope to redeem his wasted life.

As the old man began to write, he surrounded himself with what he apologetically called his trinity: violets, the Virgin Mary, and aquavit. The symbols — the first two of which refer, respectively, to nature and culture and the third of which refers to the heartening, but poisonous, liquid to which he was first introduced by Thygonius in the robbers' den — all tie Martin to the past and sustain him as he grapples with his story. They help him and force him to understand the past and himself correctly, but they also signal the fact that judgment is at hand. Very close to the end, when the town is literally burning around him, Martin feels that the Virgin Mary, to whom once he had denied his service, is letting the fragrance of violets completely engulf him. This seems ominous, since it may suggest that his attempt to gain redemption is doomed to dwindle into the nothingness of nature. Just before his death, both his symbols and his sense of humor and irony abandon him. He is alone and destitute, and he is afraid; although he does not fear death, he fears that his renewed cultural activity, the writing of the chronicle — his belated struggle against nature and nihilism — will not be preserved. He states that, if his story is destroyed, he will be burning in his own hell.[15]

It may seem reassuring that the nature of Martin's fear has changed. He is no longer possessed by the fears of the nihilist, but by those of cultural man; but whether or not he is to be granted the redemption he so fervently desires is up to his readers. It is the reader of the chronicle — the reader of *Lucky Kristoffer* — who passes final judgment on the artist and decides whether his life has been meaningful or utterly futile. A book must be read and understood: it must serve culture; otherwise, the artist has no justification whatsoever for his life and work.

CHAPTER 5

The Thornbush

I *Introduction*

THE Thornbush (Tornebusken [1946]) consists of three long, thematically related stories: "The Easter Bell" ("Paaskeklokken"), "The Midsummer Festival" ("Midsommerfesten"), and "September Fog" ("Septembertaagen"). The first of these stories, like Hansen's first two novels, takes place in a farming community and treats a struggle between opposed personal values, but the story's frame of reference is one of religious symbolism rather than of ideological dogma. The second story, like *Jonatan's Journey*, presents an intermixture of the magical and commonplace and focuses on the ambiguity of evil. The third story, like *Lucky Kristoffer*, deals with the confusion in values of men who are about to engage in war. In all these stories the problems of good and evil and of art and the artist's role figure prominently.

With the three stories of *The Thornbush* Hansen returns to the modern scene. Although "The Easter Bell" may superficially seem realistic, the other two stories show Hansen to be experimenting radically with fictional form. He uses form as an instrument for obtaining perception and, thus, for superimposing order upon the complexity of modern existence. *The Thornbush* is in fact one of the most important examples of early Modernistic Danish prose, and it therefore deserves detailed treatment.

II *"The Easter Bell"*

The story of "The Easter Bell" begins with the ringing of a church bell. The sound carries with it an idealistic promise that stirs the minds of various characters into sympathetic vibration. Many of these people are preparing for church, and two of them on a nearby farm are preparing for a mutual seduction. During the service the seduction is accomplished, but the relationship is forever terminated by the escape of a bull that takes the life of the young man. That morning's events bring about a culmination of the desires of some people and a turning point in the lives of others.

The reader is introduced by the author to the area and weather, and then, by the ringing of the church bell, to the other characters. Born on that wave of sound, the reader is carried to the characters, ushered into their minds, and made witness to their hidden and most heartfelt desires. One of these characters is a miserly, corpselike old man whose life is supported by his love of his bank book and his suspicions of his progeny, who live at Linde Farm and who — he feels — do not respect his wealth enough to make really serious plots against his life. A second character is a Mr. Nielsen, an irritable teacher who nervously wishes to blame his wife for every mischance of wind and weather. His general feeling of frustration is deeply rooted in the loss of his gift of a beautiful singing voice and is expressed in pedantry. His wife is tired of striving to be more than the milkmaid she once was and is happy simply to elude and forget her husband's implied accusations and criticisms. A young teacher, the Marxist Per, enjoys waiting on his pregnant wife and looks forward to playing the church organ at a tempo too fast for Mr. Nielsen's singing. Per's wife, Grethe, reluctantly remembers and longs for a lost love named Villi, but she also longs to grow to love her husband fully. The bell is sounded by the sexton, saddler Olsen, who takes an artist's pride in his ringing but who is seriously ill and fearful of losing his position. He is watched by Johansen, the churchwarden, who is a mason by profession and a socialist by persuasion. Johansen takes pride in honorably carrying out his apparently inconsistent duty of caring for the church and of working toward a day when religion will be dead in the hearts of the people. The sound of the bell also affects the occupants of Linde Farm, the heirs of the dying miser. Marie, his daughter, is a woman with an iron will and deep bitterness, especially toward her husband, Kristian, whose lack of strength of will disgusts her. Ingrid, their loose-living daughter, is attracted to the foreman Johan. He is an ambitious man who means to take the first step toward gaining power and position by taking Ingrid to wife and her parents' farm in possession.

The ringing of the bell seems to awaken in the characters some sort of echo, either a longing for a purity they felt in the past or an intensification of a wish to be truthful toward themselves and others in the future. The sound brings a self-awareness to those who have somehow inhibited their true desires. This is quite evident in the cases of Marie and Grethe. Marie has ruthlessly shaped her life and denied the beauty of the childhood innocence and delighted wonder that once was hers. She

The Thornbush

is said to be a woman who will not give way to emotion, but one who wishes to do only that. She had carefully chosen Kristian as her husband, for in her pride she had feared having a man as strong as herself. Twenty years ago, when she found Kristian to be lacking in manhood, in wilfulness and sexual desire, she rejected him once and for all. She looks forward to her own growing ugliness as a revenge upon her sexual feelings, which she considers to be a weakness. In the foreman Johan she sees the strength and will, the calculation, ambition, and selfishness that attract her, and she desires him . . . for her daughter.

Grethe realizes that, unless she can truly love her husband and meaningfully serve her family and community, she may suffer the fate of Mrs. Nielsen or, it seems implied, that of Marie. Grethe feels that only through an understanding of the suffering of others can she learn to love her husband, to have him become that which matters in her life. Grethe meets Johan on her way to church and momentarily loves him because she recognizes something harmful and dark in his eyes, something within him against which her presence might help him. The news of Johan's death causes a similar expression to appear in Per's eyes: his glance, one of wonder and searching, reveals a loneliness that moves his wife to love him.

Grethe, in her honesty and youth, seems to be someone through whom several of the others are able to acknowledge their conflicts. Just as Johan and Per can mutely communicate their loneliness to Grethe, so Mrs. Nielsen is able to voice her marital frustration to her. Even Johansen, a man who always bears his personal conflicts silently, feels he can tell Grethe about them. At the ringing of the bell the atheist Johansen has seen the spirit of his dead son playing in the graveyard, and the man has confided this to her. The appearance of the son's ghost has driven Johansen, like an outlaw without sanctuary, even into the church. He has not been able to remain there, but he has finally been able to speak of his son to someone else.

Both Johan and Johansen have sprung from the poor and have some feeling of sympathy for the social advancement of the poor. Each is a strong man and a lonely man, and each is somewhat shunned by his fellows, who feel that his actions in helping others are suspect, for each protects and works for that which he would conquer. In Johansen's case this is the church and, thus, religion in general, and in Johan's it is the social class of his employers.

Johan, who is about to win both Ingrid and Linde Farm and who, moved by the sound of the bell, constantly asks himself whether Ingrid is good enough for him, accidentally meets Grethe and feels that she would have been the right woman for him but that it is too late to realize such a dream. In this decision he resembles Marie, who could perhaps have married Johansen but who chose the weaker Kristian in order to achieve position and power. Ingrid knows that she is but a step on Johan's climb to power and that it is not she herself, but the help she can provide, that matters to Johan. She realizes that she is no longer the sort of woman he aspires to and only wishes he had come into her life earlier.

Just before Johan's meeting with Grethe, he had seen something shining like a star in the road's gravel. After he had spoken to her, he picked it up and found that it was only a piece of glass, but he kept it anyway. It is symbolic of both his personal and marital aspirations. Johan, with his self-assurance, ambition, hard determination, and peculiar isolation, seems to draw women to him. He plans however to command men and to have a solid footing in life; but his goal, the mystery within him, is to have a lot to risk when the unknown, but real, gamble of life begins. That game of chance comes sooner than expected, and it is fully satisfying to Johan, for his wager is not only Ingrid and the farm but also his dreams and very life against a raging bull.

While the drama of the Easter service, which speaks of death and resurrection, is taking place within the church, the drama of Johan and the bull takes place on the farm nearby. Johan, like the Easter Lamb, faces death in behalf of others, but Johan seems to do so primarily in order to overcome it personally, and although fatally gored, he believes he cannot die.

Just as the minister plays a role in church and stages a drama in which he is a substitute for both the believer and the unseen presence of God, so the melodramatic farmhand Börge sets the drama of Johan's death in motion. Börge bitterly and jealously enacts the part of sacrificing himself (because of Johan's success with Ingrid) by trying to handle the bull alone. Börge plays the part both of his own spectator and of another unseen presence that Ingrid has sensed at the farm. The unseen presence in the church seems to promise life, whereas that at the farm promises death. Johan's death is brought about not only through his attempt to protect Börge, the returning congregation, and Ingrid, but also in an attempt to cleanse himself of doubt in a ritual battle. The game of life becomes, through the bull fight, a drama of death in which Johan dances out to meet the agent of his destruction. That drama ends in physical misfortune for Johan, who — like Mr. Nielsen, the sexton, Börge, and the minister — is representative of the artist. Although Johan himself may exhibit limitations, his art — his death — opens the way to catharsis and rebirth for others.

The Thornbush

At Johan's death a rejuvenated Kristian feels that he has received his farm and his daughter back again. Marie's iron-hard control breaks. She feels the peace of deep sorrow and can cry like a child. Marie seems to be reborn to suffering. A stunned Ingrid, who was willing to love Johan unrequitedly — an act likened to lying naked on ice and trying to transform it with her love — now calls herself his widow. She receives the only thing Johan has had to bequeath her: a sharp piece of glass. It may now be a sign of her own maturity of vision.

Johan wanted to have high stakes to risk in a final gamble, but the assurance of material attainments was already meaningless to him, and he longed to take part in a war. His concern was with himself and the role he could play in the world, a role that recognized no permanent bonds. He met the bull gladly in combat as his true partner and fate, and as he lay dying, he saw only himself — as a wild, young, rising bird.

Johan's isolation from others and the community of human spiritual needs suggests one more symbolic parallel with Johansen. Johansen respects the church not only because it is the work of the hands of dedicated men, but also because it is the place through which all dead must pass. He does not attend the services but cares for the church and the graveyard. Johan and Johansen shared a respect for death, for it could never be legislated against or planned for but would always be present. This belief in death's power (like Johan's belief in himself) is the opposite of that of the spirit of the church. To embrace its grounds, but not its spirit, might seem inimical to the believers, and it is reminiscent of the legend Hansen was later to treat in a book named for it: *Serpent and Bull*. In the legend a serpent prevents the congregation from attending the church, the source of spiritual renewal. A bull is raised that kills the serpent and frees the church. The association seems strengthened by the name of the farm's being "Lindegaarden," which to the Danish ear could be suggestive of a snake pit.[1] Marie who had usurped control of the farm resembles a pagan priestess, and her father, the old miser, resembles a dragon that guards his treasures and that was pierced by the ringing of the bell as by a spear. Johan, the farm's heir-to-be, was said to duck from the sound as from a blow.

Johan's fate may parallel that of the sacrifice of the Easter Lamb, but that parallel ceases with Johan's death, for it is his very death that, like the serpent's, opens the way to the spiritual renewal. Contrary to what was to have taken place, the drama of death and rebirth has unfolded at the farm through the death of Johan and the rebirth of Marie, whereas that of love has occurred at the church between Grethe and Per.

Johan's actions must be understood on two levels of meaning: the symbolic and the physical. On the latter level his actions seem indeed praiseworthy. As Johan daringly played matador to the bull's rage, Ingrid voiced the secret desire of all who admired the self-contained Johan: "If only it were me."[2] If, however, one is to judge the symbolic meaning of the scene, one might use the minister's criterium of performance: when other people are aware of the poetic in one's actions, those actions are false and lack God's reality, God's poetry, which is truth.

III "*The Midsummer Festival*" — The Author and the Reader's Story

This novella is structurally Hansen's most cryptic and complicated work. In order to investigate it one must distinguish between three levels of fiction: there is an author who is writing a story; there is an author who is writing a story with the help of an imagined woman reader; and there is the story that they write and whose characters reflect the author and the woman reader. The time levels are also varied: the unnamed author is writing his story during World War II; the reader is reading the story after that war; and the story itself takes place before the war.

The story the author and the woman reader have written occurs on the day of St. John's Feast and starts with two women, the twenty-two year old Klara and the thirty-four year old Alma, who are on their way to a town festival. Alma's bicycle has a flat tire, and when a young man named Georg stops to help fix it, Klara is as affected by him as though she had been physically seduced. Georg sends the two women to an old farm for water. There, they feel that they leave the reality of this muggy day behind them and enter an almost enchanted world. Refreshed, the women return with the water, only to find that Georg has gone. He who has telepathically sensed his dying grandfather's need of him hurries to the old man's bedside. Georg believes that there is something his grandfather wishes him to do. The dying man, bothered by the music of the festival, merely has Georg close a window and then sends him off to the festivities. Georg leaves believing that his grandfather still wants him to do something.

In the description of the festival scenes swiftly change. If the merrymakers Klara and Alma and their dates, Holger and Klaus, are realistically treated, those about them are not. The curious fact is that nearly all the men are named Georg and are connected with the entertainment. The Georg who helped the women, the protagonist, seems to bear some kinship to all these men, but he is particularly interested in

The Thornbush

talking to one of them, a seriously injured Negro boxer who is a pacifist and loves flowers and whom Georg encourages to fight far beyond his physical endurance.

After watching the boxing matches, Georg goes again to visit his grandfather. This time, when leaving, Georg takes with him his inheritance, his grandfather's pocket watch. It is dusk, and suddenly shy of people and light, George tries to hide in back alleys and backyards. When he can no longer escape, he calls on the name of his grandfather and grows so small that he is able to squeeze through the grate of an air duct. Soon afterward he flies out to a tree near the sea. Here he catches a rook that can talk to him and puts it inside his jacket and brings it with him back to the festival.

The two couples, now sitting at a table in the festival's gala ballroom, are thoroughly miserable. Alma and Klara are irritated with each other and the men. Holger is jealous, for he believes that Klara is interested in Klaus, who, in turn, sits studying the bodies of the women around him. The four decide to go to the open-air dancing pavillion, and there Klara sees Georg. They dance; she tells him she wants to give herself to him, and he rejects her. She runs out into the woods, with Holger running after her. After some time the two are united as lovers, while a nightingale in a thornbush sings their wedding song.

Georg invites Alma and Klaus out into the woods to look for flowers, but Klaus speaks disparagingly of Georg's family and leaves. As Georg and Alma sit on Blood Hill, a place touched either by God or Satan in ages past, Georg tells her about his family, for he hopes that she will be able to help him understand his dying grandfather's wish. Georg first tells her about his father, who was innocent of crime but was accused, imprisoned, and finally convinced of his guilt. He thus flouted justice and became a criminal with regard to the law. Georg and Alma talk of minor and major crimes and the mystery of suffering. He distinguishes between two kinds of "sacred crime": the destruction of oneself for others and the destruction of others for one's own sake.[3] The greatest perpetrators of these crimes are Christ and Satan, who are as alike as twins. Georg divines that Alma is about to commit the sacred crime of suicide, and he declares himself to be a criminal, not only because he has been a writer — which is being a thief — but also because he has conducted minor experiments in the causing of suffering to others. He points out that he has already made the Negro and Klara suffer. Georg now begins to question Alma about the husband and children she has forsaken. Georg, who is looking for an omen of his grandfather's death either in the pocket watch's stopping or in his feeling free to rape Alma, suddenly begins to count the seconds between the lightning flashes and the thunder claps of an approaching storm.

Alma is beside herself from the tension growing between herself and Georg. Georg accuses her of no longer being ready for suicide, but of loving him instead. She admits that what he says is true and that she is suffering as though being reborn. Georg declares that in their life together he will make her suffer in every way he can. Alma then astounds him: she says that she intends to return to her family and, thereby, to help him against himself.

Discovering that his grandfather's watch has stopped — the supposed signal of the old man's death and Georg's spiritual doom[4] — Georg throws it into the sea. He then admits that he has cared nothing about Alma and that he can no longer hurt her but that he cannot bear that she has found out. He wishes for war and says that he can call forth war. He declares that there is one old and powerful being that never dies but vainly seeks the miracle of his own salvation in the endless suffering of others. That being — Satan — can use a man like Georg. Alma declares that she will always believe in Georg and will continually call for "the other,"[5] Satan's antithesis; thus, the good can never totally die out in Georg. This seems to be the miracle of salvation that Georg himself might need: the persecuted's forgiveness of the persecutor. He leaves, and as she leans crying against a tree in the rain, she hears him shouting that he understands.

Before turning to the coauthorship between the author and his female reader, which takes place during Georg's wished for war, the perceptions that the protagonist himself calls forth must be more closely scrutinized, for the writers of the tale suggest that Georg reflects the author.

Georg is described primarily through his effect upon others. Georg's glance causes people a disquiet and uncertainty that totters between love and fear. He causes them to view the world and themselves in a revealing and often degrading light. The clearest example of this is Klara, who perceives that she has posed alluringly before him and is ashamed of it. When she sees Georg for the first time, she is emotionally seduced, and that fact affects her view of life and herself. She feels an icy dread and senses the cold incomprehensibility of life. Its beauty and promise, like poppy blossoms, seem to become poisonous and stupefacient in fruition. Beyond the flower of life's promise lies its consummation, a sexually described, but terrifying, existential void. It bores into her, demands that she fill it, and sucks her toward extinction.

She then experiences a moment of intense sweetness in the recognition of her own womanhood and the knowledge she has gained; like the not yet finally matured promise of life itself, she has become a "full flowering fate."[6] The fruits of maturity still await her, but her body already seems awake, larger, heavier.

To realize that one has a fate is perhaps a sweetly satisfying experience that seemingly reasserts life's promise, but the end result of that fate may still be a terrifying desolation. Klara's experience has endowed her with certain attributes, and these are exaggerated in Alma. Alma is described as being, psychologically, a thousand years old and naked. Her ancient soul lies disgustedly within her lazy body, which sleepily enjoys the stranger Georg's nearness. Alma wishes weakly and indolently that she were only summer air, which might "be driven out above a lake . . . out into cool nothingness, or that she were hay, flowers, a little fly . . . [something] satisfied with being what it was."[7] The more mature and lethargic Alma is almost ready to acquiesce to the attraction of that annihilating emptiness which Klara is just mature enough to sense. Alma's wish to be something satisfied with itself, like a fly, is ironic, for a subsequent scene deals with a dungheap and its flies. The scene is described in erotic terms, whose somnolence is suggestive of Alma herself.

The sunlight is oppressive, and as Klara and Alma approach the dungheap, its rank odor seems humiliatingly personal, but pleasurably sensuous. The dungheap is described as a lazy, sensual dream blanketing a wild, nerve-quivering desire. It is indicative of an aroused subconscious that spasmodically jerks beneath a drug-induced slothfulness, and the drug seems to be the fruition of nature. Some of the intoxicated insects near the dungheap are dying from excessive abundance, whereas others are seemingly seeking to be consumed. Like the festival itself, the dungheap is described erotically and orgiastically.[8]

The insects spasmodically swarm without reason. Their movements are a dancing out of their insatiable desire to revolt against their insignificance. The insects seem to draw lines in the air in an attempt to form an all-important picture or pattern. The subject of the picture, which has never been completed, appeared before time itself. The perfect picture would be the "liberated cosmic thought [that] could change the world,"[9] but the cosmic mystery that the insects would picture is itself all-changing and is bound to their every movement and hidden within their desire.

The movements of the insects seem to represent the creative impulse, whether it takes the form of sex, art, or civilization. The impulse to change tries to express itself in "thoughts" of cosmic significance, but the impulse arises from nature and is limited by nature, which transforms everything. Nature, then, governs the world and the creative impulse. Since nature transforms everything, it can never be properly or finally pictured, and the thoughts of limited beings can never be liberated to change the world.

The life of the farmyard is contrasted with that of the dungheap. The women feel as if an invisible watchman has motioned them into the farmyard. Everything there is deteriorating and, if judged by outer appearance alone, would seem unpleasant enough to be lying in wait for the enactment of some crime. That crime is merely the emotional seduction of the women into appreciating the spirit of the farm.[10] In this farmyard they feel doom's greatness, beauty, peace, and divine promise. The farm seems to be a dying spirit in bloom. Time, thoughts, and the heart are different here from those of the world outside, and the actions of the flies suggest that even they have a sensible mission. The farmyard has one all pervasive scent: that of cool, refreshing water.

There can be said to be four occupants of the farm: a tipsy and fragile old water pump; an aged, irritable watchdog; a sleeping and work-worn old woman; and a fatally ill old man. Although the man must struggle with the angel of death in his sleep, he is mild and calm, and his calm causes Alma and Klara to bloom and to be considerate and innocently childlike.

The two women have been sent to the farm for water, and the water pump is almost the spirit of the farm. In time past it both refreshed and healed. The old man tells the women that his grandmother gave her energy and life to find this water. Now he, her grandson, is also quite ill, but he talks cajolingly to the pump and tenderly works it for the benefit of the two women. The pump seems to represent the spirit of self-sacrifice that refreshes the spirits of others and that eases or heals their suffering. Its spirit is also that of the farm and of the past generations who have lived there, as well as that of the old man and woman who now so unselfishly seek to help each other.

The spirit of this past culture is nearly dead, but its peace, gained through an acceptance of fate and a suffering for the good of others, is in sharp contrast to that death sensed through the eroticism awakened in Klara by Georg. Alma's latent desire for extinction is given impetus by the goodness of this soothing experience at the dying farm. It is the peace inherent to the death of self-desire — and not yet the painful

The Thornbush

hope intrinsic to selflessness in love — that appeals to her. Georg has provided Alma with the means to an insight into the acceptance of suffering; he had told Alma that it would be good for her to accompany Klara to the farm, just as he was later to tell her that it would be good for her both to watch the injured black boxer fight on and on for the sake of his family and to help Georg himself understand his dying grandfather's unexpressed wish.

Georg's grandfather, who at times seems to Georg to be but a voice shrouded in mountain mist, has Godlike powers, but he is dying. Georg's magical powers, which are partially dependent upon, and limited by, his grandfather, assume an ominous significance. When Georg flies about in the dark, he is suggestive of a demonic spirit, a vampire, or a bird of prey. He brings a sense of death with him to the people he meets and has a tangential relationship to those people and places that bear death within them: his grandfather, some of the carnival side show keepers, the Negro boxer, and the farm. Georg is intuitively attracted by both death and suffering. He may enter other people like a possessing spirit, but he cannot understand those who — like the sick Negro or Alma — are strong enough to suffer for others. Georg may affect changes in other people, but he cannot himself change. It is evident that his insight is limited and that he resents this limitation. Georg is intent upon understanding everything, but to do so he must take everything apart to study it. He admits that reason and reflection have led him nowhere and that, against his inclinations, he has had to go beyond reason and approach symbol and mystery. Georg is attracted to Alma not only because she wishes for death, but also because he can use her to understand the mystery of suffering.

Georg relates suffering only to crime. This assumption of the interrelatedness of the two concepts implies that Georg recognizes but one act, the criminal, and sees suffering either as the result of crime or as its punishment. The fact is that in a world where all that one has had to believe in is dead or dying — from Pan, to grandfatherly gods, to the spirit of past culture — suffering may seem meaningless. Georg has said that to accept guilt and suffering when one is innocent is to destroy the spirit of the law. He who does so, like Georg's father, would bequeath to others either a lawless world or a world bereft of "human" moral values. Alma who contemplates suicide and Georg who contemplates crime may seem to be inheritors of this nihilistic view. Although Georg may insist that the division between good and evil is arbitrary and that Christ and Satan are as alike as twins, his concern with "the criminal" and his evocation of these figures imply that his attitude transcends the nihilistic. The concept of the criminal testifies to the existence of the law. Both Satan and Christ are said to commit acts of a sacrificial nature, sacred crimes, and in suffering to seek the redemption of the self or of others from suffering.

To seek redemption is to try to subscribe to meaning in an otherwise amoral world governed by a suffering that serves no understandable purpose. The attempt to impose meaning on the world is artistic, and since Georg has equated the criminal with the beautiful, the artistic becomes both the means to crime and the sacred crime itself. The artistic either may nihilistically eliminate the distinction between good and evil or may indirectly try to reestablish that distinction. Georg has declared that one should most fear that which calls most strongly to one's feelings. For the swarming, striving inhabitants of the dungheap — like those of modern civilization — it is the cosmic mystery of purposelessness that calls most strongly to their feelings and that even dictates their efforts to impose on it an artistic form. Whether the cosmic mystery is called purposelessness, desolation, or suffering, it seems to be in the nature of things and to call forth a creative reaction to subject it to a design and, thus, the imposition of meaning.

Georg's many postulates are perhaps indicative of his own blind longing to understand the mystery and to change either himself or the world. When he can no longer hope to change himself or to retain Alma as his victim, he decides to serve Satan, who is eternally doomed in his striving for redemption. Georg thus implies that he knows such striving to be in vain, but that he longs for a redemption from his plight. The Christlike spirit that prevails in the farmyard is that which Alma finally assumes: through self-denial she shall express her love for Georg and give him new hope. This act is one that limits his power to pain her and thus limits his power to do evil. Her love for Georg has given her the will to live, and her concern for him has given her the strength of self-denial. Suffering gives Alma life, and it is a gift she shall try to return to the demonic Georg. It would seem that to live is to suffer, for it is the instrument of that traditionally called good and of that called evil, both of which seem to be indistinguishable from the cosmic law that dictates one's fate. What Georg finally may understand is that to accept suffering in behalf of another is to succeed in imposing a meaning on life.

IV *"The Midsummer Festival"* — *the Author and the Reader*

The author has started to write a story, but he finds himself frustrated by a lack of knowledge about ordinary things. The picture of an old woman, now long dead, pities him for sitting up so late to write Christmas cards. An authoritative voice, whom the author calls a critic (and who might be called a conscience), accuses the author of wasting his time in vanity during this critical period of war, which demands something far more. The author defends himself, and a voice, that of "the sick God," reminds him that no one has asked him or is forcing him to do anything and that he can wait. The author wants to continue now because he would rather not. This division in the author's desires is reflected in his own mirror image that turns its back on him. A male reader joins the critic in dislike of the author's work and leaves, as the author, begging him to stay, points out how necessary it is to have a reader.

An author and reader are like Siamese twins, alter egos, man and wife, or sadist and masochist, and the author's words must first be heard, then quicken in the reader. Without a reader an author is free not to write, but with one the author is like the prophet Jonas, who was unwilling to preach and was swallowed by a whale and, thus, endured a living death to preserve him for his mission.

This flood of analogies has served to attract the attention of a woman reader, and the author demands that she remain to play the part of the whale and, since she has asked, to find out who the sick God is. The author explains that in writing this story he is dependent upon the reader Alma. He is like a secretary for the writing of the story, and if she feels him finally to be unnecessary or a detriment to it, she must continue alone. Although Alma accuses him of being a woman hater and a prude, he believes that — in this age of the disintegration of all formerly held sacred — women alone have resisted pessimism. They excel in committing spontaneous acts of ruthlessness and in giving them a holy touch (sacred crimes); and such acts, he indicates, are what writing or creativity is all about. Perhaps because of the inspired dedication of women to the ruthless, he expects Alma to know much more about God than he does himself. The author has once made a promise to God but, like Jonas, has postponed it and must now make it good. He finds that there is no return to the blessed state before that promise was made.

The reader must swear on the New Testament to the author that what he is writing is true, and then the process in which they create can begin. The author immediately feels he is in a bad, damp, disgusting place; he has been swallowed by the whale that prevents his escaping his duty. This living death is one the author must endure when entering the minds of his characters or those of his readers. Alma's oath is actually taken to ensure his ability to write his way out again; it is the promise of his rebirth when this period of damnation, imposed as a result of the author's own rebellion against his promise, is past.

The coauthorship begins in earnest, but it is not harmonious. Alma is critical of the author's various technical tricks and, on the whole, quite perturbed by the way he manipulates her into identifying with the characters in the story. As the writing proceeds, the parallels between the two story levels become more and more apparent. The female reader fleetingly resembles Klara and ultimately becomes Alma, and the author shares a striking similarity in purpose with the men who are present at the festival and, ultimately, clearly parallels his protagonist. The sick, coughing God, who drily and unflatteringly comments on the author's attempts to carry out his promise of writing, has his counterpart in the dying grandfather, whose wish Georg is not able to understand and fulfill.

The author suggests that he himself is the band leader at the festival; his music, which sets the very pulse beat of the dying grandfather and to which all the characters figuratively must dance, now sounds through the woods instead of Pan's. Although the grandfather's heart beats in tune with the author's music, it plagues him just as the author's thoughts plague the sick God like flies. The sick God calls the author a trickster and a band leader with an infected wand.

During the coauthorship the reader asks the author why he writes, and he responds rather facetiously by listing a number of reasons, many of which are actually illustrated by the activities of the various Georgs. The author's many reasons for writing are demonstrated throughout the work to be the following: to express the biological spiritually, to represent the elevating or great and holy, to substitute art for unrealizable desires, to disclose the sham of the absurd and wonderous, to unmask hellish forms of blood-thirsty idealism, and to remind readers of the cultural past.

The author declares that art expresses the human through truth and beauty, and it seems that he believes he can achieve these qualities in the work through Alma's help and honesty. Like Georg, the author understands much about the darker aspects of life and can affect others, but the ability to portray an ultimate insight that would justify his writing escapes him. He bluntly points out to Alma that the modern myth is that of Job's book: no justice exists, and the innocent suffer meaninglessly. Although both heaven and hell have now been declared nonexistent, hell cannot die, for it exists in both the individual's thwarted ideal of justice and in his perception of the world's evil. It is this hell that author and reader recreate, the nihilistic state of mind in a culture where gods are dead or dying. The author's words about this personal form of hell remind the reader of her guilt toward a young lover she once failed. As she leaves crying, the author pretends not to understand her and wildly raves on, until the sick God, repeating God's question to Cain, asks him where his brother is. The author, thinking himself to be surrounded by the spirits of those wronged, envisions his guilt for the arrest of friends who have been active against forces he himself has not opposed. He must face the fact that, if his writing does not serve good against evil, he is responsible for the fates they suffer. The author's immediate response to the sick God's accusation and to his own ethically imposed artistic challenge lies in the story of the boxing tent.

Although the black boxer, Georg Washington, is physically broken, he stands up to all challengers in order to support his family. Those who fight against him are also named Georg. They fight because the crowd blood-thirstily demands it and sees the match as a national, racial, or spiritual struggle: it is supposedly one between the Hero and Daemon. As the sick God implies, the tent-owner is like the author; the owner has staged this unnecessary conflict to stir the worst emotions of the crowd, which, like the Negro, is his dupe. There is no good or bad side to this struggle; there are only men named Georg destroying themselves. The tent-owner is the sort of secret sadist and exploiter that causes war in the name of some hellish idealism.

This passage, like others about the various Georgs, fulfills one of the writer's reasons for writing: he does so in order not to do anything worse. The description is a faithful reflection of the negative aspects of society and art, and it serves the good only by calling forth a wish for something better. The author continues the coauthorship with more and more hesitation, for the virtues of friendship, love, helpfulness, and sacrifice that Alma advocates are prostituted ideals to which the author will not testify; he does not understand them or want them, and he will not write about them. His own thoughts plague the sick God like flies, but God says that such is the nature of flies. When God is forgiving of the flies, the reader draws an analogy between flies and men to which the author immediately objects. He will not excuse men from guilt and responsibility; they are neither helpless nor unable to distinguish between good and evil.

After the author's refusal to describe Klara and Holger's union (love is something he does not want or understand), Alma takes over the telling of the conclusion of the story of Alma and Georg on Blood Hill. The author has foreseen this — and planned for it — from the beginning of the project. He has said that her heart, unlike his own, is not corrupt. It is her heart that must now be responsible for the end of the story, and she must continue without further intimacy with, or help from, the author.[11] When she turns to the sick God for understanding and assistance, she finds that He has disappeared or died or has never even existed, except as an illusion produced by the author for her benefit, as perhaps for his own. (The author will no longer testify to the existence of a source of friendship, help, and understanding.) The author, like the sick God, now disappears leaving Alma, like Jacob, to wrestle throughout the night with one who wounds and blesses her, one who is discovered to be God. Within the context of the composed story, Alma struggles with Georg, the alter ego of the story's creator — one who represents the God of suffering and who prophetically preaches destruction. Alma the reader has however struggled with the author directly before the writing of the end of that story. If Jacob was wounded, renamed, and blessed by God, Alma too has been wounded, renamed "the woman," and blessed by the author's allowing her to write the ending of their story as best she can.[12] She does so by preaching the possibility of the redemption of another through love and self-sacrifice, concepts the author has scorned but whose examples he has pointed out to Alma as sources of inspiration (the farm, the boxing tent, and Blood Hill).

Alma the reader has fulfilled the two duties the author set forth for her at the beginning of their coauthorship. She has found out who the sick God is, and he is a fiction of the author, who is himself the choleric creator of this fictional world. She has played the role of the whale for the supposedly Jonas-like author, but since the god to whom he has given his promise to write is his own created fiction, it would seem that Alma has been taken in by the author even with regard to her role as the whale. She has instead been imprisoned in her role of "the woman" by the author, who Leviathan-like has cast her forth, at last, to preach her sermon of possible hope to the damned, the readers of the completed tale.

V *"The Midsummer Festival"* — *the Author*

The author is a man sitting alone at night in someone else's house. His country has been occupied, and some of his friends have been arrested. He is conscience-stricken and feels that something special is demanded of him in this critical age. He writes a story that he opens to the criticism of an imagined reader and, seemingly, of God Himself.

The story is however created by the artist in his own negative image and mirrors his consciousness of the death of dependable things in which to believe. Only suffering itself — the very nature of the universe — is left. The division between right and wrong seems uncertain, and good and evil resemble each other. He writes a story to analyze himself as a manipulator of men; the reader as one to be manipulated; and goodness as a dying cultural belief. The writing of this story is, in itself, evil to the author, but the purpose of the story is to find a form of redemption for man in a nihilistic universe. That redemption is merely a romantic fiction unless the author can believe in his own creation, Alma, the transformed reader. From the author's point of view, she does assume that independence required of a true-to-life character, for she takes over when the author's music — symbolized by the heart-beat of the dying God — stops.

Alma, finding strength in her compassion, has been seduced by evil into trying to redeem it. This is the hope expressed by the author's lengthy story, the Christmas message that the old woman in the portrait had suggested at the beginning of the tale. It is a message of promised redemption, but it is one told only in human terms.

The author makes an ironic comment on his own message. If someone writes a book for a supposedly good cause, he will receive an ovation of the better citizens. Such an event may be satirized in the author's conversation with a member of the town's festival committee. The committee has organized the festival in order to earn enough money to honor one of its citizens with a monument. The money is earned in the side shows and beer parlors erected for the lesser citizens' enjoyment. The worthy cause is supported by the prostitution of high ideals and by the corruption of the morals of common people and the infliction of tragedy on them. This is precisely what is implied about the work of art in its depiction of some people and its seduction of others (its readers) for the promulgation of its message. The promise of redemption exacts its sacrifices. Only if real readers, Alma-like, were willing to act on such a message could art be justified, for it would then express that longed for, world-changing thought for which the artistic impulse strives.

VI "*September Fog*"

"September Fog," the third story in *The Thornbush*, is as highly experimental in form and as cryptic as "The Midsummer Festival." "September Fog" is comprised of two intricately interwoven events, with similar themes, in the life of its unnamed protagonist, the "writer." The present action takes place just before World War II. The story is that of poorly trained and poorly equipped Danish troops waiting for the inevitable, the invasion of their country. The troops are on maneuvers and have been quartered at various farms around the countryside. The story is told by one of these men. The writer, to escape his thoughts of what the future contains, has spent the night reading a book by Scribe, a French writer of comedies.[13] The night is cold, and fog enshrouds the countryside like an evil fate. There is a call to arms; the men rush to their equipment and stand ready to face what is to come. They face only their own disappointment, for the inevitable has not yet arrived. There has been a false alarm. The men march through the fog until daylight when maneuvers are to begin.

One of the men, number forty, is not only late in arriving but also angry, argumentative, and dangerous. He has been a pacifist and a practical, sensible, and faithful man, who has now become mad, reckless in his affair with the engaged daughter at the farm where he has stayed. He has grown afraid of himself: he knows that he will continue to destroy everything for his own fiancée, Sonja, and yet he does not know what he is doing or why he is doing it.

As the soldiers discuss their precarious situation and try to explain it with terms like "a Satanic lust for war" and "honor," the writer remembers one who, during World War I, took poison because he could not understand. The story is the writer's own.

The boy's father has been called out at night, and the boy, wrapped in a blanket, stands calling to his father as wagons pass in the dark. Later the soldiers marching by day through the town all resemble the boy's father. The other boys run behind the troops and chant a song: "Mallebrok died in the war/In eighteen hundred and sixty-four."[14] When the troops have passed, the boy is as angry and as hurt as if his father really had been there and had ignored him. In seeming retaliation, the child implicitly defies parental authority: he lies about his having permission to join some older boys, but they desert him when his lie is discovered. He then goes to meet the younger children, who begin to discuss the bravery of the Danish soldier. When the boy's best friend scorns and fails him by joining in teasing him about his lack of bravery, the boy, who has longed to go to war, demonstrates his unflinching courage by eating the blossoms of the laburnum tree, which are thought to mean certain death. For the boy, these blossoms seem to become the fruit of the tree of knowledge. The child crawls under a thornbush to await death. There, he thinks of the sorrow his friends will experience when they learn of his death and of the meeting he will have with his grandparents in heaven. His grandmother will be angry with him for his premature arrival there, and his grandparents will make it evident that both the boy's mother and father, like people in many generations before them, are doing their duty by enduring this difficult time of war. The grandmother will declare that God can help them. The boy tries to avoid the unthinkable, the sorrow of his mother who will have lost him just as they both have "lost" his father. The boy cannot answer his mother's calls, for he knows he is guilty of something terrible: he has abandoned his duty to the living. His family has carried out this duty in the face of defeat since the Napoleonic Wars. The boy feels that God is angry, for He does not help him. Suddenly the boy feels that "someone" is with him beneath the thornbush and is no longer afraid. His remembrance of the night he called to his father as the wagons passed assumes a dreamy immediacy. It seems that his father was in one of the wagons, just as he has been in the town this day and left his boot prints everywhere. He has now gone away, and all is left in silence.

The foregoing scene, which ends in silence and growing darkness, concludes the story "September Fog." The boy is forsaken as he had feared, and his guilt over the eating of the blossoms is eased and forgiven by the only spirit present, that of death. The child's father, like the heavenly Father about whom the grandmother would remind the boy, has been everywhere but is nowhere to be found. This final scene, which seems to bear witness to the physical death the child had anticipated, must be evaluated, retrospectively, to depict the death of his childhood belief in a personal God.

As an adult the writer's childhood desire is fulfilled, for he is a soldier, and he is one with a very special philosophy, which he reveals in lengthy reflections. The reader is told that death is something man does not take into consideration, and thus the reality he experiences is a false one. When something happens that acquaints him with death (as the disappearance of the father suggests to the boy), it is said to be like a yell echoing from the pit and the blow of awakening. The person sees his past reality as being strange and illusive; only his weapon, defiance, and death are solid realities. Death is no longer an enemy, but a helper, and (like the boy under the thornbush) he who is about to die finally feels unafraid.

If the death that one has accepted (whether one does so under a thornbush or in war) does not occur, all becomes foggy and dim. An instinctive attraction to death is all that remains, and man is left in a ghostly state, in which mundane reality cannot intrude upon him. This ghost of a man is dangerous, for he seeks a justification for his wish to cause either his own death or that of others. Being a helpless prey to the attraction of death is the demonic.

The great and demonic is repulsive in its historic forms (for example, Fascist ideology), but it thrives in men's lives as fear of the good, true, and real.[15] Its foglike agents — ease, self-idolatry, and unreality — have infiltrated men's very beings; thus, they may harbor within them an inclination to idealize the demonic. If such men count on being spared by accident in the blind game of fate, they are less than men and become mere numbers. Like the writer, they are men who may turn their backs on the espousal of a simple belief in justice, honor, and freedom, for they know that these are concepts that must first be tested in suffering. By mentioning these concepts and the very necessity of suffering, the writer suggests an antidote to the ghostly, nihilistic state. The reader is told that, if man is to hold fast to mankind's true hope, he must face the reality that he will die. To know this is to stand at the center of reality, "a burning and consuming place."[16] Mankind's hope, the lesson that the boy should have learned under the thornbush, lies in the unification of life and death so that every moment may be perceived to be a part of eternity.

The burden of life is seen to be a harder one to bear than that of death. One old veteran of the Dano-Prussian War of 1864, about whom the writer thinks when remembering his childhood, is said to have been a brave man who would have sacrificed himself for cause or comrade but who could not stand the emotional cost of retreat and defeat. He became a peculiar old scold from the frustration of having to endure them. The duty both to protect others and to endure defeat has been a recurrent reality. It is a duty that man must carry out and that, if met unflinchingly, can never spell spiritual defeat. If man denigrates this duty by longing for death or war — by entertaining the satanic impulse — he becomes destructive to himself and others.[17]

One must ask whether the protagonist, the writer, is fulfilling his duty or succumbing to the satanic impulse. When the story opens, the writer has been reading Scribe supposedly in order to escape the reality about him. Suddenly cognizant of the silence around him, he realizes that he had not even previously been really aware of the existence of his surroundings and feels as if he himself had not really existed. He has smoked throughout the night and filled the room with a demonic fog. This fog, like that of the countryside, surrounds everything like death. The writer at first tries to avoid the new intrusiveness of the objects about him. He shares his room with a sargeant and envies his sleep, which erases reality: "fear and trembling."[18] The writer recalls the melody "Mallebrok" and his childhood experience under the thornbush. He seems to see an endless train of marching men who are ghosts from the past, just as he sees a thornbush that is the ghost of the grave he sought as a child. The writer now tries to concentrate on the objects of the room in order to enjoy the postponement of the reapproaching unreality. His smoking, however, causes the fog to thicken, and the objects about him begin to change. His bed seems to be the ill-omened ghost ship *The Flying Dutchman,* upon which he will sail forever.

When the new reality of the alarm comes, the writer is pleased, but he does not seem to believe that there is any real, immediate danger. He writes as if he understood the feelings of his comrades, but as if there was a distance between his understanding and desire and theirs. He does not want to miss a thing, and he is taking notes. The writer, who is ready to portray the experience of this night, has discovered from his reading that comedy has the same basic theme as tragedy, the theme of retreat. The writer fears an additional comic theme, immediate surrender. The men are dilettantes who do not fear superior forces and weapons so much as the disclosure of their own ineptness, which may cost one another dearly. The writer is a dilettante carrying out his official duty: to inspect, to take charge of protocol and the men responsible for the machine gun, "the death machine."[19] Like the other soldiers, he is a man who has heard the "cry from the pit," but when the alarm proves to be false, all the men march like a train of ghosts through the fog that envelopes the country. The writer gets them to march to the tune of Mallebrok, a mad, evil, scornful melody whose tone is primitive, spirited, and racing.

If the men are portrayed as now marching to the writer's beat, he may imagine their ultimate destination to be the thornbush, his symbol of a longed for death. The thornbush is however an ambiguous symbol, for it signifies a bitter tragedy that may hold a promise of life. The thornbush was said to have furnished the thorns for Christ's crown. It is also said that a mother pressed such a bush to her heart when she searched for her dead child and that the bush bloomed and leafed in mid-winter, for a love that will embrace pain for another renews life.[20] The bush of the writer's childhood was finally felled and burned on St. John's Eve to drive away ghosts,[21] but that bush has itself become a ghost haunting the writer. For the writer, the bush has symbolized guilt, the tragedy of both a disappointed death wish and a loss of faith with the loss of "the father." The writer might be said to have lived as a ghost ever since.

The child's grandmother had assured him that God could help. That

Father, like his earthly father, is supposedly everywhere, even when He cannot be found. He would provide courage for some men to meet death and give others the courage to face life; He would thus deliver them from their demonic inclinations and their ghostly state. The writer points out that, when God spoke from a burning bush, it was to declare Himself and to give Moses the mission of delivering his people.[22] This allusion suggests that, for the writer, the thornbush has come to represent the promise of man's deliverance through the pain and duty he willingly bears for the sake of others. As a child, the writer came to associate his father with that promise of deliverance through duty. The soldiers then seemed to resemble the boy's father, and when the boy finally did fleetingly see his father on leave, he resembled them, the men of the country, the defenders of the country. As the father loses his special significance, the country itself begins to partake of it.

The child's experiences bear fruit in the man just before the coming war. The writer has likened his immediate experiences to locked jewel cases to which he has no key. They can only be described from the outside, for their secret or meaning is hidden from view until he has paid dearly in experience for the key to reveal their significance.[23] Both his childhood experience, which has been locked from view, and his immediate experience on the night of the false alarm have however combined to furnish the writer with a key to his ghostly state. His experience under the thornbush has taken him decades to understand, and his understanding of it and of his present situation still seems questionable.

As an adult, the writer has not experienced God everywhere, but rather the patrols of the demonic. The lesson he was to learn under the thornbush, to experience life and death as one, a part of eternity, is ambiguous, for that is surely what one does as a ghost. The remembrance of his childhood experience may have helped somewhat to disperse the psychological fog of evil surrounding him, but part ghost he seems to remain. He has remembered those works which, to him, are in alliance with the fog: Marx's *The Communist Manifesto* and Kierkegaard's *The Concept of Dread*.[24] The former is said to have let loose a mighty force that is active now in mortal enemies; the latter is said to appeal to those few who have eaten of the tree of the knowledge of good and evil and have assumed guilt for everything. The guilt-ridden writer can offer no consolation to people like "Forty," but he feels their identity with the country and perhaps, unhappily, with himself; and he can add to literature and history a third "comic" theme: the self-destructive melodrama of guilt that can turn into tragedy for others. He may write a warning born of the experience of his own haunting.

VII   The Thornbush: *A Comparison of Three Stories*

The three short stories that make up *The Thornbush* represent various stages in a cyclic drama. The stories move from spring in "The Easter Bell," to summer in "The Midsummer Festival," to autumn in "September Fog." The action of the first takes place from morning to noon, that of the second from noon to the middle of the night, and that of the third from the middle of the night to morning. The scene changes from the traditional milieu of the past in the farm and village; to the more modern, transitionary period in a provincial town; to an unstable present with a complete displacement of men, as soldiers, from their traditional milieus.[25]

Time is measured ritualistically within the three stories. The frame of reference in the first story is the religious, the church service, and the action culminates simultaneously with the sacrament of the Eucharist. In the second story there is a temporally varying cultural reference for the rites of sacrifice: the old farm culture with its quiet, personal sacrifice; the town fair with its ritual drinking and stylized, artificial sacrifice in the boxing ring; and fabled Blood Hill with its timeless sacrifice. The last story's time reference is that of the life of a single man, but his personal experiences are reflected in the sacrifices and fates of other men, past and present, and in the fate of the very land. The three stories may also be seen as representing occasions for three sacraments: the Eucharist, matrimony, and extreme unction.

In form, *The Thornbush* becomes more and more experimental. The first narrative is told in the third person, and its characters are treated seriously by an omniscient author who can enter their minds at will. The second story is partially told in the third person, but its author interrupts the action to discuss his problems and to voice his opinions very nearly as in dramatic asides. The characters are treated ironically and sometimes even facetiously, but there are certain characters (for example, the ailing farmer and the Negro boxer) whose minds are sacrosanct to the author and never entered by him. He finally limits his role to that of "scribbler." The last story is told in the first person by the writer himself, who, as protagonist, actually carries on an inner monologue over his experiences and memories. He appears only to be guessing about what is going on in the minds of the other characters, and he defines his role as being merely a "reporter of protocol," of whose meaning he may be oblivious. The recurrent artistic need to impose order on the world seems to be limited by the artist's own inability — or unwillingness — to deal directly with certain attitudes toward the human dilemma (for example, that of the acceptance of suffering in behalf of others), and his limitation manifests itself in his role's diminishing importance to the reality he describes.

Many of the characters in the first story have counterparts or partial counterparts in the second story (for example, Per and Holger, Börge and Klaus, Grethe and Klara, Alma and Marie and Ingrid). Other comparisons between the three stories are of primary significance on a symbolic level. All three stories contain characters that have mythical significance. The miserly grandfather at Linde Farm in the first story has his parallels on two story levels in the second: Georg's dying grandfather and the sick God. All three are unable to lend more to the action than the magic of their spiritual presence for good or evil. All have some desire that is uncomprehended and unfulfilled by their heirs, whose questionings and care plague them. The long-suffering Georg Washington and Georg's Christlike father in the second story and the little boy's father in the third have all assumed suffering willingly in behalf of others. The ailing farmer of the second story shares a similarity to Johansen of the first story and to the old veteran of the third story. Both Johansen and the farmer have the symbolic similarity of being dedicated guardians of a source of inspiration, of a holy place, in whose peace and healing they cannot partake. The frustrated veteran is also a guardian of the peace and inspiration of a holy place, the country itself. In contrast to these men who keep the spirit of the past alive, the protagonists seek death in the midst of life.

The works' protagonists all share a longing for power, which they hope to attain through the pain they inflict upon others. In the first two stories, the protagonists' longings call forth antithetical longings in others. Johan's selfishness and indifference radiate an evil charm that affects the lives of Grethe, Ingrid, and Marie; and his presence and death cause them both suffering and a rebirth to life. He himself is finally changed by his momentary meeting with Grethe, someone he cannot have, and his quest for power seems to become almost a matter of indifference to him. He meets death proudly and gladly, as a worthy adversary and partner. Georg seeks a destructive power over others in order to understand the nature of crime and suffering. He affects the lives of Klara and Alma; and he, in turn, is averted — at least momentarily — from his goal of serving the power of evil by Alma's refusal to stay with him. She too is reborn to suffering. The author who, like Jonas, has set out to predict destruction has been averted from his goal

The Thornbush

by the reader Alma, who insists upon the hope of salvation being added to the work. She is reborn from indifference to active, painful participation in this work about life. The writer of the last story, whose childish anger — toward those people and situations that have pained him (especially his father's absence) — has caused him to avenge himself on others, seeks his own death. This is a criminal action that superficially resembles his father's moral action (just as Georg's action has superficially resembled his father's). The child has lived through his experience, but it has led not to rebirth, but to a ghostly existence. He actually belongs to the fog (just as Georg belongs to the night) and expects not so much to undergo any change himself as to record the changes in his fellow soldiers who are about to meet death. He is left in a ghostly state, but one that contains more understanding than was his at the beginning of the story. The writer is parallel to Johan, who sought death; Börge, who did not find it; Georg, who sought to understand through others the difference between the actions of himself and his father and who longed for war; and the author, who is haunted by his own need to preach the destructive.

The theme of the three stories is the evil that seeks suffering and death. In the form of selfishness and indifference to human needs, evil calls forth suffering in people, a suffering that may however lead to their rebirth. If the suffering is voluntarily accepted by the sufferers (for example, through their desire for the good), their suffering may transform evil itself.

Death may be brought about by a character's own attitudes, but its immediate and ambiguous symbols are taken from nature: the bull, the flowers, the fog. The symbols of death are not negative in themselves but seem to be mysterious emissaries of a force that is concealed behind the natural. It makes nature as dangerous as a wounded bull; it causes the unending dance of the dungheap; it stands behind the fog: it is the great and demonic. It is encompassed by the symbol of the thornbush, which combines good and evil: suffering, death, and a rebirth to new suffering. In these three stories man is awakened to his participation in this cyclic drama by sound: the Easter bell; the festival band; the mocking, haunting tune of war. Hansen chose Nis Petersen's poem "Cyclus" (1944)[26] to preface his work and to awaken his readers to that same drama:

....

> One thing is certain: that battle
> (we need not call)
> waits upon us all,
> — hands us its crown;

> — the crown is of thorns;
> — the thorns shall flower,
> sweet, bitter flowers;
> — the flowers shall wither;
> — the leaves shall fall;
> — flowers are the first!
> the fruits are all;
> — fruit loves the battle;
> — the battle gives us thorns;
> — the thorns shall flower,
> sweet, bitter flowers.

Just as the settings of the stories have changed with the seasons from planting to fruition to harvest, the fates of the protagonists have reflected this change as well. Johan has received the crown; Georg's crown has flowered; the author's has born fruit; and the writer's fruits are a longing to go to battle. The protagonists of *The Thornbush* all long for war. The battle they long for is one in which good and evil seem indistinguishable, for not only may evil serve good by causing its rebirth, but also good may serve evil by redeeming it. These possibilities for redemption may be the inspiration behind this labyrinth of a book, whose basic tenet of the unending cyclic drama might otherwise seem monstrous.

CHAPTER 6

The Partridge

MANY of the themes of *The Thornbush* are shared by *The Partridge* (*Agerhönen* [1947]); in fact, the two collections of stories were originally planned as one volume. Like *The Thornbush*, the latter book is tightly structured: it is composed of three sections, each of which contains four stories. The first section recalls childhood and the old culture; the second treats the mature person's existential crisis; whereas the third, with one notable exception, offers visions of death.[1] As in *The Thornbush*, realism is eventually replaced by a modernistic form with mythical overtones.

In both *The Thornbush* and *The Partridge* the pit of despair, reached by so many roads, is thoroughly depicted; but the darkness of the vision is accompanied by the hope that a painstaking mapping of this inner no-man's land, where good and evil have lost significance, will lead to the very negation of this destructive state of mind. The symbol of this hope seems to be an insignificant little bird, the partridge.[2]

The first story, "The Partridge," is that of a farm family which valiantly struggles against being overcome by poverty during World War I. A quiet mood of desperation prevails in the chilly, but spotlessly clean, living room in which the parents and children are spending this stormy winter night. They hear an ominous thud against the door — a similar sound once signaled the father's being called into military service — but when the father opens the door, he finds only a storm-blinded partridge that has flown against it and now lies dead on the doorstep. The mother prepares the bird for a meal, and they all partake of it with up-lifted spirits. Irrational as it may seem, new hope for the future has been born.

The solemn tone of "The Partridge" gives way to an initial lightheartedness in "The Owl" ("Uglen"). A ten or eleven - year - old boy tells of his visit to an old watchmaker, who neglects his paltry business for his grand project of revealing God's plan in all history, science, and wisdom. The old man plans for the boy to continue this work, but the boy, who wants to finish Jules Verne's *Captain Grant's Children*, only half attentively listens to him. The boy dreamily longs for the glittering adventure of the future, and yet he contentedly experiences the world around him. The story achieves its special tone through the young narrator's feeling of having the world and time before him. The story is viewed from still another perspective, that of the now mature, wistful narrator who sees only a barren field where the old man's home once stood. The summer landscape has grown wintry, and the spontaneous, robust mood of the child has given way in the narrator to that somberness whose shadows had sometimes darkened the old watchmaker's eyes. Only the hooting of the owl remains the same. Nature and the passage of time have swallowed up both the old man's cultural project and the boy's unproblematic relationship to the world.

The boy of "The Owl" was an avid reader, but Mattias of "The Book" ("Bogen") is an addict. As he trods home from town, he is quietly jubilant, for he has borrowed a book about world history. Although he knows that he will be late getting home, he cannot let the book alone and immerses himself completely in the mighty drama that unfolds before his burning eyes. When he finally gets home, he is totally exhausted and is put to bed. As he dozes off, he feels that he is Christopher Columbus catching his first glimpse of a new world, and Mattias can completely identify with Columbus, who sinks down on his knees and tearfully thanks God for the gifts He is bestowing on him. Little Mattias has also discovered a new world, the magnificent world of learning that beckons to him from the bright future.

"Early Morning" ("Morgenstunden") is also idyllic. It conjures up a mood of lovely, brisk summer mornings with their scents, sounds, and altering light; but primarily it sensitively reveals a farmboy's ambivalent fascination with the other sex. One early morning a farmer, his son, and a fourteen - year - old boy — through whose eyes the story is seen — set out to clear reeds from a creek. The labor demanded in this collective effort is strenuous, but the boy takes pleasure in it because he feels competent in his work. After the job is done and the sun has risen high in the sky, the three sit quietly together, while eating and enjoying their morning's rest. Suddenly a couple appears, a vagabond and a tall, handsome woman. They share in the food and drink, and they joke with the men, but the strangers spoil the mood for the boy. When the woman is about to leave, he looks up at her hatefully; his eyes are met by her clear, soft glance, which seems to divine all his feelings. He is reminded of his nightly dreams of fair bodies, his half-realized and fearful desire of women; but he refuses to look after her as she walks away. This brief moment between the boy and the woman has however initiated him into the realm of mature sexuality, for he feels that he has now been given eyes with which to see the world.[3]

These four stories, some of which have a strongly autobiographical touch, are impressive in the authenticity of their descriptions of milieus. The stories are told from a point of view very close to, or identical with, that of the child, and they register either the child's spontaneous and expectant relationship to the world around him or youth's delight in life and its possibilities. The initiations into the mature world, as rendered in "The Book" and "Early Morning," seem unproblematic and filled with promise, but the intruding voice of the author, especially in "The Owl," divulges a knowledge of the transitoriness of youthful perception. This duality of viewpoint may add to the stories a slight touch of sentimentality — an attitude foreign to the child. In spite of the poverty so realistically depicted, childhood is clearly perceived, in hindsight, to be a paradise lost.

In section two the mood changes abruptly with the first story, "Sacrifice" ("Offer"). In a detached tone a chilling, brutal drama is related. The setting is one of the past, a rural parish threatened by both plague and starvation. The people of the parish have vainly tried all means to stop the plague, and they now solicit the advice of a witch, who suggests a human sacrifice. Two small orphans, brother and sister, are sent into a field in which a deep grave has been dug. All the parishioners are assembled; some are nervous and others are drunk; but the bailiff's wife, Anna, leads the two children down into the grave, in which food has been placed for them. She gently explains the meaning of the sacrifice to the little girl, who quietly accepts the knowledge of her fate, while her younger brother eagerly reaches for the food. Anna steps out of the grave, and the men storm forward and wildly fill it with dirt. When the deed is done, the bailiff looks for his wife but cannot find her. Someone has seen her walking down toward the lake, and the bailiff remembers that once, in happier times, she had told him that he would find her there if things went awry. He rushes down to the lake and sees her body lying on the bottom. The story ends with a few words that recall the beauty of the summer day: "It is quiet in field and lake. The sun smiles, smiles on everything."[4]

The legend upon which Hansen based his story declares that the plague indeed stopped,[5] but "Sacrifice" makes no such consoling concession. The title is devastatingly ironic: although the people of the parish agree to the deed, their conscience-ridden behavior shows that they are actually committing a murder rather than a sacrifice performed in the proper ritualistic spirit. The compellingly beautiful witch could suggest such a sacrifice because she is representative of a pre-Christian era in which such ritual acts were deeply meaningful to all members of the community. Now, only Anna seems to embody the cultic spirit that could make the sacrifice acceptable. She has made the little scapegoat accept her lot, but when Anna sees that no one else shares her sense of responsibility, she is emotionally thrust into utter isolation. She then seeks death.

"Sacrifice" is a bitter protest against those people who betray their communal responsibility of carrying out the sacrifices that seem necessary to preserve life and culture. Such a betrayal cruelly sacrifices those who, like Anna, assume that responsibility, for to them it makes the sacrifices meaningless and therefore unbearable. The burden will always be too heavy for the individual to bear if he alone, instead of the whole community, is to assume the crushing responsibility of having broken society's ethical code and especially if that infraction of the code has not resulted in the desired change.

Nature's indifference to whatever occurs signifies that the community will receive no relief from the plague; and, as Thorkild Björnvig suggests, this Job-like accusation against nature may actually be extended to the creator of nature.[6] Meaning can only be superimposed upon existence by a culture that assumes full responsibility for those acts by which it attempts to control nature. This is not the case in "Sacrifice."[7]

Unbearable death is also the motif in "The Harvest Feast," but in this case spiritual paralysis is eventually transformed into an austere consolation. The region's farmers celebrate the harvest with a hearty dinner, which is accompanied by the local minister's obligatory speech and blessing. Meanwhile a small boy is being lethally plied with liquor by a brutish farmhand in the servants' quarters. Upon discovery of this cruel act, the minister is rushed to the scene, and when the boy's father arrives and carries his son's body away, the minister follows him. When the father bitterly asks, "Can you bring him back to life?"[8] the minister realizes that he is totally incapable of giving the man any consolation. The minister goes home to his wife and launches into a violent self-accusation that broadens into an anguished cry against the injustice of life itself. The Lord's servant, who would demand an accounting of his Master, will not accept as valid the usual answer of the church, that God is testing man through suffering.

In this moment of angry, frustrated despair and relentless honesty, the young minister is helped by his wife, who quietly packs some necessities together for him to take to the poor, mourning family. When he comes to the cabin, the father repeats his cutting question, but this time the minister answers, "If you can join me in believing, Jesus Christ will reawaken him."[9] The father, hitherto dry-eyed and angry, breaks into tears, a sign that he has been given "the first, terrible consolation."[10]

Both Björnvig and Wivel point out that the two antagonists, the minister and the father, share the same position.[11] Both have felt fury and utter helplessness, but both have also come to share the knowledge that neither of them possesses the belief that can call the dead back to life. When the minister's reply turns the tables on the bereaved father, the two men become united in their powerlessness. In this fellowship is the grain of consolation that rescues them from their spiritual paralysis. The stark mood of noncathartic tragedy in "Sacrifice" is ever so slightly relieved in "The Harvest Feast."

"The Waiting Room" ("Ventesalen") is closely related to "The Midsummer Festival." In both, the nature of nihilism is analyzed through a person who has arrived at the outer limits of meaninglessness. The protagonist — "the confessing woman" — has much in common with the tired Alma, but this woman has traveled so far into spiritual limbo that she, like Georg, perversely enjoys seducing others into following her. The setting is a waiting room in a railway station shortly after the end of World War II. The protagonist sits waiting for a train, and her spoken and unspoken confessions reveal that she has left her husband and children behind to find a man who once was in love with her. She has however been "a traveler" for so long that she feels most at home when rushing toward some destination that she knows is of no significance. She thus feels perfectly at ease in the dingy, nondescript waiting room, which emerges with its cast of travelers as a symbol for the modern crisis-ridden mind. She may seem desperate, but it would be more correct to call her bored, with others as well as with herself. She finds a grim satisfaction in both her ennui and her knowledge that truth does not exist. Although she rejects any meaning in life, she nevertheless feels a contradictorily motivated urge to reach out to people, and she decides to address a homely, quiet woman sitting next to her.

The confessing woman's inner monologue shows that her wish for contact may also express itself in a desire to contaminate people with her own malaise. She does not have to force herself on most of her fellow travelers, for they share her state of mind, but she wants to harm those few who are different from her: the only one in the room she does not understand is the woman sitting beside her. Like other impure souls in Hansen's writings, the protagonist perversely looks for momentary entertainment in an attack upon someone who, as she instinctively knows, does not experience life on her nihilistic terms.

As the two women engage in a halting conversation, it becomes clear that the quiet woman is expecting her son to come home from the war — but in a casket. For the confessing woman, this knowledge is an impetus to evil; in her thoughts she viciously lashes out at the men she has known and fiendishly swears to destroy the man whose help she is about to seek. As her lust for spiritual destruction grows, she turns on her neighbor and savagely attempts to break her spirit. She convincingly points out the meaninglessness of the bereaved mother's situation; curses God; and confesses that, before she left home, she had killed her own children in order that they, at least, would not have to live in this world of falsehood.

Her game, however, is a two-edged sword. Motivated by evil instincts, she has dared to break her isolation, and although she does not know it, she has now made herself vulnerable to counterattack. Her listener does not leave, and she is not crushed; instead, like the minister in "The Harvest Feast," she unexpectedly responds and breaks down her opponent's defenses. The quiet woman refuses to believe that the other has murdered her children and even suggests that there is one person who can help the protagonist. This is a reference to a young man whom the confessing woman had mentioned meeting in the resistance movement and who was later shot. This young man, whom the confessing woman has not dared to besmirch with her spite, fought without any grand illusions, but with a sense of responsibility that could serve as an example for those people who survived the war and who found that peace offered no solution to their personal existential problems.

The confessing woman feels utterly confused and surrounded by riddles that her mind cannot solve. She has been broken by the unassuming remarks of a woman who has refused to give up her responsibility to life, even in the face of what many would deem to be meaningless suffering. That this seemingly insignificant and weak woman has such spiritual strength — reminiscent of the Negro's in "The Midsummer Festival" — is evidenced by *her* confession just before the train pulls in. She admits that her son's grave is unknown, but that she wants to put some flowers on the coffins that are arriving. She asks if the other woman will accompany her, and the answer is "yes."[12] The protagonist's willingness to participate in this ritual act shows that she has changed. She has also given up mentally slandering others and now thinks compassionately of her husband. The nihilistic spirit has been exorcised.

Through the choice of setting and of nameless protagonists who engage in a spiritual battle, this lengthy story becomes symbolic of the cultural situation. The confessing woman represents the modern person lost in nihilism, and through the portrayal of her state of mind, the nature and effect of nihilism are presented in disturbing detail. This destructive attitude, an abstract concept so often discussed by philosophers and cultural critics, is hauntingly presented here in terms of its day-to-day reality. The protagonist's transformation reveals however that the destructive impulses on the part of the nihilist can be redirected toward a painful rebirth into a life of meaningful suffering.

"Night in March" ("Martsnat") is strongly autobiographical.[13] It tells of a son's thoughts as, one night in March during the war, he keeps vigil by his dead father's coffin. In spite of the realization that his father has led a meaningful life, the son nevertheless associates his father's death with the horrifying deaths in concentration camps. The son feels weighed down by the world's evident lack of justice, and the thought that the dead are now one with nature offers him no comfort, for he knows that nature makes no distinction between good and evil and promises only extinction.[14] The accusation against nature in "Sacrifice" is re-echoed, but its desperation is resisted. The son stresses that in man's ignorance he knows nothing about death; death may be life or rather it *must* be life. Although the son's words seem to suggest a belief in resurrection, he puts his faith instead in a meaningful relationship between the living and the dead. Since past generations have worked for the sake of the present one, it must reciprocate by proving that the life of its forefathers has been of consequence. When one asks for his own life to be judged, he is asking for the verdict of the living spirit of those now dead. The son opens the door to the quiet night of the March landscape and feels that his father is standing behind him. It is as if they exchange thoughts and, together, look toward the sky where the wild geese are in flight. This gripping final scene implies that the son senses the validity of the conclusion he has reached.

"Night in March" thus terminates in the protagonist's feeling of relief and consolation, but whether or not it can be shared by others who have entertained the same dark thought of life's injustice is questionable. Hansen asserts that in order to be meaningful his answer must be true for others as well. This demand may make the reader balk, for the highly personal answer offered may seem like a desperate pseudo-solution that fails to be convincing as soon as the poetic force and seductive power of the text's language fade. This reaction on the part of the reader (a reaction he may have had to the two preceding stories as well) would hardly surprise Hansen who (especially in "The Midsummer Festival") often voiced his own suspicion of the well-wrought phrases and clever, manipulative artistry that make the false ring true. Such poetic solutions to fundamental dilemmas may ease the mind temporarily, but they do so only until the artistry loses its impact and the questioning again starts.

The remarkable fact about these stories is that the rebirth theme does not seem to be a hollow postulate. The reason may very well be that Hansen never presents the transformation in a romantic light. The transformed person does not receive static bliss, but suffering, and his lot in a confusing world demands a difficult and taxing moral commitment In fact, through rebirth — which at times seems too mythically loaded a term to be the *mot propre* — meaningless suffering is actually transformed into a suffering that is deemed meaningful. Meaning is established through an interaction with both the living and the dead.

The first story in the third section, "The Soldier and the Girl" ("Soldaten og Pigen"), seems to start in a Hans Christian Andersen world. A picturesque train is comically rattling along the track. The passengers and the train officials are sharply and humorously depicted. The main character, a soldier returning from war, has quite an ironic bent of mind, but his playful words reflect the fact that life has lost its significance for him. As he points out, he is a soldier who cannot get out of uniform. Like so many returning warriors in fiction, he "has been in hell"[15] and returns to civilian life as a member of the living dead. He stops the train and walks across an empty field to an old marl pit that is used as a dump. Here, among defunct things, he feels at home, and he throws his medal into the water, stretches out, and goes to sleep. His act strongly suggests death, for he seems to become one with the empty, quiet ground. After dark he awakes and hears the voice of a girl who had so desired life that she was fearful of it and had drowned herself in the marl pit. The two engage in a tender dialogue that has a soothing effect upon both of them. She is comforted by his presence, and he feels discharged from his warrior mentality. In the moonlight his medal seems to float to the surface of the water and to melt there.

This concluding image suggests rebirth, but the associations of rebirth cannot cancel out those that connote death. The touching dialogue between the soldier and the girl may indicate that the soldier, an inhabitant in the borderland between life and death, has finally crossed over to the realm of death. He unmistakably gains peace of mind, but it may be the kind of relief that only his extinction can proffer. For one who has committed acts with which he cannot reconcile himself, death may seem to be temptingly like its opposite, life. The rebirth motif becomes ominously ambiguous.

With "The Soldier and the Girl" and the following story, "The Fathers" ("Fædrene"), empirical reality is left behind for mistier regions of the mind. In "The Fathers" an old man, an unworldly philologist, totters through an autumnal landscape shrouded in rain and fog. As so often in Hansen's works, such a setting signifies fatigue, confusion, and death. In fact, the old man is lying in a hospital bed somewhere, but his mind is unwittingly traveling back to his place of origin, the farm that his family has owned for generations. He finally meets his forefathers, each of whom appears younger than his son;[16] and at the old man's request, they allow him to stay with them. Death is thus seen as a rejuvenation and a meaningful reunion with past generations. The old man's senility, which manifests itself in forgetfulness, frustration, and confusion, finally takes the form of a childlike eagerness to please and trust in his elders.

Death, however, may be something other than a reassuring, mythical homecoming, for this wandering is only an untrustworthy dream in the mind of a dying man. Even the dream is unsettling, for the strange fact is that the longer a man has been dead, the younger he seems; thus, a dwindling into nothingness may actually be death's nature. Only in man's memory of past generations do the dead still live, and when memory fails, they become one with nothingness. This suggestion, which posits the idea of extinction against the idea of rebirth, seems furthermore to take precedence in the story's very last lines, in which the old man is said to be not only blind but invisible.[17] Since this may be his actual moment of death in the hospital, "The Fathers" leaves the question of the nature of death ultimately unanswered.

"The Birds" ("Fuglene") strikes a different and lighter note. In tone and characterization it is reminiscent of *Jonatan's Journey*. Its protagonist, Espen, is of the smith's mold, an honorable fellow whom it is easy to tempt, but who, though slow in keeping promises, is very responsible and acts as a guardian of others. In the story Espen goes to work for a "wise fool," a minister, and does his best to put this employer's neglected land back to good use. Espen is initiated into sex through the willing offices of the minister's flirtatious daughter, who soon leaves him for other, more debonair cavaliers. The minister is finally forced to leave his position. Espen, who sees a spiritual strength in this apparently weak man, eggs him into continuing his calling on the road until, at last, the minister fearlessly meets death. Espen finally returns to his father's farm and digs the well that, for years, he had promised his parents.

The characters are compared to birds, and they fly in strange, unpredictable directions, which to them are meaningful but of which society does not approve. The minister may seem like a Don Quixote, but in spite of his nearly complete lack of practical sense and his poor sermons, he is a person who can teach people to experience life spontaneously and joyously. He is also a kindred soul to Father Mattias, in *Lucky Kristoffer*, who once characterized God as a humorist. The implication is that life's humorists are closer to God than any of the sober probers into its mysteries. Neither the minister nor Espen is tormented by the confusing question of good and evil. Each meets life with acceptance.

"The Birds," which blithely seems to present characters that have a nearly ideal and unproblematic relationship to existence, takes place, rather expectedly, in the lost land of the old culture. These "birds" may seem far from the modern, complex world, but as the author concludes in *Serpent and Bull*, a bird in flight can be seen even when the sun has set: "It is illuminated, although the light has faded."[18]

In "The Birds" Hansen pays homage to the mythical past, which embodies that meaningful existence which later times only grudgingly and imperfectly could grant their people. After this superb and inspired intermezzo, "The Man from the Earth" ("Manden fra Jorden") renews the somberly ambiguous vision of the third section. The narrator remains nameless because, one must suppose, he has forgotten who he is. Like so many of Hansen's other characters who have lost their grip on life, he is imbued with a sluggish indifference to the struggle of making heads or tails of life. He finds himself standing in a harvested field; and as he aimlessly walks on, like the protagonist of "The Soldier and the Girl," he discharges himself of all his acquired, but useless, knowledge. He admits that none of his knowledge can tell him whence he has come or whither he shall go. The mood of spiritual death is enhanced by his finding a dead and decaying partridge. As if reacting in dull awe, he responds by taking off his shoes and leaving them behind.

He then heads for a distant forest, in which he sees a cow licking out the form of a naked, hairy man from the roots of an ash. The protagonist realizes that he must fight this man, but he remains as detached and as impassionate as before. He loses the struggle and unresistingly lets the man shove him into the hole beneath the ash and heap dirt on him. He finally sees the stranger go off in the direction of the shoes and the dead partridge. He notices the beauty of the ash, and in the hope that the little tree may thrive, he falls asleep.

The cow's licking out a barbaric man from the roots of the ash clearly refers to the creation myth in old Norse mythology;[19] thus, death and rebirth are juxtaposed. Although the tired wanderer has struggled against his attacker, he blissfully accepts his fate, which may be a fulfillment of his own death wish. Death, a reabsorption into nature, may seem like a wondrous sleep for the man who is no longer aided by, or cognizant of, cultural values. The man in this story exemplifies the extreme consequences of that fatigue which so many of Hansen's nihilists embody. This man gives expression to none of the restless passion, the lust for destruction, or the concealed desire for redemption that is otherwise characteristic of those desperate protagonists. In fact, he has left even desperation behind and wishes only to sleep in the earth. The view of death that was so forcefully rejected as meaningless in "Night in March" is now perceived to possess compelling beauty.

The men's portrayed switch in roles may however signify rebirth in the individual. The old and tired in him dies as the young and vigorous comes to life, victoriously takes over, and sets out to retrace the old self's steps. A transformation has occurred that may imbue culture with new life, but it is questionable whether it is possible to vest much cultural hope in the victor, the reborn man. He is a man without forebears or tradition, and in Hansen's works such a being is normally judged to be dangerously close to nature and, thus, oblivious to any distinction between good and evil. This new man emerges as a striking contrast to those seemingly weak characters who secretly possess the spiritual strength that constitutes and protects culture. The new born man is a brute force, the negation of culture. Surely, this creature may become humanized, but that will also entail his learning the vanity of acquired knowledge and his returning one day to be reburied under the ash. This circular view of cultural striving makes nature the final victor, which fulfills the death wish inherent in culture.

Although each of these stories deserves to be read and discussed in its own right, the composition of *The Partridge* implies that the stories are used to depict the stages on life's way from childhood to death; it is a passage through exasperating years during which the individual must wrest a sense of purpose from life. In the child's anticipation, maturity is not seen as being a bitter struggle, but an exhilarating journey toward knowledge and fulfillment. As this anticipation is replaced by actual experience, most of the characters lose the young person's unproblematic relationship to the world. When knowledge proves insufficient and values defunct, a nihilistic attitude threatens to engulf the mind. A precarious hold on life can however be regained by those people who save themselves from their spiritual isolation by reestablishing a fellowship with others. They learn that the fate of suffering is one they share with others, who can give them a sense of meaning and to whom they must respond in kind. The nihilist then becomes an "ethical pessimist"; this transformation or rebirth, which both *The Thornbush* and *The Partridge* portray, is a stringent remedy against the modern lack of sustaining values.

The meaning established in life is one that must be extended to death, and such a text as "Night in March" forcefully argues that the spirit of the dead must be reborn in the daily existence of the living. Other stories in *The Partridge* point out however that death ambiguously suggests extinction as well as rebirth and that the individual who finds himself in a morally confusing world may betray his spiritual fatigue by a wish for extinction. This nihilistic impulse manifests itself by the protagonist's desertion of culture for an attraction to nature. The thought of extinction, so horrifying to the cultural mind, becomes equated with harmony.

Both *The Thornbush* and *The Partridge* contain complex and irreconcilable ambiguities, and thus both works emerge as quests for understanding.

CHAPTER 7

The Liar

THE Liar (Lögneren [1950]), based on an unfinished short story called "The Ice Breaks," was Martin A. Hansen's last novel.[1] The story takes place on an island called Sandö shortly after World War II and actively encompasses three days — from late afternoon of Friday, the thirteenth of March, until the evening of Monday, the sixteenth — in the life of its protagonist, Johannes Vig. The narrative ends a year later with an epilogue that sums up the events of the intervening months. The account begins as a diary in which the naturally aware, highly poetic, and literate Johannes examines his activities, hopes, and fears. He does so in a chronicle both illuminated and obscured by allusions to the Danish classics, Icelandic sagas, Nordic myths, and the Bible. He addresses an imagined, young friend and calls him Natanael as an indication of his honesty.[2] Since the fictive Natanael proves to be curious and ready to pronounce judgment, Vig must explain himself either by justifying his actions or by calling them into doubt, and he cautions against saying his own name — Johannes Vig — too fast, for the syllables may slur, causing his last name to be pronounced *Svig:* Fraud.[3]

The facts of the story are puzzling, and the motives behind the protagonist's actions and his interpretation of events are only hinted at during the course of the story. It is not until the end of the account that the reader is able to evaluate all that has been told and to ascertain its significance for the protagonist.

Some important past events are gradually revealed through Vig's account. Vig, who had been a student of literature, had loved a young woman named Birthe. She forsook him for another man, and Vig gave up his studies at the university to study education at a teachers' college. Although some years later he found that he could win Birthe back, he eventually fled from the mainland and took up the position as teacher on the island.

Vig has been on the island for seven years. Among his first pupils were three whose fates became intertwined with his own. Annemari Höst, the bright and beautiful daughter of the owner of the general store; Oluf Olufsen, the son of the fisher Johan's stern widow; and Niels Jensen, Oluf's quiet young friend. Annemari and Oluf began to go together, but Oluf's mother, Marie, disliked the young girl, and the courtship became increasingly problematic for Oluf. Annemari became pregnant, and she seemed to hope that this fact would force Oluf to make a decision. One day — rather late in Annemari's pregnancy — Oluf and Niels, both engaged men, set out in a boat on high seas and capsized. Niels drowned and Oluf swam a phenomenal distance to safety. When Oluf returned, he was guilt-ridden over his role in Niels's death. Oluf became apathetic and listless, and even though he and Annemari have remained engaged, they have never married. Oluf has since continued to fish during the summers and to work in a factory on the mainland during the winters.

At the beginning of February a young engineer named Harry arrived on the island to study the economic feasibility of shipping out chalk. He has begun to court Annemari.

In early February two men set out in a boat, through forming ice, for the mainland. When their boat hit a floating mine, they were blown to bits, the accidental victims of a war now past. One of the men, Erik, the best fisherman on the island, had tried to save Oluf and Niels at the time of their accident. Because of the impassable ice Johannes Vig, in his capacity as vicar, has held the church service for Erik. The ice has continued to surround the island for forty days.

Vig's account opens just as the ice is about to break. He gradually reveals himself to be not only the island's schoolmaster, vicar, postmaster, and tax accountant, but also its good Samaritan, conscience, guest, hunter, drunk, and evil spirit; and he finally becomes its historian, naturalist, and martyr. During the few days covered by his account, Vig frets about what Annemari will do when the ice breaks and Oluf returns. Vig maintains that he dislikes the coming of spring, for it will disturb his peace and quiet and involve him in the lives of others. On Friday night, when Annemari brings him supper, she mentions Harry, and Vig pointedly reminds her of Oluf. She asks Vig whether he intends to dance with her at the Sunday night spring ball at Næss Farm, and she asks to borrow the necklace that he keeps as a memory of Birthe. Vig pretends to be unable to find the necklace; and when he again mentions Oluf, Annemari leaves in anger. The next day she forces Vig to read a letter that she has written Oluf in order to break their engagement. She leaves the letter with Vig to be delivered when the ice breaks. She is obviously anxious to let him know that she is free, but he refuses to accept that fact until the letter has been delivered. She then questions Vig about his rumored relationship to the married Rigmor of Næss Farm. Annemari accuses Vig of deceit in both his words and actions, maintains that he has been the cause of her own unhappy relationship with Oluf, and finally refuses the necklace that he now offers her. His behavior has been continually frustrating to Annemari, especially since he has stressed his age and dodged all her attempts to make him reveal his true feelings for her.

Saturday afternoon Vig walks about on the island. He buys two bottles of liquor and then visits the wealthy Frederik of Næss Farm and flirts slightly with Frederik's wife, Rigmor. Vig next goes to tell the parents of one of his pupils that their son, Kaj, must be treated for tuberculosis and must be sent to the mainland on the first ferry. By the church Vig accidentally meets Harry and takes an instinctive liking to the young man. Vig nevertheless tries spitefully to upset Harry by telling him that Annemari has broken her engagement, a fact that she has told only to Vig. Vig has felt like an evil spirit in his treatment of Harry; afterward, as Vig drinks the altar wine and plays Bach on the church organ, the sheer, incomprehensible beauty of the music causes him to realize not only that he is a sinner but also that he will lose his toy, Annemari. He breaks down and cries, and he feels that his only friends are his hunting dog and a seallike head of death sculpted in the church choir. In a strangely unreal and emotionally divided state, Vig starts on his way home. He stops however at the inn, and there he meets the barmaid Elna, who unhappily tells him that she is pregnant. That night, the sleepless Johannes watches the ice break.

On Sunday morning Vig contemplates the peace of a death that is free from mortal cares or idealistic obligations. When he conducts the church service, he feels first as if he is an entrapped Jonas and then as if he is possessed by the devil himself — to seduce the congregation through the recitation of a biblical text (Luke 11:24 - 26) over the unclean spirit that constantly returns to possess the man from whom it is driven. Vig at last breaks the evil enthralment in which both he and the congregation are held mutually captive. It seems to him as if he receives a blow from the departing spirit and hears the sound of the flight of a snipe.

After the service he has dinner with Oluf's mother, Marie, and while looking through her photograph album, he conceives the idea of writing an all-encompassing work about Sandö. On impulse he had arranged for Kaj's father, Anders, to earn some money for Kaj's treatment, and Vig again reminds Anders to cut down the lovely trees surrounding the schoolmaster's quarters, trees that had sheltered Vig from the outside world. Vig then returns to the school, and while feeling that the work he is about to write is the product of the vanity and deceit with which his life is filled, he senses that the schoolroom accepts and commends him.

Vig's heartening discovery is interrupted by a visit from Harry, who accuses him of exercising a sickly control over Annemari, the control of the past. Elna visits Vig next, and he sacrifices his cherished isolation by offering her the position of his housekeeper so that she will have a place to have her child. Later, Vig finally decides to attend the spring ball at Naess Farm. There, he confides in Rigmor his feeling of dedication to the school and arranges Kaj's transportation to the sanatorium. Vig then tells Annemari a tale of past self-denial: he had nobly renounced the possibility of an affair with the married Birthe. Having spurned Annemari through analogy, Vig takes his leaves.

School is dismissed at noon on Monday, and Vig prepares the post for the incoming boat. When Oluf has finally arrived and serenely read Annemari's letter, he says that he has expected Annemari's decision and knew their parting was inevitable. He then mentions his own plans to invest in a fishing boat and to become a sea captain, and he wishes the astounded Vig luck. Vig rushes off to find Annemari, who is packing to leave with Harry. Vig realizes that he is too late, and angered by her pity, he tells her an ignoble version of his reconquest of Birthe and his subsequent rejection of her. He gives Annemari Birthe's necklace as a farewell curse. Vig, a hunter who has shot only seals, leaves to hunt the snipe, a migratory bird thought to appear on the same day that the text of the unclean spirit is read in church and a bird to which Vig has likened Annemari, himself, and the transitory in man's fate. Vig has arranged for Frederik to take the sick Kaj to a sanatorium, and now that Rigmor is at the farm alone, Vig goes there to seduce her. This act, born of his anger and wounded pride, makes her love for him seem meaningless. Later, nature appears as ominous to Vig as if Leviathan had just swum past. He regrets his cynical treatment of Rigmor, and when he stumbles upon a snipe, he rushes back for her. The frightened woman must join him on this hunt, and when he finally manages to shoot a snipe, he gives it to her as a pact between them of his own belief in her ability to make her life meaningful.

Natanael, like the reader, is told in the epilogue that on that same night, as Vig stood on Nærbjerg Height, he realized that he was a man who could not change. He then dedicated himself to a life on the island.

The Liar

Afterward, accidentally meeting Oluf near the church, Vig tried to assume his own share of the guilt over Niels's death: Vig had encouraged the young men to sail out to confront death.

Even more astounding to the reader than Vig's revelation of his guilt is his admission in this epilogue that the whole account has been written long after the action. This admission, along with the avowal of his inability to change, demands a reevaluation of all he has told. Vig reveals that in July he had shot his hunting dog and faithful companion, Pigro. He declares that Rigmor was the woman whom he had really cared about and that, since the snipe hunt, he has helped her to develop a belief in herself and her life by keeping away from her.

Vig has heard from Annemari and has tried to ease the ugliness of their parting. Elna has had her baby and rules as the "authority" in Vig's household. It seems that Oluf and Elna may marry; and Vig dreads the coming of his own complete loneliness, which he must bear without wine, without women, and (now that he must bid farewell to Natanael) without the escape of a poetic confession. He has written the words "The Liar" across this chronicle and has turned to writing an account of Sandö's past and natural history.

To understand Vig's actions this "unchanging" man's philosophy must be explored. His intertwined views of the divergent perceptions of youth and maturity, hunting, sexual desire, and the role of the aesthetic are basic to his actions, and are all dependent upon his view of nature.

Nature is something Vig has long studied in many of its aspects: plants, fleas, birds, topography. Nature as a larger concept is something that he finds to be alien to man and destructive of his culture. That larger nature consists of the cosmic, about whose laws one, Job-like, knows nothing. It is something great and beautiful, but completely foreign, unapproachable and ungraspable, preternatural. The capricious, icy sea and the island itself are a part of nature in its broader aspect. The sea may look as if Leviathan had just swum through it, but the island is itself a Leviathan,[4] one harpooned and bound by culture: language, the mind, the spirit. The island is a Leviathan that must be constantly reconquered by each new generation. This cultural activity gives the island its daytime appearance, but it has its nighttime aspects, too: it is a monster that devours men, families, generations, until all is forgotten. It is death and its seallike head is pictured in the church. This sculpted head is the foremost member of the congregation for the minister or vicar leading the service and is counterpoised across from the crucifix, the symbol of resurrection, a cultural longing.

On Nærbjerg Height Vig felt that his fate was bound to the island.

He did not belong to the island as one born there and having roots there, but rather as one embedded like a spear in the island. He thus draws a parallel between himself and the thought of resurrection that he has described as a harpoon in the body of the island. Both the spear and harpoon are weapons used against nature; their usefulness is in limiting nature, and they are products of culture. Culture is a question of major concern to Vig, and religion itself becomes a question of culture, since the conquest of nature is the "spiritual."

Nature must be subdued in whatever way it is possible to do so. This may be achieved in many ways. It may be done by plow or pen. If living man is not to disappear without a trace, he must preserve knowledge; and this Vig decides to do through his work about Sandö. He finally becomes a dedicated servant of culture in order to give his life a measure of meaning.

Vig, who occupies so many positions of trust in this small island society, constantly refers to himself as a guest, a stranger, a refugee in life. Men pass by like migratory birds. All men and, ultimately, the island itself are but moments in the stream of time. Vig has found that respite from feelings of homelessness is gained either by acquiescing to a wish for death or by acquiring a feeling of awe over tangible reality. Vig believes that this discovery constitutes the critical dilemma of youth. Looking back on his own youth, Vig describes youth's longing for purity and truth. The youth sees nature for what it is and seems to find that purity and truth are incompatible — even within himself. He looks at a spring day and sees the sexual, the dead, and the rotting. He also senses, antithetically, nature's unfathomable and unreachable ultimate beauty, a beauty that has relevance perhaps only from the point of view of the creator of the world. The young man becomes intimate with thoughts of death. The mature man no longer understands the concepts of truth and purity. He can no longer see life's great contradiction, and he speaks of what he has learned in life. His knowledge, however, consists merely of forgetfulness, ignorance, and little lies and deceits. In the songs of birds and the budding of plants, he hears and sees the beauty and promise of resurrection in nature; yet he has forgotten that he himself cannot always be a part of it. The mature man can experience awe, but it is an aesthetic experience from which the truth of impurity has been edited.

Vig would deny the mere enjoyment of nature's beauty, for he demands an appreciation of it through the acquisition of a respectful knowledge about it. This knowledge is based on truth, which must include the darker aspects of nature, and is therefore different from the mature man's lie, which sees purity and beauty but has suppressed certain truths in order to do so. Vig's insights into nature are however at odds with his cultural strivings, for he knows that culture is a passing phenomenon. Vig still attempts to awaken awe in the school children over all those things that exist and that, if valued by his pupils, may become meaningful in their lives. In spite of his own dark knowledge he tries to teach them an appreciation that is in furtherance of culture and to give them a knowledge that will temporarily bind nature.

Vig, as a guest, a stranger in life, has "youthfully" wished for "peace and quiet" and that feeling of belonging whose ultimate form is the grave. He has taken several approaches toward attaining them. He has tried not to be involved in the demands of those around him, and he has finally hunted out and killed the bird of sorcery, the snipe, which he had come to vest with connotations of his own recurrent evil and sexual desires. The killing of the snipe, which seems to signify a cultural inclination, also symbolizes a death wish. Consonant with his assumed role of cultural defender, he has hunted the seal to destroy it and, thus, what it symbolically represents. Although Vig feels that nature must be bound in order temporarily to overcome its destructive force, he paradoxically feels himself still to be intimate with its visage of death, the seallike head in the church choir. This is an image that, like his hunting dog, Pigro, he calls friend. Although Vig is the propagator of culture within the school, he is vacillating in his dedication to culture in his personal life. He is divided between his manipulative, intellectual desire to support the views of the mature man and his emotional affinity to those of youth. All his actions become paradoxical in their significance to him . . . and to the reader. Nowhere is this more evident than in the connotations surrounding his hunting. He "hunts" both for what he would treasure and for what he would destroy.

Vig, the hunter, has sent out the shadow of past guilt and doubt to pursue others (like Annemari); but at the end of his long account, he has likened himself to one who has always had doubt and disbelief like dogs on his trail. He has also likened the past to dogs on the scent of game. The skeptical Vig cannot escape living his life as a prey to doubt, whether it is doubt about his own past — self-doubt — or doubt about the nature of life itself — religious doubt. Vig has called himself a dilettante in belief, an unbeliever who believes what he does not believe. In the face of tragedy and death (at Erik's funeral) Vig has recalled the biblical assertion that the past, which has been, is and will be, for God seeks the eternal return of that which has been banished.[5] For Vig this seems to be borne out by the ever-recurrent views of his youth, the guilt from his past, the repetition of events in his love life, and the repetitive condition of nature itself. Vig, the hunted, becomes the hunter seeking a solution to his predicament. Just as he sometimes tries to escape the ugly and impure by glossing it over with a higher significance, he tries to transform man's helplessness and fate into something meaningful.

Vig sees those who suffer undeservedly (Kaj's mother or the biblical, hounded Job) as well as those who act evilly to do harm and to destroy (himself or the devil) as somehow being proofs of God's existence. At the extremity of meaninglessness one finds the battle ground of two powers,[6] which might be called good and evil, purity and truth, life and death, man and God, or culture and nature. Through the victims of misfortune Vig senses God, who seems to be the ultimate hunter (one whose Leviathans can never be understood by man). For Vig, this God is nature's master, and evil is the usurpation of His power, that of inflicting tragedy on others. Vig, the hunter, has usurped this evil power over the fates of others (Birthe, Oluf, and Annemari). Although evil — or nature — may seem to be the ruling principle in the world, Vig maintains that goodness does exist *in man*. Vig, who would bring out this goodness (as in Rigmor), shows a humanitarian bias that is an idolatrous dedication of himself on the altar of the cultural (just as he has accused others — like the engineer Harry — of self-dedication on the altars of the political, scientific, or technical). Vig, the servant of culture, realizes that his dedication to culture is an act of deceit, an act that seems ethical but is aesthetic. It is a renunciation of the true for the good and the beautiful.

If one should trace Vig's development, one must bear in mind his final recognition about himself: he is a man who cannot change. He can however pretend to change, and this energetically pursued pretence is the cause of his vacillation. As a young man he was disappointed in his love affair with Birthe. Whether, upon meeting her again, he nobly disappeared from her life, or he took her, destroyed her marriage, and forsook her is immaterial in face of the fact that he did not want her.[7] He has later explained that he came to the island because he was not mature enough for his former position. He had not been able earlier to give up his paradoxical, youthful demand for truth and purity, and he sought an escape from his conflict by accepting a cultural role on the island.

Vig has assumed the role of teacher in the community, and he has tried, spiderlike, to bind his students emotionally to the island. He exercises an "ethical" seduction of others, through the aesthetic, for the spiritual: he makes it his duty to awaken awe for the perpetuation of culture — which is for him both the "spiritual" and the purpose of schooling. In fact, in his private life, Vig seems to try to fuse the concepts of the aesthetic and the ethical into one. In the role of schoolmaster he could not have the young Annemari, and when she started going with Oluf, Vig found himself at odds with his own earlier, youthful position: he was now the older man who would be competing with the sonlike Oluf. Vig began to mold the lives of those closest to him, and although he succeeded in forming them aesthetically, they reveal the dubiousness of Vig's ethical stance.

Vig believes that the aesthetic in the form of the saga is one of the facets of culture longest to endure the ravages of time.[8] The saga often depicts the heroic in the face of death, and Vig has encouraged Oluf (who perhaps suspects the attraction between Vig and Annemari and who is desperately torn between the wishes of his mother and fiancée) to test his strength against death as a sign of maturity. Oluf and Niels have dared the elements by sailing out into a storm. In Oluf's reckless attempt to forget his dilemma by seeking a meaning in some form of the aesthetic, he has gone to sea as if called by a myth. At sea, when faced by death, he has become its agent, for he has unintentionally killed Niels in order that he himself might survive. When they have capsized, Oluf learns the lesson that Vig had failed to teach him: to overcome death one must tragically ally oneself with it. Oluf accomplished his mighty swim because he had to flee from his own active evil and from his guilt over Niels's fate. Having come to grips with death, Oluf seems no longer to care about the aesthetic — the myth that calls him — or the doubts he has previously entertained. Johannes Vig has not allowed Oluf to admit his guilt, and the silence Oluf has had to endure, while living on as a hero of surpassing strength and bravery, seems to have broken him. Just as the ghost of Niels pursues Oluf, so Johannes's guilt over Oluf's passivity — his emotional paralysis — becomes a ghost of the past pursuing Johannes Vig. Oluf and Vig are in parallel situations, but Vig has found that, although one may bitterly have to ally himself with, and be spiritually paralyzed by, death in order to overcome it and its personal form, desire, one can conceal that fact beneath the aesthetic view that denies both death and desire. Vig has sacrificed truth on the altar of the aesthetic and has helped to create the saga of Oluf. This act foreshadows Vig's later creation of a saga for himself.

During Vig's stay on the island he has attempted to create an aesthetic view of life. He has pretended to negate that immediate aspect of nature, personal desire, which is ever-recurrent and inconsiderate of others, and he has attempted to give it an aesthetic form: he would assume an ethical role and, thus, create the saga of Vig. No matter how noble his role may appear, his constantly fluctuating emotions show that it is an assumed one. There is no true evidence of his spiritual paralysis when he denies his ability to act with regard to his "toy," Annemari (and he has proved the lengths to which he *could* go by his encouragement of Oluf to face death). After the boat accident both Vig and Oluf avoid their desire for Annemari. Oluf and Annemari remain bound to the island in a sort of limbo, and Vig resumes his aesthetically ethical stance and his hunting.

Vig hunts the seal, which represents not only death but the death-dealing in his own nature as well, for he knows that he is part warlock, part devil. The second aquatic symbol of nature is the Leviathan-like island that Vig would harpoon with culture and that he calls an ancient matriarchy, once ruled from Næss Farm. He thus associates the island with the realm of woman's influence, and the island becomes representative not only of death but also of that desire which Vig sees evidenced everywhere in nature. He cannot directly overcome the island, but he can overcome that second sexual symbol, the snipe. He has a snipe in his schoolroom, and he identifies the snipe both with his own sexual desire and with Annemari, who is like a bird that is shot and held in his hand.[9]

The threatening arrival of Harry is the impetus to Vig's present crisis. When Annemari lets Vig know that she cares for him by showing him the letter she has written Oluf rather than showing it to Harry, Vig refuses to accept this knowledge. He believes it has been her game to encourage Harry, just as she once had perhaps encouraged Oluf, in order to make Vig jealous enough to act. Vig refuses to be under her influence, and he hides behind his ethical behavior. Johannes wants neither to lose Annemari nor to win her through those means that she, Birthe-like, leaves open to him.

Rigmor and Oluf have become pawns in the game between Annemari and Vig, a game that has lasted for Oluf for almost seven years. Vig furnishes Harry with the information he needs to win Annemari, for Vig tells him of her letter to Oluf. Vig does this because he wishes to maintain his solitude even if it means losing his toy, Annemari. He has dreamed of peace and quiet, a lack of involvement in the affairs of others. If he is a guest in life, he means to enjoy it in passing. His youthful discovery of the falsity of purity and love has allowed him to play with aesthetic reformulations of life, whether they are implied in his retelling the tale of Birthe or are present in his revising the more recent events in the lives of Oluf and Annemari. In the creative act of molding not only his own life but the lives of others as well, Vig plays with the divine power of forming the fates of others; thus, within a religious frame of reference he assumes a satanic role, one made up of lies and seductions.

After telling Harry of Annemari's letter, Vig sits drinking the altar wine and playing Bach on the church organ. The music reveals a higher world of truth and beauty that is unapproachable and unknowable for Vig. His dog, Pigro, returns from his daylong sexual adventure like a satanic imp to his master. Weeping, Johannes sits with the representatives of those things he really does understand: the head of death in the choir and the hunting dog of desire and past guilt. The evening in the church is the drunken sabbat of the warlock, the priest of nature, a power inimical to the church.[10] When he leaves, it is as if he rides a spirit horse and has become some ghostly haunter of the island.[11] He feels divided, renewed, younger. Vig has been reminded of the insight and demands of his own youth.

Sunday morning finds Vig yearning for a peace free of either earthly or transcendental longings. The former is a longing whose object (Annemari) he does not want, and the latter (like Bach's music) is one he cannot attain. Longing for the everlasting peace of death, Vig leaves for the church.

In the church Vig feels that, like Jonas when swallowed by the whale, he is in a living coffin that preserves him for a duty he does not wish to perform. Like Jonas, Vig has no desire to preach to the doomed that they might be saved. When faced with the unvoiced demands of the churchgoers, his perception of himself changes from Jonas, a prophet held captive by a divinely sent Leviathan; to Loke, the Nordic troll spirit of the divine; to Satan himself, another terrifying agent of the divine. The growing expectations of the people, when they are about to become spiritually united as a congregation, seem alien and threatening to Vig; what he senses to be ugly but true, the mortality of the congregation and their desire for seduction, causes him to view himself, within the Christian context, as being demonic, impure. This sense of the ultimate incompatibility for man of the true and beautiful belongs to youth.

The expectations of the congregation, which demand that Vig be seductively soulful, make him feel like a market town entertainer. He suddenly finds himself possessed by the spirit engendered by the congregation for its own self-enchantment and corruption.[12] This spirit slyly overpowers the person toward whom it is directed, makes him feel stronger as a man, and then through him seduces those from whom it originated. It is a spirit that enhances the unimportant man and makes his earthly stay appear to be meaningful; that grows out of a common tradition — a hope of grace; and that uses the language of poetry to create a common bond. Vig's refusal to be soulful is a partial defeat of this aesthetic seduction. He refuses to elaborate on the biblical text about the unclean spirit, which — once driven out of man — suffers and returns with seven others to dwell in that man once more and causes his end to be worse than his beginning. In the text it is said that one cannot drive out evil with evil, for Satan's house, like any house divided against itself, could not endure.[13] Vig then uses one aspect of Christianity to drive out the other. He asks Line (Erik's widow), the only uninfatuated member of the congregation, if Christ has helped her. At her nod the spirit possessing Vig seems to flee and to strike Vig as it goes. Shortly afterward Vig identifies the slap ringing in his ears with the sound of the snipe.

Vig has said, at the end of his account, that he recognizes God's nearness only when He strikes him. The spirit sent forth by the congregation would surely seem to be representative of man's secret hunger for the metaphysical, for meaning through the aesthetically mystic. This may be the divine spirit as the congregation wishes it to be, but it is one that corrupts belief. This unclean spirit is born of man's pride, which demands grace of the immortal. The spirit strikes Vig as it departs, and it is exorcised by Vig's reminding the congregation, through Line, of the existence of undeserved tragedy and death and the simplicity of a culturally advocated acceptance of suffering.

If, at the beginning of the service, Vig's actions have been dictated by the philosophy of youth — and he was then like one made dumb through the possession of the evil spirit biblically alluded to — his possession by the spirit of the congregation has been in keeping with the aesthetic self-seduction of the mature man and has demanded soulful outpourings. At last Vig seems to reassert a view more compatible to that on which he bases his teaching: although suffering and death are man's lot, a simple belief in culture (that is, a stoic acceptance that one's fate is purposeful) can dull their sting.

Although Vig feels that his decision to write a work on Sandö may be born of vanity and although he describes his manipulation of the fates of others as an attempt to pass the time by one who is a stranger, a momentary guest in life, the school — where his use of deceit and carnival techniques are appreciated — forgives and blesses him. Johannes feels that he is accepted by, and belongs to, the school, and that after-

The Liar

noon he tells Elna that she may move in as his housekeeper. This is his attempt to burn his bridges behind him, for there will be no room in his household for either Annemari or Rigmor. He feels the wild joy of youth, since he is being truthful about his not desiring them. At the ball he tells Rigmor of his dedication to the school, and he tells Annemari not only of his past, noble withdrawal from a possible affair with Birthe but also of his decision to have Elna as his housekeeper.

Annemari has accused Johannes of being cold and passionless. When, on the next day, he suddenly finds that he has lost control over Oluf, who seems free to act for the first time in six years, Vig's resolution of the night before immediately reveals itself to be another lie. He rushes out to win back his pupil and toy, Annemari, but discovers that he is too late to win her on his terms. He reacts with both passion and malice. He now tells Annemari that he had won Birthe from her husband and deserted her. Vig gives Annemari Birthe's necklace as a symbol of Sandö to wear about her neck, a symbol representative of his own curse, the loss of love, the truth, and nature's infliction of suffering and death. He also promises her a snipe.

In cold passion Vig then goes on his snipe hunt. The snipe is associated in his mind with unrestrained sexual desire and the unclean spirit. The fact that the snipe may also be associated with spiritual renewal first occurs to Vig later. His hunt brings him to Rigmor's bed, where he coldly conducts his second sabbat. He calls himself the devil and her a witch. When she grieves over life's meaninglessness and his destruction of their friendship, he explains that meaninglessness is what life is all about and implies that the hounding of Job, his suffering and helplessness, is descriptive of man's fate. When Rigmor says she loves him, Vig's determination to harm and corrupt her is broken.

Upon leaving Rigmor Vig notices that the sea looks as if Leviathan had just swum through it. He then catches sight of a snipe and rushes back to get Rigmor so that she may accompany him on the hunt. Just before dark Vig shoots a snipe and gives it to Rigmor as a pact between them. It is a sign of his belief in her ability to start her life anew. He declares that life in modern civilization is lived in the pursuit of happiness but that one must perhaps choose a stricter law.[14] He asserts that, although evil seems to be life's ruling principle, goodness and warmth, purity and light exist in man — and, it seems implied, can redeem him by his good works.

Vig conducts a private ritual for Rigmor who, like the congregation, has expected him to represent something more than the empty and meaningless. Poetic language is the means of carrying out this mutual spiritual seduction, and this time, in contrast with his actions in the church, Vig uses that language.

Rigmor's declaration of her love for Vig, an admission of her vulnerability and her dependence on him, had earlier brought the school to his mind. Vig has now resumed his aesthetically ethical role through his wish to give Rigmor an attitude toward life that, in turn, would furnish her with a role in life, just as he gives the children such a role. The student must however be convinced of his teacher's belief in what he is teaching, and so it is with Rigmor and Vig. Vig belongs to Rigmor because of her profession of love for him: she has embraced him just as the school has, and he is bound to them both. Both are able to profit by his ways.

Vig's rite of killing the snipe for Rigmor's spiritual renewal is the sort of act that seems basically demonic to Vig, for it entails his spiritual seduction of another. Vig has recalled the biblical assertion that a realm divided against itself will be desolated; and by employing an evil means to achieve a "supposedly" good end, Vig destroys, through his own form of the demonic, the evil side of truth: that unclean spirit which is the eternally returning desire for seduction. He thus causes evil to destroy itself, and his shooting the bird becomes symbolic of his own willingness to conceal the dark side of truth in order to promote the cultural.

After Vig's pact with Rigmor to serve by self-denial some greater law — that of accomplishing something, of creating something — in order that all may not seem meaningless, Vig and Pigro go to Nærbjerg. There on the highest stone, which Vig imagines to have been a sacrificial stone upon which others have been slain in honor of a great force of nature, he awaits the sound of wings in the growing dusk, for such moments bring over him a sense of being in the power of the divine. Vig understands that his fate is bound to the island, and he determines to make a choice.

The myth that calls Johannes Vig is the wish to accomplish something. By killing the snipe and dedicating himself on the sacrificial stone, Vig has allied himself with death in order to overcome it. Vig's familiar spirit, Pigro, his "snipe hound" — representative of himself as a bringer of death, doubt, and guilt — grows ill. When Vig shoots Pigro, he symbolically destroys a part of himself and demonstrates that a phase of his life has passed. The unchanging Vig, who must always be, by nature, devious and sly, has turned his destructiveness from others and directed it wholly against himself.

The Liar

The year spent in the writing of *The Liar* may be Vig's version of the heroic swim carried out because one is pursued by past guilt. Both Vig's continued writing of his account of Sandö and his continued abstension from life are perhaps of help to others, but he has trapped himself in the aesthetic role. Vig may raise the spirit of youth, Natanael, to converse with, but Vig's diary is in itself an exorcism of his past in the name of culture. Although his new account (one primarily in celebration of the island's past and its natural characteristics), like *The Liar* itself, was originally a means of escape into the aesthetic role, that role now assumes the character of a duty that, for Vig, must be an end in itself. Vig has dedicated himself to culture, even though it is a god in which he ultimately does not believe.

For a person like Vig, the "thinking" person, acting according to the dictates of feeling alone leads to evil results, and not acting at all leads to a feeling of meaninglessness. Vig is a man who is unable to share in a metaphysically positive aesthetic vision of life, like that which Christianity represents to man or that which the ungraspably sublime music of Bach represents of God. For Vig, the vision productive of awe is that of the sunset rather than the sunrise, that of the knowledge of pain rather than the experiencing of joy, that of rebellion rather than submission. He is unable fully to accept both life and death, for death is his ultimate vision, and he sees all life in terms of it. In his past pessimism he has toyed with creating small aesthetic stories about life, but he has lost both his influence over his main puppets, Oluf and Annemari, and his own controlled noninvolvement. Losing his minor Godlike role — his demonic role — he has tried to assume a new, saintly role for the sake of Rigmor; but he is unable to give it a positive meaning on a personal level. Such a pretense about life may be a premature form of death. Vig's lot is one of intense longing. Across the whole account he has written the verdict of himself, "The Liar," and the latter part of that account is as much one of his own self-seduction as it is a seduction of Rigmor.

Vig has placed himself in an intolerable situation, and his suffering he attributes to God. Vig declares his lot to be that of Job who, being hounded by Satan, wanted death, man's ultimate fate. He could not understand that he in any way deserved his past suffering, but he accepted it, for he could not know God's purposes. The God to whom Vig thus refers has not promised man eternal life but has shown that tragedy and death may be man's lot. God's question to Job, which Vig remembers and which illuminates the problem for him, is whether Job could loosen the belt of Orion (also called The Hunter, after Nimrod). For Vig this question implies the vastness and unknowableness of creation, in which suffering and death are apportioned parts. Hunting assumes cosmic, mythic proportions and, like Leviathan, is an inescapable part of God's plan of what "will be."

Vig's situation is one he has created himself, and his final deception is to see himself as suffering a God-inflicted pain. With the illusion of God's punishing him, Vig tries to create for himself a "state of wonder" through pain and, thus, to achieve a "feeling of belonging" for as long as life lasts. Vig attempts to transform his belief in the indifference of a god of nature into a belief in the God of the Old Testament, a God who would exact proofs of man's submissive belief in Him, a culturally determined God. Vig, the author of his own misfortunes, tries to be the revising editor of his own true vision of God; this corruption of the truth — this slander — is truly satanic.[15]

Although Vig has brought about his own situation, his own suffering, he is similar to Job in that he is no longer an active agent, but rather a deflector of the evils of life against the origins of destructiveness. Against the seeming lack of pity on the part of such a God, man has only his own goodness and his belief in that goodness upon which to fall back. Although Vig encourages others to believe in the rewards of goodness, he himself would prefer life to take the form of a wild, short battle, and he likens his lonely fate to the skull of the pagan Skallagrimsson.[16] Just as an axe could not penetrate that skull, no weapon of suffering is able to affect Vig's fate. He seems to imply not only that his lonely fate is partially a product of his own mind, but also that, no matter what may be the dictates of his emotions, his mind is unimpressionable and, thus, so is his fate.

If the writing of *The Liar* has been a proud escape from truth carried out in behalf of culture, Vig's writing about the nature and past of Sandö — also an aesthetic act, but one dedicated to truth — is a purification of himself from pretense. Vig's writing a faithful depiction of the nature of Sandö, the very name of which in Danish suggests truth and transiency, ironically seems to be almost his attempt to recapture that vision of nature and nature's god which to Vig has represented death, but which may now represent to him the only form of life guaranteed to man. Vig's preserving this knowledge, however, is in itself a cultural act. Vig is a man apart, one who has not attained the peace and quiet of which he has dreamed, for he has challenged truth — and, thus, God as the author of truth — with man's version of beauty. Vig is an artist who has wished to write not only his own saga but that of the victory of culture over nature as well; yet, nature has taken its revenge, for he is as a man entombed by longing and without the peace of death itself.

Vig endures his self-inflicted pain; thus, an act that is personally and philosophically negative becomes publicly positive. Like his schoolroom example of the explorer Brönlund who dutifully wrote of his surroundings until his death by freezing on a polar ice field, Vig, who says that he has been icebound for forty years, now waits out his time dutifully describing Sandö for those who may follow. From a distance, Vig's suffering seems dimmed, and only the beauty of his acceptance of his fate is reflected. Vig's descriptions of nature may however present the beauty of a world as emotionally inaccessible to others as the music of Bach was to Johannes Vig himself.

And the reader? The reader — like Natanael, who would get to the bottom of things, who would understand the motives behind them — is dismissed. There is perhaps nothing more for Vig to say, except that, that is how life is.

Natanael has served Vig both as conscience and as listener. He is present as a substitute for the book's reader. One may accept the fact that the reader is the writer's conscience, to whom the writer both appeals for understanding and from whom he must receive his judgment; but one must add that the reader may also seem to be the writer's dupe as well as his conscience and his student as well as his mentor. The reader, that ever present — but inarticulate — extra character who is manipulated by the author, must always play the role of dupe before he may assume that of judge. In most instances it is a harmless enough arrangement based on a really quite pleasant gentleman's agreement. If, in the case of *The Liar*, the reader identifies himself with Natanael, while accepting Hansen as the author of the work, the contract remains a pleasant one. Since, however, Hansen allows his pen to be guided by Vig — an author, an excellent teacher, and a professed liar — the reader's transition from the role of dupe to that of judge is severely hampered. The reader cannot escape having Vig's words, those of a sly pedagogue, ringing in his ears: "It is art, Natanael, that I care about. To slyly ease them on until they themselves sort of surprise the meaning in the equation."[17]

In some ways *The Liar* seems to complete the cycle of *The Thornbush*. One of the main symbols in the last short story of that trilogy was fog, and the opening scenes of *The Liar* are enshrouded in the fog of late winter. The seasonal cycle is completed as the story line once more moves toward spring. If death was the wish of the protagonist, the "writer," of "September Fog," to overcome death is the wish of the writer Johannes Vig, and he does so ultimately by a depiction of nature in his work. He binds it with the mind and attempts to make it a part of culture through the work he has written to portray its enigma.

The Liar parallels *The Thornbush* in a number of ways. *The Liar* and the first two stories of *The Thornbush* each contain two contrasted cultic scenes. In the stories, the rite in nature spells death to the past lives of the three protagonists, and in each story a younger woman, who is attracted to the protagonist, is allowed to go her way, whereas an older woman, who is tired of life, is reborn into suffering. The protagonist of *The Liar*, in his capacity of vicar, schoolmaster, and devilish manipulator, has been enlarged to contain facets of Johansen in "The Easter Bell," some of the side show barkers in "The Midsummer Festival," and the unchanging Johan of the former story, the manipulative "author" of the latter, and the emotionally confused and isolated "writer" of "September Fog."

If the "The Midsummer Festival" and "September Fog" were both the literary products of their protagonists, so is *The Liar*, which also resumes the conversation between author and fictional reader begun in "The Midsummer Festival." The "reader" of that story and Natanael, the substitute for the reader, in *The Liar* are left to make what they can of the stories when their respective authors are finished relating them. The reader must make the final judgment, the final interpretation, and thus assume the final telling of the story.

The protagonists of all four tales seem to bear out the assertion of the author in "The Midsummer Festival" that peace is also war. It is a war waged by the nihilistic modern protagonist to discover meaning in life through suffering or death, which are the elements he recognizes as being true about life. "The Midsummer Festival's" final, apparent optimism is taken up for reexamination in *The Liar* and found to be an attitude possible for the author to give others, even though he may never be able fully to share it. The reader is left to discover whether or not that optimism and the art that produces it are justified.

The symbols of *The Liar* link it closely to *The Thornbush*, for the birds and the ghosts of past guilt all reflect aspects of the protagonists themselves. Perhaps the final symbol relating the two is the thornbush itself, whose replica in miniature may be Vig's pen, which — he fancies — when planted, might flower and leaf if there is truth in what he has written. Annemari had hurled the pen at the floor near Pigro, and it stood quivering there like a harpoon.[18] The pen is truly the instrument of culture. When *The Liar* opened, Vig had already filled twenty notebooks about Sandö; when the story closed, he had written five more and *The Liar,* the story of himself and of other people living on the island. It would be difficult to say which work's "truth" would cause the pen to bloom; but after the writing of *The Liar,* for Vig to write of nature may well feel to him like having to embrace nature's thorns in the hope that its promise will burst into bloom.

CHAPTER 8

Apples of Paradise, The Conch, *and* Aftermath

I Apples of Paradise

Apples of Paradise (Paradisæblerne og andre Historier [1953]) was the last collection of short stories to be issued by Martin A. Hansen himself. Both this slender volume and the posthumously published collections include excellent pieces of fiction but still do not measure up to the unique quality of *The Partridge*. Two of the most significant texts in *Apples of Paradise* are the title story itself and "The Ostrich" ("Strudsen").

In "Apples of Paradise" a boy contentedly spends a long afternoon at his grandmother's little house, but when he sets out for his home at night, he suddenly decides to take a shortcut across a creek that is covered by treacherously thawing ice. He makes this choice because he has come to feel that his life is unbearable. Before leaving for home he has talked to the suspicious, crippled, old gamekeeper who lives in a part of the boy's grandmother's house, and on the way home the boy has met a former schoolmate who seems to be destined for a miserable life. The grandmother, with her unshakable belief in God's Providence, is clearly contrasted with these two figures, who represent fear, isolation, and purposelessness. When the boy contemplates his own future, he imagines it to be as bleak as the lives of the gamekeeper and his schoolmate, and this supposition makes the boy indifferent to what will happen to him and angry with those who love him. In a defiantly careless mood he tries to cross the ice. When the ice seems to give, he suddenly receives a shove that helps him to struggle up the opposite bank of the creek. He storms off in fear, but when he finally regains his composure and his defiance once again prevails, he wants to lose his way in the foggy darkness. He scatters a few crab apples his grandmother has given him, and as he searches for them, he realizes that he no longer knows where he is. In panic he bounds off across the plowed field, stumbles, and loses most of the apples. Crying and fumbling about for the apples, he discovers that one step further would have hurled him into a treacherously deep marl pit lying directly before him. Flushed with shame, he finally regrets his defiance and, aware now of where he is, walks in a direction from which he will soon see the lights of home.

The story is told by the boy, and through his thoughts and associations the narrative gains a rich, symbolic texture. As long as the boy is possessed by gloom, the landscape continually reminds him of the old gamekeeper; but when the boy is miraculously saved from certain death by the apples of paradise, the scent of the field seems to him to be that of his grandmother's home. The vital attitude of the old culture, represented by the grandmother and her gift of apples, has saved him from a self-destructive despair.

"The Ostrich" also reveals a great deal about the obstinacy of children, as one long summer afternoon a boy and his little sister hunt for an imagined ostrich. They do much that is forbidden, and although the boy, a mighty hunter, will celebrate his birthday on the following day, he will undoubtedly receive for his erring ways this day an unpleasantly warm welcome from his irate parents. The story is both humorous and idyllic, but like the preceding one, it testifies to the allure of the dangerous and forbidden.

"Our Lady's Hunter" ("Vor Frues Jæger") retells a Norwegian hunting yarn about a lazy, but capable, bear hunter who, rather against his inclinations, finally fulfills his promise to the Virgin Mary to kill a bear for her. He manages this feat within an abandoned church in a region that has been totally depopulated by plague, and he thereby opens the area for resettlement. This humorous tale unpretentiously celebrates the theme of culture's conquest of nature through the offices of a fairly shifty character, who nevertheless has a grudging sense of moral commitment.

"Tirad" is thematically closer to the focal point of Hansen's works. The setting is the peninsula of Stevns during the twelfth century, when hundreds of churches were built in the newly Christianized Denmark. Tirad is a church builder, and after the consecration of the building, he carves the two words "Tirad rist" (carved) into a wall. The village is attacked by Wends, and although the onslaught is beaten back, Tirad is captured. He may be doomed, but as an old man points out, "he created the church and he carved the runes on it. Tirad is here anyway."[1] An artist who works for the spiritual needs of his community, for culture, cannot die; and his works, like the Danish churches, will continue to symbolize strength and justice and to protect the country from the barbaric invasions of the future.

Whether the most significant stories in *Apples of Paradise* recall childhood or history, they are celebrations of the sustaining strength of the old culture and are unclouded by the doubts born of modern complexity.

II The Conch

Hansen had planned to publish a new volume of short stories in 1955, but his wife and Ole Wivel had to act as its editors. Hansen had wanted the book to be named after its first story, "The Countenance" ("Aasynet"). That title was to suggest the book's thematic relationship to *The Partridge*, for "The Countenance" bears a close resemblance to the title story of the earlier book. The setting of "The Countenance" is once again a farming milieu in the throes of economic crisis, and the story's cast is once more those closely knit family members who battle against bad luck and share an experience that they take as an omen of better days to come. Unfortunately, the story lacks the immediacy of "The Partridge" and carries a tinge of didacticism and sentimentality.

"The Sin" ("Synden") expresses with gusto the human urge to give in to dark, irresponsible impulses. In this humorously related instance such a desire for sin is shown to be the result of a too single-minded devotion to ethical purity. For a long time a little boy has jubilantly looked forward to the day when his family will move out to their own farm. In order not to anger God the boy has consistently been on his best behavior; and when the anticipated day finally comes, he sorely needs to wallow in sin. His inner tension finally erupts into a fierce and nasty fight with two other boys; although he wins, the beautiful day drowns in his bitter tears. There is nevertheless little doubt that his indulgence of this urge for the wildly excessive has been deeply satisfying to him.

"The Righteous One" ("Den Retfærdige") is a story that Hansen revised several times.[2] It is a monologue in which Manuel tells about his parents and the dissolution of their marriage. His father, Vilhelm, employed as a stonecutter, was a talented sculptor who could envision extraordinary works but dared not rely upon his own judgment. He, therefore, had to make sure that his wife could "see" something in his half-finished sculptures. When she responded positively, he would neglect all else to finish his work; otherwise, he would destroy it, return to his job, and act the part of a good and dutiful father. As the years passed, however, Vilhelm gave in to more and more frequent drinking bouts, and although he and his wife undeniably loved each other, the relationship between the two became strained by their growing mutual resentment.

The story clearly analyzes the question of the costs of art in terms of human relationships. Art demands much of its priest, for it does not allow him to fulfill the needs of people who rely upon him. He isolates himself, exploits his family, and he increasingly suffers from the recognition that his indulgence in art makes them suffer. He still cannot give up his art, for such a choice would destroy him. Consequently, the tension in the family grows until it reaches the breaking point. As so often before, Manuel is sent to the inn to fetch his father. His father is with some other men, and one of them, who maintains a pretense of being righteous and just ("the righteous one"), cunningly manipulates Vilhelm into inviting them all to his home. When Manuel's mother warns Vilhelm that this visit will bring them all unhappiness, he ignores her. The men engage in a card game in which Vilhelm loses most of the furniture and, eventually, even those sculptures that his wife had helped him create. Vilhelm once again pleads for his wife's help, but she has given up her exhausting struggle to preserve the family. Afterward, Vilhelm stops going to the inn; then he moves away, never to return. Art has caused a distance to grow between him and his family and has finally estranged them completely. Vilhelm has been destroyed — or has destroyed himself — not only as a father and a husband but as an artist as well.

As Manuel and his mother sit quietly listening to the card game in the adjoining room, she asks him if he, like his father, would "find people in stone."[3] Manuel firmly rejects the idea and lives up to his promise: he becomes a good family man; and although he may inherit his father's gift, he uses it merely as a means to entertain his children. Still, he gives the impression of being a man made impassive by artificially imposed limitations. His totally understandable reaction to the past has been a flight into normalcy, which, for the artistic mind, exacts its price.

The grim lesson of "The Righteous One" is that, no matter what choice the artist makes, he will be damned. Vilhelm destroyed and was destroyed by the hard demands of his art; and Manuel, in his renunciation of art, is spiritually petrified. For the artist who is caught up in the struggle between art and life, only conflict or spiritual paralysis is feasible.

A parallel can be suggested between the artist's spontaneous moments of creation and those moments of yielding to wild, dark impulses, which are featured in "The Sin." Both instincts allow an intensity of experience and momentary fulfillment that is otherwise unobtainable.

"Haavn" takes place one deadly cold winter during the war years.

The protagonist, Haavn, is a cantankerous farmer who is involved in perennial strife with his community. He stubbornly clings to past custom and may represent an ugly caricature of the old farm culture. He is self-righteous, petty, and — like the gamekeeper in "Apples of Paradise" — suspiciously watchful of the world. One icy morning, when he finds his most valuable sow frozen to death, he momentarily gives up and contemplates setting the farm afire. He feels like a demon who has caused the desolation of winter, and with perverse joy he envisions the farm and its animals ablaze. In this moment of simultaneous despair and indifference, his long dead grandmother seems to haunt him and angrily scold him for repudiating his family, the generations of farmers who would never have committed such a sin. Haavn is a changed man. Although he knows that the dead animal is supposed to be turned over to the wartime authorities, he decides to boil the sow in order to produce the soap so sorely needed by the community. During a raging blizzard he struggles to the town in order to procure the necessary ingredients for his project. The next morning, shortly after his work has begun, it is interrupted by his neighbors who have gleefully come to witness his defeat when the official truck arrives to haul away the dead animal. Haavn, however, stands up to the government agents, and since they dare not accost such a bloody and forbidding figure, they must beat a retreat. Haavn returns to his work.

Haavn's continuing with his plan may seem ludicrous, since the community has turned against him, but (as Björnvig points out) the transformed Haavn needs no tangible reward.[4] In his darkest moment, when he was about to forsake his duty as a farmer, he was saved by the spirit of his culture's age-old tradition — speaking through the specter of his grandmother; he is now reintegrated into that culture. He, who had earlier imagined his grandmother's spirit to be merely a malignant sprite that wanted to work his downfall, was himself then but the ghost of the degenerating old culture. He has now returned to the living. His foolish, illegal project symbolizes his liberation from crippling isolation. With "Haavn" Martin A. Hansen exemplifies his thesis that the values of the past can offer meaning and guidance in the modern world.

The same deeply rooted feeling of responsibility toward the past and present is also at the core of "The Messenger" ("Budbringeren"), which is set in Norway during World War II. A school teacher has been asked to deliver a cryptic message to some members of the resistance movement in a distant region. Half-delirious from a lack of food and sleep, he stumbles through the wilderness until he comes across an old farm. Its occupants are long dead, but strangely preserved, and to the dazed messenger they seem alive. He stays with them for several days and washes them and tidies up before he leaves to carry out his errand.

The story's eerie, dreamy quality may make the sanity of the protagonist doubtful; but in his overwrought state he discovers *his* errand in life. He promises to return to the dead and to recultivate their land, which has been slowly invaded by nature. He exuberantly allies himself with the spirit of the farm, for that spirit is to him a source of healing and life. The farm finally reminds him of his duty to get his message through to the embattled living.

The strength of the old culture as a force in the modern individual's life is clearly brought out, but not without the intimation of a conflict. The protagonist's total devotion to his newly found mission seems to obscure his responsibility to the living, who await his urgent message. "The Messenger" suggests that a preoccupation with the past, which grants the individual meaning, can endanger his sense of the urgency of the present. The man's acceptance of the authority of the dead engulfs him so completely in the past that he appears to be its own ghostly messenger.

The concluding story of this volume, "The Bridegroom's Oak" ("Brudgommens Eg"), strikes a similarly disturbing note. Its motif is well known from folklore: a man visits the realm of the dead for a few moments, but upon his return he discovers that he has been away many years and has grown old.[5] The story is narrated by an old man who tells what once happened to his grandfather, Per Nilsen. Over a hundred years ago, when Per Nilsen served on the minister's farm, an old man suddenly appeared out of nowhere and strangely asked whether the wedding guests had risen yet. He seemed to be oddly youthful and quite exuberant, but when he caught sight of a tall oak, he immediately began to wither. Upon being questioned by the minister, the old man explained that on the morning following his wedding he had left his bride to escort to the grave a dead compatriot whom he had invited to the feast. As they were about to part, the groom asked whether he could visit the realm of the dead. His friend took him along, and they wandered through dreamlike regions; but when the bridegroom had to wait alone to be ferried across a river, he was suddenly beset by terror and rushed back. He had found himself standing again by his friend's grave and had happily walked home on that lovely morning to greet his bride and the wedding guests. Although at first everything was familiar to him, he suddenly saw the tall oak that he himself had so recently planted. As he told the story, the old man grew calm and meekly accepted the passing of the years since his wedding. Shortly after his receiving the sacrament in church, he fell dead near the large tree.

The groom's story was, of course, not easy to believe, but he offered enough proof for Per Nilsen to trust him. The minister was less inclined to be convinced, and he was apparently so disturbed by the event that he falsified the account of the old man's death in the church annals. He also let Per know that it would be better if the story were not told, but Per did not agree and passed the incident on to his son after the minister's death. One may ask why the minister wanted to suppress the story, and the answer must be that this shaken servant of orthodox belief could not cope with incidents that seemed to bespeak life's purposelessness. He insisted upon there being a meaning in every occurrence in life, and twice he intimated that some day the good Lord would reveal His purpose in allowing such a fate to befall the old man.

After realizing that time had indeed passed, the old man had offered a drastically different view of life: "Misfortune is like a clear day; you can see far."[6] Misfortune clears one's senses, and one sees one's lot for what it is. Those terse words moved Per Nilsen to pass the story on to his son, and it is obvious that Per put more trust in the old man's harsh insight than in the minister's consoling words. The old man faced the bitter fact that a human being's life can be utterly wasted, and both Per Nilsen and, implicitly, the minister, who attempted to conceal the story, seem to have agreed.

Björnvig notes that the story is difficult to interpret, for although the young groom sinned against life by following his dead friend, his punishment is inordinately severe.[7] In fact, the human being's claim to justice in life seems to go unheard, and the only knowledge that this dark tale imparts is that life is painfully short and can easily be completely wasted. A mood of unalleviated sorrow permeates "The Bridegroom's Oak."

III   Aftermath

Aftermath: Last Stories and Sketches (Efterslæt. Sidste Noveller og Skildringer) was edited by Ole Wivel and Thorkild Björnvig and published in 1959. A number of stories from the 1930s are well told but are only potentially indicative of the tone and themes that bear Hansen's special touch. Two stories in "Aftermath" stand out: "The Homecoming" ("Hjemkomsten") and "The Gardener, the Beast, and the Child" ("Gartneren, Dyret og Barnet").

"The Homecoming" is the story of a soldier's return home after the Napoleonic Wars, but this horseman, now riding through the landscape of his youth, may easily be identified with all the disillusioned warriors to whom a homecoming has given scant relief.[8] He seems to be a dulled and indifferent man, and he scarcely reacts when he is told that his younger brother has married his fiancée and taken over the family farm. The warrior returns home in the dark, and his former fiancée shrinks back from him in fear. When his brother lamely tries to make excuses, the soldier impatiently brushes them aside and leaves. Before his inner eye the foggy night becomes a fertile summer landscape, the life he could have had; but the fog then transforms itself into marching and battling armies. As he curses bitterly and starts to ride off, he hears steps hurrying behind him and his mother's voice calling his name.

"The Homecoming" is not symbolically shrouded in total darkness, for the ever demonic fog is not allowed to swallow up the soldier. He may stay on and cultivate the land, and he may even marry a young girl he has met earlier in the day, but these consolations are still meager. The times have dealt cruelly with him, and he will not soon forget his experiences. To the young girl who likes him, he explains, "One has seen a lot of cursed filth, but one gets used to it. That is not so good, Lisbeth; one gets used to it."[9] This disillusionment and the indifference it breeds destine the soldier to be spiritually isolated. The constrictive feeling of great loss — the loss of love, peace of mind, and a sense of purpose and belonging — speaks from "The Homecoming."

"The Gardener, the Beast, and the Child" has the same nightmare quality as do many of the stories that depict the inner landscape of the mind, but this text seems initially realistic. It is twilight, and the narrator is tying up roses in a garden, while his little son, Egon, is playing a short distance away. The gardener's thoughts belie the scene's inherent idyllicism. He feels indifferent to his work, and he wishes that he could take one little step to the side, become a boy again, and be free. When his son approaches him, the gardener hides in the darkness, and the frightened boy rushes off. The father calls after him, but softly, as if not wanting to be heard.

The gardener is possessed by one of those inner demons that, in Hansen's writing, so consistently represents the lure of nihilism. His state of mind is signaled by the falling darkness, which — like the fog in other texts — marks his indifference to the role and responsibility he has chosen in life. His gliding into the surrounding darkness is, as Björnvig has pointed out, the gardener's negation of his own identity; and his little step to the side now makes him one with nature.[10] Nature is tellingly pictured in terms of decay: the roses look to him like mushrooms; the air seems clammy and dead; the "wet flowers shine palely, voluptuously, indecently"; and he likens his own life to "a quiet water with worms at the bottom."[11] Nature attracts him — the erotic nuances in the description are subtle, but unmistakable — and his longing for it is accompanied by a wish to drowse, by a lack of memory, and by an inability to comprehend language: "Your child, they say, I don't understand that word. I understand nothing."[12] The gardener here joins ranks with those many other figures in Hansen's works who reject responsibility, and he allies himself to all that is destructive to life and culture.

As the man watches the boy disappear into the darkness, he is startled by the shadow of a big animal that seems to leap off in the same direction. He grabs a spade and storms after the boy; but even when shouting the boy's name, the gardener has not rid himself of his indifference. His pursuit leads him to an area that must be seen as symbolic of the gardener's mind. This space had earlier been occupied by a garden center (the crumbling foundations of the hothouses can still be seen), but its decay has become so pronounced that the place is now filled by a jungle of tangled weeds. The stages of decline are clearly indicated: once culture ruled, and nature was tamed by busy gardeners; but then destruction occurred (the tall houses in the background seem to have been hit by bombs), and the place was turned into a dump filled with the debris of culture; finally, the area has been overcome by a jungle of tall weeds. The place thus becomes a consummate symbol of a negative development both within culture and within the mind. The decline of culture and the supremacy of nature have much in common, for in their effect on the mind, they are identical. Nature, like a culture without values, neutralizes everything. Everything is of equal importance, which is to say, of no importance.

That such a state of mind is dangerous is evidenced in the story by the fact that wild beasts (a wolf and lionlike animals) prowl the grounds for prey. Their presence indicates an absence of humanity, and the gardener feels that, when he stares into these animals' eyes, he sees himself. He knows that he must fight these beasts, but he feels a strong desire to be like them and to live by their law. He greets the wolf thus: "We look at each other, the beast and I, and I feel a deep sympathy for it, . . . a desire to go down on all fours and to drink together with the wolf. I would like to kill you and to be killed by you."[13] The man feels free, but he also feels that his freedom is poisonous. He must take one further step and forget everything, for only forgetfulness liberates one totally. This wish for a complete annihilation of thought, which he even extends to a wish for madness, is a masked desire for the peace that only death can bring.

As the gardener still continues to search for his son, he is divided between contradictory impulses, which have apparently poisoned his life and which now have finally been brought out into the open. When

Apples of Paradise, The Conch, and Aftermath

he sees two lions tearing into a dark shape, he goes to attack them even though he expects to be slain; but that expectation is also attractive: "Now it is happening, now you will receive peace, now you will forget."[14] The lions, however, look at him with dishonest, shifty glances that are like his own and skulk away. Their booty was merely the carcass of a horse.

The gardener now fears only one thing: "Out of the darkness and the silence a being will come who is even more horrifying to meet than the beasts."[15] This is the boy, in whose eyes the gardener will meet — as he explains — "a deep and painful knowledge, the wonder of death, which I cannot endure to see and yet must see. Which I never shall forget, for I shall never forget anything."[16] The gardener is no longer drowsy or indifferent, and he fully realizes what his little step to the side has cost. He has irrevocably changed another human being and must assume the responsibility for this sacred crime, which he has committed in his demonic desire to give up all responsibility. Although he is still tempted to retain his freedom by keeping silent, he calls out his son's name.

The story ends with a spiritual transformation, one that is not uncommon in Hansen's work, and as in other texts, this transformation is preceded by a minute and unsettling study of the nihilistically inclined mind. Two oppositely inclined forces in the mind — those that Hansen projects into, and symbolizes through, nature and culture — are brought into confrontation in this nightmarish text. With compelling force Hansen shows how tempting it is to forget all trivial responsibility for a life in total, wild, destructive freedom. This freedom is deadly in character and must be rejected by the cultural being. In this story a rejection takes place, but it occurs so late that the gardener has already set his mark upon his innocent victim and must always live with that guilt.

CHAPTER 9

Essays and Leviathan

MARTIN A. Hansen's profound cultural engagement is expressed in the numerous articles that came from his hand throughout most of his career. They vary greatly in subject matter but, together, give an excellent impression of what Hansen meant by the tradition of the past and by the modern spiritual crisis.

In 1948 Hansen put together a volume of essays under the title *Thoughts in a Chimney (Tanker i en Skorsten)*, and in 1950 he published a book-length essay, *Leviathan*. *Midsummer Wreath (Midsommerkrans* [1956]) and *Aftermath (Efterslæt* [1959]) appeared after his death. Later, two collections were issued that overlap with the previous volumes but that also contain new material: *At the Crossroads (Ved Korsvejen* [1965]) and *The World Novel (Verdensromanen* [1966]). These collections treat, respectively, literary and historical subjects. *From the People's History of Denmark (Af Folkets Danmarkshistorie* [1959]) and *Martin A. Hansen and the School (Martin A. Hansen og Skolen* [1968]) are also compilations of essays on two subjects that had particularly intrigued Hansen.

I *The Essays*

The following discussion of Hansen's essays will be thematic rather than chronological, and it will be structured by the author's own compositional principle in *Thoughts in a Chimney*, since this collection's composition is clearly indicative of his interests. The first essays in this volume deal primarily with his childhood milieu on Stevns and the waning of that culture. His reflections quite naturally assume a historical perspective, and this perspective often expands to include more than the immediate past, for Hansen reaches back to those ages from which the old farm culture originated. Using this added historical insight, Hansen then turns to his own times and analyzes the war years and their aftermath. Although in the historical and biographical essays he is often close to narrative rendition, in those that deal with the contemporary cultural situation he becomes quite analytical and, at times, cryptic. This difference in approach is explainable: when he wrote of the past, he could conjure up what he envisioned as having been a lost cultural synthesis; but when he wrote of the present, he engaged in a quest to create such a synthesis in a world that seemed to defy such efforts. Through a careful attempt to chart the contemporary spiritual atmosphere, he has tried to devise a way out of his age's postwar pessimism and nihilism. In some of these essays Hansen studies the effect of the cultural crisis on contemporary literature and, at the same time, gives illuminating insights into his aesthetics.

The very first entry in *Thoughts in a Chimney* brings out Hansen's quintessential experience of the contrast between nature and culture. The essay is entitled "The Plow" ("Ploven"). This age-old tool is viewed to be one of those instruments that formed nature into "mellow plateaus and soft waves." It tore away supremacy from "raw and mighty nature" and transformed the wilderness into landscape. Hansen judges such labor to be one of those decisive cultural acts that check "vengeful nature that would prefer to make us all into plants."[1] Like so many of the other texts, "The Plow" rings out a warning against man's inclination to see purity in nature and to identify with it, for such an identification entails a brutalization that may end for him in a nihilistic form of barbary. In another essay, "Old Friends" ("Gamle Venner"), Hansen calls horses old friends, not only because he has handled horses in his youth, but also because, for centuries, they "have drawn the land from wilderness and savagery."[2]

To cultivate land makes the unknown and threatening known and safe, but in "Astern" ("Agterude") Hansen admits that man only knows well that piece of land on which he either has worked by the sweat of his brow or has shed his childhood tears, and that is a very small spot.[3] To Hansen his childhood region, Stevns, clearly is that spot. Although Hansen cannot be called a strictly regional author, his works can be seen as an attempt to make that small geographical area familiar to the reader, so that he will experience the old culture of Stevns as a symbol of all those cultural values that can fend off nature, especially when nature begins to manifest itself in "the wildest regions of the mind."[4] What originally was a personal experience of childhood in a waning farming culture gains symbolic significance and becomes myth.

Many of these childhood recollections may superficially seem quite simple and clear-cut. The events of the past are conjured up with such a keen sensitivity that, had not the voice of the older man intruded, the time span between actual experience and later recollection would have been very nearly eliminated. Everyday existence, compellingly festive even in its ordinariness, comes to life in such a manner that the reader intuitively grasps that, no matter how difficult life at times could be for Hansen as a child, he nevertheless grew up in a world that furnished him with a genuine feeling of security. Especially through his characterizations of the various members of his community, notably, those in his nearest family, one senses the fundamental harmony of his childhood world. As "Double Portrait in a Carved Frame" ("Dobbeltportræt i Karvskaaren Ramme") especially reveals, those people possessed a deep-seated sense of justice; worked hard for their often perilous existence; and yet felt strongly responsible for others in the community. In spite of their poverty they knew that life ought to be lived in a hopeful, joyous manner.[5]

The essays on Stevns and the old culture can be read as "fictional homecomings" that serve to sustain Hansen in his pursuit of purpose in the diffuseness of the modern world. The language of these pieces may be humorous, lighthearted, solemn, or nostalgic; but no matter what their predominant tone, they are deeply reverential and basically ritualistic in character. As "Legends in September" and "Old Friends" show, the writer knows that he is performing a symbolic act in order to gain contact with a world that is irretrievably lost to him. In this act there may be some joy, for by being an outsider he can recognize the past for what it was and understand it more fully and more clearly than before;[6] but there is also a sense of a heartrendingly great loss, for he will never again be able to experience life with the native's spontaneity. A disturbing note creeps into some passages, and it gains strength from the fact that his visits to that setting of the past are often made in solitude: The reader almost seems to be listening to a disembodied voice that, ghostlike and lost in dreams of what once was, haunts the land.[7] Since the restless ghost appears in Hansen's writings as a demonic force allied with nature, there is something unsettling about his fictional and actual returns to Stevns. As in so many other passages, Hansen's official program and staunchly positive attitudes are undercut.

Hansen began seriously to engage in historical writing during the first somber years of the German Occupation. In "The Dark Ages" ("Den Mörke Middelalder"), "The Sibyl and the Virgin" ("Völven og Jomfruen"), and "The Axe" ("Öksen"),[8] he focused on the often deprecatorily portrayed Catholic period in Danish history and the immediately preceding, widely adored Viking Age. In the latter he finds, as noted in the first chapter, a spiritual atmosphere that has its modern correspondence in nihilism and barbaric individualism (both presumably expressed in Nietzsche's teachings), and Hansen asserts that the advent of Christianity freed the Danes from that degenerate age. The new culture gave man "that meaning in life which is probably modern man's most horrifying lack."[9] In the common enthusiasm for lusty, seafaring warriors, one sees a projection into the past of wishful thinking, caused by a general enthralment with the seductive idea of the "natural" human being. What one hereby judges to be natural was more nearly the manifestation of barbary and destructive individualism, for if one takes a close look at the renowned Viking chieftains, such as King Svend Estridson in "The Nordic Caesar" ("Nordens Cæsar"), one will find a rigid, unconstructive imperialist.[10] The Vikings "could conquer, but they could not make the fields grow."[11] For people enduring such actual and spiritual oppression, which had resulted in a desperate pessimism, Christianity emerged as a liberator. A culture was born that made societal beings of the Danes and that embodied those values from which the old agrarian culture gained sustenance.

The core of that culture was a fervent belief in justice, a belief that was passed down through generations. According to Hansen in "The World Novel" ("Verdensromanen"), his father's generation still had a confidence in history: a belief in the eventual victory of justice.[12] Upon Hansen's departure from the old culture, however, he could no longer share in that optimism. His view, as Björnvig points out,[13] was cyclical rather than evolutionary; nonetheless, Hansen adamantly rejected the determinism inherent in the cyclical concept. He might view history as a repetitive process — as his strong, albeit indirect, parallel between Viking and Nazi supremacy indicates — but that did not make it permissable to deem cultural striving to be futile.

In Hansen's advocacy of the old tradition, he refers to some of the cultural heroes of the past, and although they may have been mythical, the tales about them project the kind of values that have made such a figure as Prince Uffe an integral part of Danish history. In "The Uffe-Poet" ("Uffedigteren") Hansen celebrates the seemingly half-witted Prince Uffe who saved the realm from subjugation to foreign rulers; and Hansen sees qualities in him that would guarantee society both freedom and spiritual health.[14]

In Uffe's amazing and abrupt metamorphosis from a mute hulk into an expert warrior, Hansen discerns a hope for a similar transformation in men who may suddenly realize that culture must be defended against those who violate the principles of justice. In the articles Hansen wrote for Danish underground publications, he admonished his halfhearted countrymen to recognize that it is sometimes necessary to transgress ordinary ethics and to use force against oppressors. To fight the Nazi menace — and to kill for that cause — was a duty.[15]

Hansen's various essays have demonstrably strong moral overtones, for it seemed to him that only through ethical commitment could meaning be wrested from life. For the man who was a member of the earlier farm culture, such a moral commitment was spontaneous; but in modern times, as traditional values have been questioned, man has been forced to engage in an agonizing search for values.

Hansen's strong engagement in the spiritual crisis in the postwar years makes it tempting to see him as a victim of history, but one will not comprehend Hansen's inner tension if one overlooks the fact that an attraction to the nihilistic and destructive had always lain in the recesses of Hansen's mind. As it has been pointed out, he understood that inner discord in terms of his parental heritage, and several texts offer ample evidence of the temptation he had felt as a boy to give free rein to those darker impulses that would make him a stranger to his secure world. In such moments the boy may momentarily have experienced that demonic closeness to wild nature which the grown man deemed dangerous and destructive. In the article "Unfinished Postscript" ("Uafsluttet Efterskrift"), Hansen himself voices such an interpretation:

There were fields, hedgerows, forest, beach, creek, meadow, fen. And [there were] two powers in all this. In the field, which man cultivated to the best of his ability, the peace-loving and the good had the upper hand; the field was spirit, sanctuary. In the "wild," the dangerous and devilish ruled, and the wild was therefore the more enticing. In creek, fen, and thicket lived something one did not see, but against which one felt an inner warning. It sometimes happened that the boy and the cattle of the meadow would suddenly storm away from the creek toward the field, the Christianized field. Nothing could be heard; nothing could be seen; but it was there: the coldness, the destroyer, the evil side of nature. Aimless, mechanical insanity; a soulless, illimitable propagation that threatens all spirit. . . .[16]

This passage effectively posits the well-known contrast between nature and culture. It is also typical of Hansen that he goes on to equate demonic nature with those destructive forces in culture and man that would destroy culture itself. Nature becomes connotative of purposeless death.

Death — or rather the attempt to make the thought of death acceptable — is often the subject matter of these essays. People who have led meaningful lives can peacefully go to their rest, but those who have not had such harmonious lives find death a problem.[17] To explain, Hansen adds in "Kindred" ("Ætten") that, in contrast to modern civilization, the old culture understood that to retain a knowledge of the dead was a duty.[18] One's own existence rested upon that knowledge, and if one rejected the authority of the dead, he would suffer a tragic fate.[19]

Hansen, as ever, refuses to glamorize the old way of life and to represent the past as a carefree, unproblematic time. In several instances he relates events of the past that have a chilling effect in their sheer brutality and horror; but it is significant that he finds that those incidents, now obscured by the passing of time, were all perceived to have grown out of the individual's obstruction of society's code.

As Hansen explains in one of his essays on the author Johannes V. Jensen, the old culture maintained a precarious existence between the poles of horror and joy.[20] Still, since that culture preserved a firm sense of values, it must be judged to have been basically harmonious and resistent to pessimism. In "The Storyteller from Vinje" ("Fortælleren fra Vinje") Hansen points out that, in spite of an awareness of the harshness of the human condition, the nameless people of the country could not be broken by tragedies; such people knew that miracles could happen.[21]

Modern man does not have such an intuitive security, for in his rootlessness he cannot cope with the fact of death, and thus the unbearable thought of death pervades his life. Through a crisis of values modern man has become ghostlike, a destructive and mournful demon.

This view of modern man is voiced in Hansen's literary criticism. He wrote several pieces on contemporary literature, in which he vested the poet with the duty of being the guardian of culture. The last essay in *Thoughts in a Chimney*, "The Eumenides" ("Eumeniderne"), depicts to what extent those goddesses of guilt and revenge made their crippling presence felt in the works that expressed the cultural climate after World War II.[22] The war had become a stark symbol of moral chaos, which darkened not only the past but also the future, and the ensuing, disillusioning peace strengthened the sense of crisis rather than diminished it. The war and, in particular, its aftermath demonstrated that neither philosophy nor political ideology could furnish new values upon which a cultural resurrection could be based. It was that dismal situation of alienation and excessive individualism which the young poets depicted, and their basic mood was summed up by Hansen with the Kierkegaardian term *angst*.

Angst, according to Kierkegaard's analysis in *The Concept of Dread* (*Begrebet Angest* [1843]), denoted that fear for which no object can be found and which, thus, cannot be eliminated. *Angst* makes the individual fear the good and draws him toward a demonic state of mind.

Several critics concur in the opinion that Kierkegaard's impact on Hansen was substantial,[23] and there can be little doubt that Hansen came to feel a kinship with that anguished sufferer who found meaning in his suffering by devoting himself fully to a mission. Hansen shared Kierkegaard's suspicion of art and could heartily agree with his conviction that no philosophical system, no man-made ideology, could exhaustively encompass existence and make the individual's life meaningful.

Although Hansen could not take Kierkegaard's final step and find subjective truth in Christianity,[24] Hansen agreed that man, in his quest to understand himself, could not rely on objective, empirical knowledge. Both authors insisted that, if man was to gain redemption from his state of *angst*, he had to exert his free will in order to choose a path that would defy the temptation of the demonic.

In spite of the troubled vision rendered in modern poetry, Hansen seemed to see a quest for redemption in the young poets' symbolic and supposedly cryptic verse. In "The Eumenides" Hansen expresses his belief in the new generation of poets through a characterization of the lyricist Ole Sarvig: "To his perception everything seems to dissolve, but in this chaos intuition finds the seed of life. It germinates; it becomes an organic structure that transforms chaos to cosmos and makes existence meaningful."[25] The emphasis of this brief passage on the transforming power of structure marks another important feature in Hansen's thinking about literature. Such essays as "The Eumenides," "The Decline of the Novel" ("Romanens Forfald"), "Himmerland and the Stories" ("Himmerland og Historierne"), and particularly "Convention and Form-spirit" ("Konvention og Formaand") — all show Hansen's growing preoccupation with form, that apersonal element in art which exists independently of the artist.[26] Hansen does not merely conceive form to be a stylistic or compositional principle, but a mystery that, although it cannot be analyzed exhaustively, is the innermost force in the creative act. This force, which he names "the form-spirit," he finds in those works of the past that have passed the test of time. The form-spirit has originated in the cultural traditions of the distant past and, thus, can transcend stifling epochal, ideological, and literary conventions and can regenerate a sense of meaning. The poet who allows himself to be guided by the form-spirit will discover that he no longer infuses his knowledge into the work but that, as if by mysterious grace, the work grants knowledge to him. The question is no longer what he wants of his work, but what it wants of him.[27]

Hansen's frame of reference for the form-spirit is mostly the older epic literature, not only the severely objective Old Norse Sagas and the medieval folk-ballad but also the supposedly simple oral tale that he had heard recited in his childhood. In the oral tale the outlook of the culture is never openly stated, and the motif is not interpreted by its narrator, who allows it to develop freely. In this sort of literature, which is neither primitive nor undemanding, the form-spirit is at work and makes of the narrator a conveyer of culture. The personal experience that once was put into these forms has now been transformed into being apersonal and universal and, thus, relevant to later generations. That this feat can be accomplished today is precisely what the young poets prove. In "The Eumenides" Hansen states, "The stanzaic form is, in itself, a part of their [the poets'] thinking. The verse-form, which they have inherited, is a cosmos that the crisis has not overtaken. In that form, this otherwise so chaotic existence has preserved its structure. By filling the poem with genuine feeling and personal experience, they can make of it a symbol for something meaningful and structured in life."[28]

The concept of the form-spirit, no matter how metaphysical it may seem, must have brought Hansen much relief, for it seemed to him that the form-spirit salvaged art from modern individualism and sanctioned the cultural function of the kind of art he venerated.

Hansen, however, did not find his task easy; although the lyric poets could find release from their torment in confessional verse, the epic writer — whose lot was harder — had to objectify his material and survey it from a distance. At times his necessary detachment turned into a frightening coldness, which could make him suspect that his creations were of a cynical and parasitical nature.[29] The concept of the form-spirit surely made Hansen's vocation more amenable to him, but as always his reconciliation with it was not total, and new qualms and problems ensued.

Prose, not poetry, was Hansen's domain, and he found it taxing to create epic art in an age that no longer had an epic tradition. According to Hansen in "Convention and Form-spirit," the demise of epic structure occurred with the rise of Naturalism in the late nineteenth century. The rigidly positivistic and individualistic outlook behind that analytically inclined literature generated a set of conventions that destroyed not only the great epic novel but also the existential thinking that the old forms made possible. Hansen was not alone in viewing

Naturalism to be a sign of cultural sickness; to many artists and critics, both Hansen's predecessors and his contemporaries, Naturalism seemed to disseminate a restrictive conceptualization of the human being. Reason and intellect came to rule, and the human being was analyzed through reductive, positivistic simplifications, which excluded any existential debate of good and evil. Accordingly, Naturalism has led to pessimism and despair, but in spite of its failure it has tended to dominate everyday thinking and to condemn any departure from positivistic thinking and aesthetics as a return to Romanticism.

Hansen admits however that there is one reaction against Naturalism that can indeed be dangerous and can actually lead even deeper into cultural darkness. Some poets flee from Naturalism's barrenness into an introverted, unrestrained depiction of the mind; consequently, they leave the real behind for unparalleled flights of imagination. This cult of the mind may inspire a complete form-anarchy, and works so inspired become dangerous forces of chaos. In "The Decline of the Novel" Hansen takes to task such impressive writers as Proust, Kafka, and Joyce. They strive for the infinite; thus, their novels can have no endings. The modern novel is decaying, since it is not based upon a cultural synthesis, a meaningful tradition, which the epic genres once had but now lack.

Although Hansen contributed significantly to Modernist prose and had found hope in Modernist poetry, he harbored suspicions of that literature's experimentalism, which could serve the forces of cultural fragmentation. As an alternative he posited a form that contained "the real" but that went beyond Realism. Such a synthesis was to be found in the past, especially in *Don Quixote,* but it was also present in those newer works in which the poet's imagination was controlled by the form-spirit, for example, in Alexis Kivi's *Seven Brothers* and Herman Melville's *Moby Dick.*[30] Such works generate an understanding of existence, for novelists who are guided by the form-spirit link themselves with the tradition of culture long past. It is not by explanation, but by narration, that epic writers project their vision and transcend intellectual perception. Although Hansen hesitated to equate their art with revelation, he maintained that "the poet knows and can express more than that about which he is capable of thinking."[31] Analytical literature creates illusions offered as truth, whereas true epic art transcends illusion and becomes a cultic experience for the individual. Hansen's concept of the form-spirit may be clarified by applying it to his own works. *Jonatan's Journey* and *Lucky Kristoffer* very nearly embody the principles he was later to develop, and *Serpent and Bull* overwhelmingly proves his ability to carry out his literary program. According to

Hansen, the last work utilizes the epic form to conjure up past traditions in such a manner as to be relevant to modern times. By never acquiescing to "private fits of crying,"[32] Hansen has created a work with *Serpent and Bull* that is in keeping with old epic fiction: the book transcends its author, achieves the suprapersonal, and gains universal perspective.[33]

The concept of the form-spirit may also be illuminated in Hansen's treatment of the authors he esteemed. One such author was Johannes V. Jensen, who had once exerted a good deal of influence on Hansen and against whose ebullient Darwinism and "biological Romanticism" Hansen later strongly reacted. Hansen nonetheless always appreciated Jensen's ability as a storyteller, and in a treatment of Jensen's fiction, in the essay "Himmerland and the Stories," Hansen found proof for his own theories concerning the creation of epic art.[34] In those stories Jensen utilized his memory of times past and moved back in time to ages that predated his own recollections; thus, in his texts, the people of the old farming culture were resurrected from their graves. Hansen found evidence in the stories that a suprapersonal remembrance and an adherence to the form-spirit of the old, anonymous, oral stories had enabled his predecessor Jensen to create unsurpassed art.

In Steen Steensen Blicher, an eminent Danish writer of short stories from the Romantic period, Hansen saw an artist who, "awed by the story's discipline,"[35] forgot himself in his engagement in narration; and with Tarjei Vesaas, Hansen's friend and Norwegian colleague, Hansen particularly established — or tried to establish — a common bond. That "Storyteller from Vinje," who (like Hansen) probed the modern, alienated mind, still resided in an old farming culture that, although it was on the wane, had not yet been reduced to an abstraction. Vesaas, along with a number of his countrymen, wrote hauntingly of human isolation, but since they all had their roots in an old and vital culture, they did not sink into "metaphysical pessimism."[36] Through their evangelically colored works they revealed instead that human fellowship could be regained. Vesaas might carry his form experiments and his awareness of alienation as far as Kafka did, but through suggestive narration and symbolism Vesaas could convincingly approach the mystery of spiritual redemption. In some small measure Hansen's wistful characterization of Vesaas can be extended to himself. Although their views on modern man and his cultural striving may be quite similar, Vesaas could express his personal peace of mind through spontaneous poetry on life's sacredness, whereas Hansen seemed to lack the necessary tranquility to do so.

The reader who wishes to gain insight into the concepts underlying

Hansen's writing will definitely be enlightened by his essays. They exhibit Hansen's attempt to give answers to all those existential questions with which his psychological make-up, his personal fate, and his troubled times had burdened him. The term *burden* is appropriate, for at times Hansen's nearly frantic attempt to form a philosophy seems indicative of a desperate search for meaning. This fact may account for the reader's discomfort; he begins to feel that he is sometimes being subjected to a restrictive reasoning that fails to be convincing. Hansen resorts to a kind of intellectual fireworks, a dazzling play of intricately intermingled concepts and symbols, which leave the reader with the sensation of having been manipulated into accepting Hansen's interpretation of life. Especially when Hansen argues most fervently for the possibility of spiritual rebirth, he may either "commit metaphor" or rely so heavily on lofty abstractions that he leaves his reader perplexed as to the meaning and validity of the views being expressed. In such passages, in which Hansen gives free rein to reflection, his prose can be intricate to the point of being florid, a style perhaps symptomatic of his striving to assert those views that he felt he personally had to accept. In spite of Hansen's conviction that the artist should be suprapersonal, some of the essays are very private. It has been important in this context to point to some of the flaws that could mar Hansen's writing, but it is quite as necessary to add that the majority of the essays — and certain parts of those against which this criticism has been directed — offer totally absorbing and illuminating reasoning.

II Leviathan

Like Hobbes's work to which Hansen refers, *Leviathan* (1950) takes its title from the monster in Job's book. This ill-omened creature had also made its presence felt in *The Liar,* and in both that novel and in *Leviathan* it clearly functions as a very inclusive symbol. In the latter Leviathan signifies the many false cultural gods that offer man a brighter future but that are actually incapable of saving him from a crisis of values.

The direct inspiration to *Leviathan* was Hansen's growing discomfort with the Marxists. Like so many of the young intellectuals, he had been close to the Communists in the 1930s but had broken with their dogmas by the end of that decade. During the war a common front against oppressors had obscured the ideological differences between the various groups within the resistance movement, but soon after 1945 that solidarity dissolved. Although Marxism bears much of the brunt of Hansen's criticism in *Leviathan,* he lashes out at all those materialistic interpretations of existence that remain the stubbornly and widely accepted trustees of truth in the modern world's anguish and confusion. Besides Marxism, he singles out for special treatment not only Darwinism but also the general belief in scientific truth; and he scourges their adherents for pretending to offer exhaustive explanations of existence, which, in fact, are only partial views or mere hypotheses. He does not deny those views' usefulness as long as they are employed purely descriptively, but he stringently opposes their advocates' cocksure readiness to interpret life ethically.

Hansen's reasoning may itself seemed flawed, but his main point, that those interpretations of life offer only partial explanations of existence, seems particularly valid when applied to Danish literature after the breakthrough of Realism and Naturalism in the 1870s. Philosophical idealism was then replaced with positivism, but the works of the renowned writers of that new movement — such as J. P. Jacobsen, Henrik Pontoppidan, or the somewhat later Johannes V. Jensen — reveal that, beneath the surface of materialism, metaphysics survived and ruled. The simple reason for that survival was that, although the new scientific theories could explain much about the human condition and much in the individual's life, they were unable to furnish man with a complete interpretation of existence or to grant the individual what he most needed: assurance that his life was not accidental, but meaningful.

Although *Leviathan* is a strongly anti-positivistic tract, it does not spare the outgrowths of idealism that seduce mankind into accepting an equally stifling view of fate. The failure of institutionalized Christianity is readily admitted, and Protestantism is stingingly rebuked for having paved the way for modern alienating ideologies: God has been made remote and life disharmonious by barren theology.

Hansen's quite encompassing attack groups widely different outlooks together as being insufficient, if not detrimental to man. Underlying his reasoning is the conviction that none of the views he criticizes serves culture. None of them enables man to distinguish between nature and culture, and each bequeathes him only a sense of meaninglessness. A civilization that falls into the popular positivistic trap of cherishing "the natural" can never gain the ethical awareness that constitutes meaning in society or in an individual's life. With a note of triumph Hansen refers to an assertion, made as early as 1893, by T. H. Huxley (Darwin's friend), that ethical progress depends not on mankind's imitating the cosmic process, but in his resisting it.[37]

The fallacy of modern civilization is that it defines itself in opposition to the past and thus breaks rather than joins in alliance with tradition.

Hansen hereby reasserts his credo that man can regain a sense of sustaining values only if he learns to view history correctly. In the past he can find a strict sense of justice that cannot be transformed by relativistic ideologies, for this sense of justice is based not upon theory nor upon moral or religious reasoning but is based on instinct, by which the rights and value of the individual are recognized.

It is with this awareness that one must write. The artist's duty is to go beyond a description of the human condition to that creative interpretation which alone can grant meaning. In this activity the artist is repeating man's age-old creative effort, which the German philosopher Ernst Cassirer expressed in the dictum: thought creates and transforms reality. The point is not that man actually forms the empiric world around him, but that through his naming of objects he conceptualizes them and thus creates culture. Hansen states in his conclusion that Cassirer's view "directed a slash against the Gordian knot" that was a blow of deliverance. After that no one could longer "doubt the validity of history as knowledge, the insight of poetry, the existential understanding of art, the calm knowledge of wisdom, or the experience of religion."[38]

Wivel has pointed out that shortly after the war, when Hansen was deeply immersed in a personal crisis that was fraught with both the temptation of pessimism and a profound suspicion of the artistic vocation, Hansen was rescued by his discovery of tradition. One passage of *Leviathan* succinctly and solemnly captures Hansen's understanding of tradition's existential meaning:

The historian is the court of appeal for the dead. Through him, those who were innocent but persecuted can file their complaint; the evil will be judged; those who have received undeserved praise will stand unmasked. The task [of the historian] is not as insignificant as people may believe; it is great, since our fellowship with the dead does not cease as long as the transcendence of culture encompasses both them and us; and in such a society justice must rule....[39]

Faced with such convictions the ideologue must fall silent, for through them he is confronted, as Björnvig has pointed out, with an unarguable statement of belief,[40] and — it is tempting to add — by that belief Hansen becomes as difficult to argue with as Sören Kierkegaard himself.

More than most works from Hansen's hand, *Leviathan* reveals his obsession with the personal and cultural situation in which he found himself. As in the other essays, the author's private dilemmas are intentionally transformed into ideas that are of cultural service to contemporary society, but *Leviathan* still seems like a very personal testimony. As Björnvig notes, there is an irony in the fact that no form-spirit seems to have guided Hansen when he struggled with *Leviathan*.[41]

CHAPTER 10

Serpent and Bull

IN 1952 Martin A. Hansen published the ambitious and monumental work *Serpent and Bull (Orm og Tyr)*, to which, in the preface, he gave an alternate title: "The Romanesque Churches and Their Nordic Old Testament."[1] Together with Ole Wivel and Sven Havsteen-Mikkelsen, who was to illustrate the book, Hansen undertook many field trips to old cultic sites in order to gather material, and this impressive and highly personal cultural history slowly took shape.[2] *Serpent and Bull* deals with the beliefs of the Danes from the distant Stone Age to about 1250, when the substitution of the Gothic for the Romanesque style in sacred art signaled a major change in the medieval mind, a change that, Hansen asserts, initiated ways of thinking that still exist.

For Hansen the project must have been deeply satisfying. He dealt with a subject matter that interested him profoundly, and at last he had the opportunity of fusing his views of the past into a synthesis. *Serpent and Bull* meant much to him on yet another level, for with that work he turned away from problematic fiction and used his creative powers in the service of history, of culture.

In his preface Hansen makes it clear that his account is based on a personal understanding of the past, one that may seem to disagree with canonized views; and he adds that he does not offer theoretical discussion, but narrative. He respects, of course, historical data (and he studied them laboriously and conscientiously); but he feels that, if the past is to come alive and to be understood, the author must rely upon his intuition and "remembrance." Wivel observes that the writing of *Serpent and Bull* was, in a sense, a homecoming for Hansen to his lost Stevns and that for Hansen to recall childhood and "to remember" ancient times were very nearly the same thing.[3]

Hansen's very personal approach to his topic is discernable in the preface, in which he recalls his childhood visits to the church of Ströby parish. He particularly remembers his grandfather's burial: After the service in the church, six strong men carried the casket out to the grave, where "he was to sleep near the church"; hymns were sung, and then the men put on their hats and "looked satisfied." Everyone participated in the wake; and people ate and were jolly, although "it was a shame grandpa wasn't there, for he liked to tell stories when so many people were seated around a table." Hansen recalls, however, another sort of death, that of a little friend; but Hansen remembers only the weeping, and it is as if he ascribes the sound of crying to the child who had suffered so untimely a death: "the lament of one who is without destiny."[4]

The two deaths are contrasted: that of the old man who had led a full life and that of the child who had had no chance to experience life. Hansen is particularly concerned with the effects of these deaths upon the living. The living can reconcile themselves to the fate of the old man who now rests peacefully in his grave; but their lives are poisoned by the haunting memory of the child who was without a fate. The thought of his meaningless death makes a restless ghost of the little boy in the minds of those left behind.

Hansen does not express these feelings directly in the preface, but page after page of *Serpent and Bull* verifies this interpretation. The book voices the author's almost obsessive concern with the role the dead play in the lives of the living. The fate of the dead and their relationship to the living are the main themes of this cultural history; thus, its perspective transcends the ages it treats and assumes a significance for modern man's situation.

In his exploration of these themes Hansen reaches back to the Stone Age, to the time when human thought first transcended nature. The hunters became farmers; consequently, the culturally significant distinction between wilderness and cultivated land arose. Man's ancestors were given the preeminence of being protectors against the destructive forces of nature that would let the harvest fail and the cattle die. The presence of those forbears was betokened by the dolmens, from which their vast power supposedly emanated. The dead may have seemed ominous, but their power was made benevolent through cultic acts carefully executed so that the living and the dead could coexist peacefully. The living could then devote themselves to their own lives without fearing restless, malevolent ghouls and without being haunted by that perpetually unsettling question of the fate of the dead.

As Hansen moves forward in time in his examination of the burial customs of the changing cultures, he shows that the beneficial balance in the relationship between living and dead was disturbed in certain ages and that this disturbance was extremely detrimental to the peace of mind of the populace. He refuses to give direct parallels to modern times, and he keeps himself very much in the background, but in the scenes that describe the living's sheer horror of the dead, there is a very personal touch. When the death cult degenerates, the dead become threatening; and as menacing ghouls, they infiltrate the existence of the living, who must shiver not only in fear of those demons that stalk the night but also at the thought of their own fates when death inevitably catches up with them.

The terror of such a relationship between the dead and the living is especially brought out in the depiction of the Iron Age, which Hansen baptizes the Milennium of Mist. The summer climate of the Bronze Age gave way to fog and drizzle, and Nordic connections with other cultures were cut off by the roving Celts, who managed to isolate the Germanic tribes for about a thousand years. Hansen sees much that is positive in that historical event, for during those ten centuries of isolation, modern Scandinavia emerged. A Scandinavian culture, based upon a stabilizing democratic sense of justice, gradually formed and managed to fend off all threatening intrusions from the more totalitarian, southern civilizations. Hansen also registers the effects of the worsening climate with approval, since it forced the Scandinavian to use his ingenuity: to bring his cattle under roof; to discover the plow; and, in short, to establish the agrarian culture that has continued to exist into the twentieth century.

Hansen, a servant of culture, observes the technological progress during the Iron Age with an almost boyish delight. That developing technology forced the wilderness to yield to landscape; man started to tame and control nature. Strangely enough that healthy development was accompanied by a conceptual poverty that left the Iron Age man and his descendent, the Viking, living in a world that must have been psychologically chilling. With the fading away of the sunny Bronze Age, which had thought of death as a liberation and a journey to a far away world, the dead from the gravemounds seemed to lurk everywhere in the damp and misty land. A new official religion, that of the Asirs, gained ground, but it was not strong enough to exorcise the ill will of those dead ancestors. In fact, the death cult may possibly have overshadowed the belief in Odin and Thor, for the religious views of the Iron Age man were marked by confusion and fear. There is actually strong evidence that human sacrifices were offered to the Vanir, the gods who had preceded the Asirs and who had degenerated into demonic representatives of blind and indifferent nature. Those sacrifices could however do little for the people who performed them, for their "nature gods" could offer them neither peace of mind nor meaning, but only fear. The horror of the age was that the realm of the dead had become identified with nature itself. The dead were doomed to walk in a rainy, cold region from which there was no promise of liberation; and that knowledge was like a fever that tortured the living. They feared those restless, sighing, malevolent shadows and trembled for the moment when they themselves would join that multitude in a dark, inescapable eternity.

In spite of the very significant cultural advances of the Iron Age, its people could not keep demonic nature at bay. That impotence, according to Hansen, makes itself felt in the poetry of Old Norse literature and particularly in the figure of Odin. In spite of all Odin's might, that brooding, unspontaneous god was tormented by his powerlessness in his knowledge that he and his order would perish. This interpretation of Odin concerns the present as much as it does the past, since Odin, in his spiritual confusion and limitations, seems to epitomize the modern state of mind. He even emerges as a consummate portrayal of the conflict-ridden, doomed creator, an artist who can understand much and, yet, who feels that his insight is too insufficient to grant him any peace of mind.[5]

Hansen had carefully orchestrated his narrative to make the advent of Christianity stand out as the very liberation of the haunted, despairing Nordic mind. With the gradual and peaceful conversion of the Scandinavians to Christianity, the dead were conjured away, and the world was once more returned to the living. Hansen wanted nonetheless to make one point emphatic: the best of heathen cultural values was actually preserved and reinforced by Christianity. The most important value that Christianity salvaged, the very foundation of the old culture, was a sense of justice, which the spiritual crisis had severely threatened. The very fact that the conversion was remarkably peaceful shows, argues Hansen, that the Scandinavians had a strong inner need for a force that would revitalize that valuable part of their culture.

In order to understand Hansen's interpretation of the conversion, it must be realized that he primarily saw Christianity as being affirmative of the here and now. The evangelical spirit of Christianity was a far cry from otherworldly pietism, which later came to judge this world as mere vanity and as only a preparation for a real life after death. Early Christianity recognized no such alienating dualism and, in fact, rescued people from the haunting and nihilistic thought of the fate of the dead and restored life to all its everyday splendor. The dead, according to early Christianity, had no fate, for they rested peacefully in the ground until they were resurrected on Judgment Day. Life was purged of its deadly demons.

Although Hansen hardly ever broke with his characteristic restraint, there is undeniable fervor in his depiction of the early Christian culture's tremendous vitality. Social rules guaranteed not only the welfare of all members of society but also a daily existence that was fully satisfying to the individual. Man was recognized to have a responsibility to be joyous and to uphold the festive spirit in the community: "There is a great deal in this that is ancient, a strong heritage now practiced to the glory of Christ. People had a solemn duty to be steadily merry and joyful. They were want to speak about many things gloomily, but joy was the basic element of the acts that sustained them."[6]

Hansen thus saw and evaluated Christianity in a broad cultural perspective: Christianity was a force that beneficially affected everyday life. Hansen was nevertheless aware that Christian dualism later asserted itself with lasting consequences. New thoughts about the afterlife of the soul, of sin and salvation, which directed the human mind toward the otherworldly, gained impetus and, once more, made death an alienating part of life. In Hansen's opinion that deplorable development was symbolized in sacred art with the replacement — in about 1250 — of the rounded Romanesque arch with the pointed Gothic arch. The Romanesque arch emblematized serenity, whereas the aspiring lines of the Gothic arch were indicative of the striving mind whose needs could not be fulfilled by the actual world. To Hansen, the broken lines of the pointed arch also symbolized a split between thought and emotion, those qualities of the human mind that had been harmoniously integrated during early Christianity. That spiritual division, which had also been familiar in Antiquity, now took root on Christian ground and paved the way for the coming secularization of the Renaissance.

Hansen captures the existential difference between "Romanesque" and "Gothic" Christianity in a consummate picture of peasant and monk, both representative figures of the age immediately after the conversion. Although both may toil in the field, the way they experience their daily work has little in common. For the peasant, the world is real: he sees no distinction between his plowing the field and his going to church, for both activities serve Christ. Daily life is a deeply satisfying and spontaneous service rendered to a familiar God. The monk's relationship to this life is entirely different: he too works well and hard, but his toil is only a duty that he executes or a penance that he pays in order to get closer to the remote God who rules far above this fallen world. For the peasant, God's realm is here and now; for the monk, this world is unreal. Both men may enjoy the beauty of this world, but only the peasant can enjoy it fully, for the monk experiences the sophisticated thinker's distance from what he loves, whether it is this world or God.

Hansen recognizes that the monk, that consciously cultural worker, taught the peasant much, but the author clearly displays a wistful sympathy for — or rather longing toward — the life of the peasant. That man, dedicated to everyday existence, gave to life a joy and vitality that the monk could never foster. It is revealing, however, that in the portrayal of those two figures the author feels a much closer kinship to the monk than to the peasant. With somber conviction Hansen observes that the robust, vigorous world of the peasant can only endure until "other thoughts win the upper hand, and every human being actually becomes a monk in this life, a guest on earth."[7] These pages of *Serpent and Bull* disclose a wish for identification with the peasant, but the actual identification is with the brooding exile, the monk who, wherever he turns, seems separated from all that is real.

In *Serpent and Bull* Hansen strongly reaffirms those cultural values that can establish a just society, in which the individual can live an ingenuously purposeful life. The book, however, poignantly shows that such a blessed form of life is doomed whenever the thought of death takes preeminence in man's mind. Both the reflective monk and the human being who shudders at the thought of death become estranged from life. That estrangement allows demonic nature to encroach upon culture, and such an encroachment essentially permits nihilistic reflections to make not only man's death but also his life meaningless. As an apt symbol for this horrifying state of mind, Hansen uses the sleepless ghost that knows no rest and denies others rest.

By rendering, in historical context, that drama which takes place in the individual mind, Hansen gave his audience not only a very personal but also a very knowledgeable and inspiring cultural history. As mentioned before, although the book avoids both explicit parallels to modern times and references to the personal, *Serpent and Bull* is both an exorcism and an invocation. This fact becomes particularly evident in the last pages of the book as Hansen turns to the old tale of "serpent and bull." This tale is one of death and rebirth, but these concepts are understood not only metaphysically but psychologically as well.

The tale of serpent and bull had fascinated Hansen for years. It appeared in many places and in many renditions, but Hansen clearly saw it as an expression of the culture that fostered Romanesque art. The tale concisely tells the story of a farming community that was invaded by a mighty serpent. It came from the surrounding forest and encircled the church so that no one could enter it. The villagers then found a young bull, fed it well for seven years, and finally brought it forth to do battle with the serpent. The two fought and the bull killed the monster. The bull took nine steps and then fell dead, but it had freed the cultic site.

The tale strikingly brings to mind the opposition between nature and culture. The serpent comes from the demonic wilderness; and by barring access to the church, the serpent signals death to culture. For those who told the story the symbol was clear; they knew that the serpent represented many kinds of death to the community, not only through withering crops and dying cattle but also through those dangerous states of mind that threaten healthy society. Death, whether it is in the form of an outer or an inner force, is anything that ravages culture.

In the tale evil makes its threat explicit by cutting off the community from the cultic place, but the worshippers are aware of the proper way to exorcise death from life. They do not abandon themselves to a crippling sense of fatalism, nor do they call for the metaphysical aid of angel or saint; instead, they turn to something as familiar as a domestic animal, nature tamed, to enact the role of saviour. Only a people resting harmoniously within a strong cultural tradition has the wisdom and strength to act in this constructive manner.

This tale concludes *Serpent and Bull*. That both the tale and the whole book are parts of an invocation becomes very explicit in the last few lines. As Hansen well knew, the ideal to which the book was devoted belonged to a lost or fading culture, but he hoped that his invocation of past tradition would serve the cultural purpose of showing modern times the relevance of distant periods of Danish history. *Serpent and Bull* ends with a poetic image: "Late in a vigorous, but waning, age the tale flies out and rises like a bird at evening. It is seen high up in the sky and is illuminated even though the light has faded."[8]

On the way toward this lyrical conclusion, Hansen had described the old Danish churches in detail, and he had repeatedly emphasized that Christianity must be seen as a bearer of many values that are heathen in origin. Understandably, he was particularly fascinated with the examples of art to be found in the churches, for, there, long dead artists were still serving the cultural tradition. In Hansen's descriptions of those creators and their creations, one senses his feeling of deprivation, since no modern artist could approach his task with the spontaneous attitude of the medieval painter who decorated the walls of the church. That artist of the past did not suffer from a suspicion of his vocation, nor did he have to struggle with making painful choices of motif or with forming a personal style. He was merely a craftsman, and he could fully abandon himself to his art in the secure knowledge that he was serving Christ.

Hansen could not share in such joyful abandon, but *Serpent and Bull* — a volume whose many facets could not be suggested in brief treatment — can be read as an attempt, an ambitious and superb attempt, to ally its author with the past and to be of service to the cultural tradition.

CHAPTER 11

Chronicles of Travels

MARTIN A. Hansen delighted in traveling. In *Danish Weather* (*Dansk Vejr* [1935]), he speaks of his "yearning for roads"[1] and notes with pride that he knows nearly all the highways on Sealand. He traveled widely in Scandinavia but never really ventured beyond those areas he considered to be Nordic in culture. His visits to northern Germany were undertaken to acquaint himself with its Danish minority culture, which was flourishing in the decade after World War II. The patriot Hansen felt strongly that this "exiled" region, now on German land, for centuries had been a bulwark against continental cultures and that the region's old fortresses had prevented Scandinavia from being overrun by forces that threatened Nordic justice and freedom.[2]

In obvious irritation Hansen lashed out, in *Danish Weather,* at those people who harp on Denmark's diminutive size. He felt that, if one seriously tries to get to know Denmark, one will discover that it is really quite large; with respect to both culture and nature each region is distinctively different from any other. That attitude is hardly surprising for a man who very nearly made a whole universe of Stevns and who found a vast cultural richness in that small region. On his foreign travels he was confronted with a nature that, as he put it in *Kringen (Kringen: Billeder fra övre Gudbrandsdal* [1953]), seemed to challenge "the best one knows,"[3] and he rose to the defense of Stevns and, unavoidably it seems, took exception to those impressions that threatened the myths with which Stevns had vested him. The endless mountainous regions, whether they were in Norway or Iceland, were especially disturbing to him in their striking difference from the cultural landscape of southern Scandinavia. When faced with the wilderness Hansen's usual reaction was to resort to history, to man's effort to overcome nature; thus, Hansen tried to make the unknown known, and in the last analysis this meant relating the unknown to the simultaneously very real and very mythical Stevns.

In three books, *Danish Weather*, *Kringen*, and *Travel on Iceland (Rejse paa Island* [1945]), Hansen describes his impressions as a traveler in Scandinavia, and at the same time, as Björnvig notes, writes works that, in character, are postscripts to *Serpent and Bull*.

I Danish Weather

Danish Weather is not purely a travel book; the author draws on his memories of many trips to various parts of the country and intersperses among those recollections a knowledgeable commentary on Danish landscape painting. The reason for these seeming digressions is Hansen's assumption that one does not see the landscape as it is, but as art has taught one to see it. Art thus acts as a means of opening the land to one's mind or, rather, of conquering the land for the mind:

It is hardly going too far to say that changing generations create changing pictures of the land and of nature, so that they are something entirely different in the eyes of descendents than in those of distant ancestors. The pictures so radically influence consciousness and feeling, spirit and culture that there is something active and creative in the process. We witness an immensely fruitful interaction.[4]

This passage not only implies that art enables the human being to know nature but also suggests that by "nature" Hansen refers here to the landscape, not the wilderness. He states that, "for art, nature always contains an anthropological and historical substance"[5] and that, ". . . through the ages it has not been wild nature that has been most inspirational for a sensitivity to nature and to culture. The cultivated landscape has performed that function, and most painters have not strayed far from it. 'Nature,' in the full meaning of the word, also includes the fields with their roads and buildings."[6]

Time and again Hansen praises the architecturally perfect farms, the age-old roads, and even the modern dam. To Hansen, the Danish landscape testified to man's cultural endeavor throughout the ages and made the traveler feel secure and at home. It is this ordinary landscape that Hansen keenly observes on his travels in all seasons and in all kinds of weather and that he sensitively portrays for his readers.

The book's last pages may seem surprising, for Hansen's focus suddenly narrows, and a personal, emotionally charged experience is allowed to close this otherwise quite impersonal account. Hansen tells about a biking trip he once took in the northernmost part of Denmark. By afternoon he had become utterly lost in a dense fog. He biked on through the lonely countryside in hope of finding directions. Suddenly the form of a church loomed before him, and he went there to rest. The experience was startling, for he felt that he had seen the church before, and he had seen it — both on a visit to this same region twenty-four years previously and in the dreams of his childhood.

The situation is quite similar to one that is often encountered in Hansen's fiction: the protagonist finds himself far from the main-traveled roads and loses his way in an all-enveloping fog. He finally comes upon a place in which he can stop to rest, and he learns there something about his fate. In *Danish Weather* the author finds both a shelter and a landmark, and he observes the old building with reverence, but his reflections typically encompass more than the actual situation. The strange coincidence of his having been there a quarter of a century earlier gives him the sensation that all the intermittent years have passed in an instant. He knows no more about the church than before; it is still a riddle, and for a fleeting second he imagines seeing, lowered into their graves, all those who have died since his last visit to this place. Then he again sees only the wet stones, the "crying tombstones."[7] Such a moment may recall to the reader "The Bridegroom's Oak," which imparts the somber knowledge that nothing may come of an individual's life and that nothing can be done to alter that tragic fact. All one knows is that life is pitifully short.

Danish Weather, which is predominantly devoted to the reassuring effect of culture upon nature, ends with the author's listening to the sounds of nature that culture can never still: the wind against the roof and among the trees and the dried grass. He hears the sound of fine sand as it touches against the roughly cut stones and slowly "wears and wears" them away.[8] The theme of life's vanity finally subdues all else; nature's eternal might is reaffirmed even after many pages have been devoted to belittling its power.

II Kringen

The slim volume *Kringen*, like several of the essays,[9] testifies to Hansen's affection for Norway and its people. The culture that he encountered in the Norwegian countryside gave him an enchanted feeling of having returned to the past, but he also seems to have traveled in Norway with some ambivalence, for the imposing scenery could sometimes appear threatening to a man who was accustomed only to "tamed" nature. In the essay "Astern" ("Agterude"), from *Thoughts in a Chimney*, this attitude toward Norway is clearly formulated by the author, who watches the coastline of Oslo Fjord as he sails away. He confesses that Norwegian nature is hard to grasp; it may inspire one with enthusiasm, but it may also seem utterly foreign and hostile to a southern Scandinavian. The myths of Denmark and Norway differ, too, for the folklore of the people of the lowlands concerns itself with history rather than with nature, whereas nature looms large in Norwegian myths. This difference, so significant to Hansen, sheds light upon his ambivalence toward all mountainous terrain. He nonetheless hurries to diminish the variance between the two cultures by adding that the Norwegian myths by no means indicate an identity between nature and mind. In fact, the Norwegian tales clearly refute the romantic notions of the nineteenth century; by maintaining a strict dualism those tales relegate the forces inimical to mankind to lonely mountain stretches.[10]

Hansen thus makes his peace with Norway; and when he leaves the country, he sees not panorama, but pageant:

> Hill by hill, endlessly. But there is not one spot in which people have not tried to get pickaxe, crowbar, spade, or plow into the ground; and where the stone gave, they clung on, stayed, and fought for their daily bread, as they were clutching the rock, battling the enemy, singing, telling stories, and thus imbuing the land with spirit. Norway's history.[11]

Norway has clearly been made familiar. It has become spiritually akin to the lowlands, to Stevns, for the two places now share in the same cultural endeavor and stand up against the same enemy, nature. It is nonetheless tempting to point out that, when Hansen sealed his peace with Norway, it was as if he included only the inhabited coastline or as if he had lowered his glance so that it would not meet the towering mountain ranges that resist human interference.

Kringen is loosely based upon two sojourns in the upper Gudbrands Valley, where the pass Kringen is located. One visit took place in the late thirties when rumors of war were persistent, and the other, shortly after World War II. Hansen's personal experiences serve as a basis for his reflections, but quite typically the perspective widens to encompass broader cultural and historical issues.

On the night of the author's first arrival, his host, an elderly farmer, performs an almost cultic act. He relates, as he had undoubtedly done countless times before, the story of Mr. Sinclair who, bent on conquest, had marched on Kringen with his Scottish troops in 1612 and fallen with all his men at the hands of the Norwegian defenders. It is with a strong sense of pleasure that Hansen listens to the tale, for the old farmer is one of those storytellers who can experience the distant past and heroic defense as if they had taken place only yesterday. The story binds the living to the cultural tradition and makes the deeds of those long dead become alive and meaningful to their heirs.

At first Hansen describes to the reader only the mood induced in him by the story and reserves the telling of the story for a later and darker context, that of the German invasion in 1940. In 1612 the intruders are halted, but in 1940 brave and fierce resistance is in vain: the German troops force their way through Kringen. A man who tells about the desperate battles recalls that a fellow defender shoots a German soldier and then says, "I shall never get over that,"[12] whereupon, weeping, he again starts firing at the enemy. Such stories, which testify not only to the individual's and the community's sense of responsibility but also to the guilt that man may reap in defense of a cause, gave Hansen a feeling of spiritual affinity with the Norwegian experience.

The daily life on the farm of Hansen's hosts especially made those summer days in Norway a kind of homecoming for him. He observes with pleasure that the attitude of those who work in the fields is akin to that which he felt once was to be found in the old farm culture in Denmark. The young people are not rebels; they work hard during the long day and even far into the night, but they find satisfaction in their labor and know how to enjoy the land around them.[13] These Norwegian farmers are still part of a harmonious culture and have not yet been exposed to the rootlessness of modern civilization. Despite the somber moments in Norwegian history registered in *Kringen*, the book primarily pictures a vacation in a waning culture and a celebration of the virtues to be found there.

Only for a brief moment do dark and bewildering thoughts surface in this work. Once, as Hansen stares into a gushing river, the wild dash of the foaming waters becomes like time itself, and a voice seems to ask, "Life is so short; why?"[14] Hansen then immediately recalls the meaningful past, the victory over Sinclair and his men: "It happened recently. A long, motley serpent [the line of troops] is gliding by high up on the road. . . ."[15]

III Travel on Iceland

In the summer of 1952 Hansen and Havsteen-Mikkelsen made their way across Iceland in a jeep in order to gather material for this long book. It contains many lively incidents from the journey and offers much information to both the traveler to Iceland and the admirer of Old Norse literature, but the reader who is familiar with Hansen's work will detect sad signs of artistic fatigue. It is as if both the harrowing journey and the land itself left Hansen with a disconcerting sense of being in exile.

Hansen looked forward to seeing the homeland of the sagas, and he offers inspiring insights into the culture that produced so remarkable a literature, but he found to his disappointment that few tangible remnants were left from that culture's golden age. Iceland, in fact, struck him as being infinitely desolate, and its natural grandeur seemed closed, foreign, and confusing to him. At times the light across the empty vistas forced upon him disturbing associations with madness, hysteria, and fiendishness.

The opening passages, which depict a tiring drive at night in harsh, wintry weather, are symptomatic of the anguish of the cultural mind lost in a land beyond culture. Hansen looks across vistas that strike him as being utterly desolate, since he can glimpse traces of human dwellings from which the inhabitants have fled. These abandoned farms bluntly reveal the fact that man's effort to overcome nature has been thwarted. *Travel on Iceland* renders many similar experiences, and Hansen's reaction is predictably the same: no impression of the grandeur of nature can outweigh his feeling of chilling loss whenever he must face culture's defeat. It is not surprising that he views less magnificent areas with much more peace of mind, for human effort has there born fruit. It is almost as if Iceland's barrenness makes Hansen look with more than usual approval on the advances of the machine-age. He admires the technical know-how of the Icelanders, enjoys the hustle and bustle of the fast-growing capitol of Reykjavik, and lyrically praises the red gasoline pumps that indicate human presence on the lonely and primitive roads.

The overawing nature of Iceland time and again forces Hansen into shielding himself with the culture of the past. That reaction on his part is more desperate than ever, and it seems that his invocation of the past serves nearly as a drug against impressions that are clearly associated with death. Although the strategy of seeking refuge in the past had worked earlier, it is now less successful, for Iceland often seems to demonstrate that man's attempt to set his mark upon nature is doomed. More hauntingly and less ambivalently than ever before, nature is identified with a form of death that offers no meaning, but rather the horrifying knowledge that cultural striving is to little avail.

Although Hansen does not belabor this theme and although the book contains many lighter moments and more comforting thoughts, the fear of the nothingness of death nevertheless remains the tenor of this account. On the very last page, culture's disappearance into nature gains dominance: as Hansen sails back toward Denmark and looks out across the stormy sea, he first imagines there the ships of the pioneering Norsemen on their way toward Iceland; but then he sees only the tall waves that, to him, now appear to be gravemounds over dead travelers. With this final picture of a nature that can never be overcome, Hansen concludes the last book he himself was ever to prepare for publication.[16]

CHAPTER 12

Conclusion

ANY reading of Martin A. Hansen's *œuvre* that probes beneath the surface must be a study in human conflict. The texts depict a quest for meaning that proves to be illusive; thus, they suggest a very general resemblance to a number of prominent, albeit very different, novelists whose works Hansen knew: Hamsun, Proust, Kafka, Joyce, and Gide. It is important however to note that Hansen reacted against the open-ended fiction of those authors, for he refused to accept flux as the governing principle of life.[1]

Hansen's quest for meaning led him to reject the religious, philosophical, and political solutions commonly offered to the cultural crisis. Like Kierkegaard, Hansen felt that such all-encompassing theories could have no significance for the single individual and would therefore leave him in moral chaos. Hansen attempted instead to bring the single individual into a relation to his past, to his forebears and their tradition, and thus to suggest purpose in a cultural fellowship: as upholders of a healthy tradition, the dead and the living would be united and, thereby, death would be transcended. That solution to an individualistic culture's crisis may be judged by some readers to be an intellectual fabrication, but it was proffered by Hansen as a very concrete historical reality: a state of consciousness that once had granted — and might again grant — the individual meaning in life and death. With that leap into the past for the sake of the present and the future, Hansen caused his thinking and writing to become suprapersonal and to assume mythical qualities.

The opposition between nature and culture was an integral part of that myth, for Hansen considered his writing to be a cultural defense against the encroachment of nature and of nature's spiritual twin, nihilistic civilization. An investigation of Hansen's work shows however that, ironically enough for its official program, nature also denoted many vital aspects of human existence, which, if denied, could trap the human being in a state of living death. As Hansen's portrayal of the past indicates, those vital aspects had once been a part of the individual's existence. Tragically, no such integration seemed possible to modern man, for whom the spiritual and the physical, the immaterial and the material emerge as irreconcilable opposites. Hansen, therefore, appears to have been both culture's insistent advocate and the modern divided world's restless prisoner.

That tragic irony is one that the most complex of Hansen's texts take cognizance of but cannot overcome; thus, they testify to an existing conflict and not to its impending resolution. The presence of this textual limitation may cause the reader to feel that Hansen's thought was molded by the dominant ideology of a specific age: the tendency to spiritualize all values and human relationships; the dependence upon vaguely, metaphorically stated concepts; the use of metaphysical terminology; and the expression of tortuous reasoning — all tie Hansen's works closely to the decades marked by World War II. It may also be that epochal limitation which accounts for the fact that Hansen's quite extensive impact on other authors has mostly resulted in a mannered and artificial imitation of his way of writing.[2]

The restricted and restrictive scope of Hansen's work may seem obvious today, and it is quite clear that, if Hansen had allowed himself to be merely simplistically didactic and supportive of his quite conservative cultural ideal, his work would have seemed dated within a decade after his death. But only a few of his texts — the too philosophically twisted of his essays and the too sentimental of his works of fiction — have gathered dust. One reason that readers continue to be fascinated with Hansen's works, in spite of the passing of time, may well be that those ideologies that are reflected in his writings have remained a part of the readers' experience of existence. Such readers will still identify with Hansen's haunted and confused characters who long for rebirth and will still share those characters' paradoxical relationship to all that nature and culture may represent. If, however, the human being were to perceive itself differently in the future, Hansen's works would be of only historical interest.

Since the realm of conjecture has been entered, it may finally be in place to insert the subjective opinion that, although such a fate may lie in store for some of Hansen's texts, his best works will never share it. The reason, quite simply, is that Hansen — who was passionately intrigued by all that he rejected and who was ever subject to the artist in himself — in his most accomplished texts transcended his own official vision and, thus, the epochal limitations of his time in history. His

Conclusion

readers must reach the consequent conclusion that Hansen's writings question the very answers they offer.

The readers' response may suggest both the failure of Hansen as a thinker who imbued his works with a cultural mission and the success of Hansen as an artist who deeply suspicioned his own vocation. It may be recalled that the protagonist of *The Liar*, in an oddly and rarely truthful moment, admits that "It is art . . . that I care about."[3] In that context, as well as in Hansen's other works, art may not necessarily mean aestheticism but rather truthfulness; and it seems that, by giving in to the artistic inclination and by not adhering strictly to a self-imposed cultural mission, Hansen created a number of works that will continue to fascinate readers. In spite of Hansen's well-defined existential positions, his readers will not escape feeling that the life he depicts remains contradictory. Notwithstanding Hansen's ideological scope, he was a dialectical writer who will undoubtedly continue to appeal to any reader who admits to being caught up in the dialectical process of existence.

It seems fair to predict that the best of Hansen's works will continue to defamiliarize reality and, thus, to function existentially in the lives of its readers.

Notes and References

Chapter One

1. Thorkild Björnvig, *Kains Alter: Martin A. Hansens Digtning og Tænkning* (Copenhagen: Gyldendal, 1964). This book's thesis has been a point of contention and departure for much criticism of Hansen's works. In *Forsvar for Kains Alter: En Kritisk Efterskrift* (Copenhagen: Gyldendal, 1965) Björnvig responds to his critics.
2. Ole Wivel, *Martin A. Hansen: Fra Barndommen til Krigens Aar* (Copenhagen: Gyldendal, 1967) and *Martin A. Hansen: Fra Krigens Aar til Döden* (Copenhagen: Gyldendal, 1969); hereafter referred to as Wivel, *Martin A. Hansen*, I and II.
3. See Aage Henriksen, *Gotisk tid: Fire litterære afhandlinger* (Haslev: Gyldendal, 1971), pp. 103 - 05; and Torben Kragh Grodal, "Sælens lyst og sjælens ubodelige ensomhed: En analyse af Martin A. Hansens *Lögneren*," *Poetik*, 5 (1972), 1.
4. It should be pointed out that Henriksen and Grodal have little in common as critics; the former is often labeled an existentialist, whereas the latter is neo-Marxist.
5. Henriksen, p. 103.
6. Wivel, *Martin A. Hansen*, I, 23 - 24.
7. *Nationaltidende*, November 12, 1944; not reprinted.
8. *Politiken*, June 22, 1949; reprinted in *Midsommerkrans*, ed. Vera Hansen and Ole Wivel (Copenhagen: Gyldendal, 1956), pp. 7 - 15.
9. To Hansen's generation Jensen (1873 - 1950), a prolific novelist, poet, and essayist, represented a robust materialism and an open reaction against religious dualism.
10. In *Lögneren* (1950) glimpses are given of the techniques of an accomplished pedagogue. Direct and poignant observation of Hansen in the classroom can be found in Ib Spang Olsen, *I Kristoffers spor*, Gyldendals Bogklub (Copenhagen: Gyldendal, 1973), unpaged.
11. Hansen published some articles and short stories in the school paper

Kæden (The Chain). His insignificant debut was a sports reportage published on August 22, 1928. See Wivel, *Martin A. Hansen*, I, 65 - 67.

12. Wivel, *Martin A. Hansen*, I, 88 - 99; II, 40 - 52.

13. Hansen's family was highly patriotic, and for generations its men had donned their country's uniform. "The soldier," a man often bitterly marked by his experiences, became a recurring character in Hansen's works. See Wivel, *Martin A. Hansen*, I, 126 - 30.

14. Hansen was always an avid reader and always quite ready to admit his literary debts. Curiously enough, he rarely mentions Hamsun, even though strong stylistic and thematic similarities can be detected in a number of their works, for example, between *Løgneren* and Hamsun's *Mysterier* (1892) and *Pan* (1894).

15. *Aarhus Stiftstidende*, March 2, 1940; reprinted in *Midsommerkrans*, pp. 53 - 61.

16. From an interview in *Kristeligt Dagblad*, January 9, 1949. Here quoted from Wivel, *Martin A. Hansen*, I, 105.

17. See Björnvig, *Kains Alter*, p. 502. Björnvig points out that personal recollection is transformed to suprapersonal memory, which is a leap into myth.

18. *Heretica*, 6 (1953), 165 - 94; reprinted in *Verdensromanen: Historiske Essays*, ed. Thorkild Björnvig and Ole Wivel (Copenhagen: Gyldendal, 1966), pp. 147 - 73.

19. After the war Hansen became one of the main contributors to *Folk og Frihed*, but the circulation of the magazine was poor, and it ceased publication in December 1945.

20. "Dialog om Drab og Ansvar," in *Der brænder en Ild* (Copenhagen: Folk og Frihed, 1944), pp. 17 - 23; reprinted in *Verdensromanen*, pp. 135 - 46.

21. Wivel, *Martin A. Hansen*, I, 196 - 97, 201.

22. The trilogy was to span the years between 1800 and the present day and to depict the members of a family from three generations. See Wivel, *Martin A. Hansen*, I, 283 - 98; and Björnvig, *Kains Alter*, pp. 259 - 72.

23. Wivel, *Martin A. Hansen*, I, 287.

24. Ibid., pp. 275 - 328.

25. Ibid., p. 307.

26. Ibid., pp. 299 - 300.

27. *Morgenbladet*, February 5, 8, 14, 21, and March 3, 1946; reprinted in *Ved Korsvejen: Litterære Essays*, ed. Thorkild Björnvig and Ole Wivel (Copenhagen: Gyldendal, 1965), pp. 7 - 33.

28. *Ved Korsvejen*, p. 27.

29. Wivel, *Martin A. Hansen*, I, 310.

30. The contributions to *Heretica* (1948 - 1953), published by the avantgarde Wivels Forlag, clearly signifies a lyric renaissance with a bent toward mythically weighted language. The writers indicated their taste by their interest in the French Symbolists, the Finno-Swedish Modernists (Edith Södergran, Gunnar Björling, Rabbe Enckell), and in Rainer Maria Rilke, T. S. Eliot, and W. H. Auden.

31. Literary Modernism, signifying a form experimentation in order to defamiliarize reality and thus force readers to perceive it anew, arrived in Denmark late but dominated lyric diction for more than two decades. One aspect of Modernism is particularly relevant in the consideration of Hansen's works: many Modernistic texts can properly be called metaliterature; that is, their subject matter is the problematic creative act, which is viewed with suspicion, since poetic, seductive language tends to falsify reality.

32. The term "ethical pessimism" is used in "Romanens Forfald," *Heretica*, 1 (1948), 24 - 35; reprinted in *Midsommerkrans*, pp. 149 - 60.

33. Wivel, *Martin A. Hansen*, II, 21 - 24.

34. See "Konvention og Formaand," *Heretica*, 1 (1948), 72 - 91; reprinted in *Midsommerkrans*, pp. 170 - 90.

35. Wivel, *Martin A. Hansen*, II, 39.

36. Ibid., p. 51.

37. See in particular "Den Retærdige," in *Konkyljen* (1955), and "Gartneren, Dyret og Barnet," in *Efterslæt* (1959). The poem "Menneske," *Heretica*, 1 (1948), 356 - 64, is an intensely desperate confrontation with the Cain nature of the artistic vocation. Hansen's few poems, published mainly in magazines or newspapers, span from the "occasional" to the very private. No collection of them has been issued.

38. Hansen bought the old vicarage in Allerslev. This village is situated in the midst of the archeologically rich Lejre region, supposedly the seat of ancient Danish kings.

39. Wivel, *Martin A. Hansen*, II, 332 - 41. Hansen's very last story, called "Gæsterne" ("The Visitors"), starkly shows that his wartime advocacy of killing informers still tormented his mind. The last draft of that story is paraphrased and quoted quite extensively by Wivel in *Martin A. Hansen*, I, 377 - 83.

40. As of yet no complete, scholarly edition of Hansen's works has been published.

41. "Sagn i September," *Nationaltidende*, October 11, 1947; reprinted in *Efterslæt: Sidste Noveller og Skildringer*, ed. Thorkild Björnvig and Ole Wivel (Copenhagen: Gyldendal, 1959), pp. 172 - 79, from which the quotation is translated; see p. 176.

42. Several critics, for example, Björnvig and Wivel — and, recently, Grodal — have dealt with this opposition in Hansen's works but have mainly chosen to view the writings in terms of other conflicts (Björnvig: the conflict between Christianity and art; Wivel: the conflict between the artistic inclination and human responsibility). The choice of making the nature-culture opposition paramount in this study should not be seen as a rejection of the other models devised for analysis of Hansen's *œuvre*, but as a critical strategy suggested by the texts themselves.

43. Wivel offers much evidence for the theory that Hansen's concept of tradition did not become fully developed until the conception and ultimate rejection of "Kains Alter"; although that moment in Hansen's life can be seen as a turning point, it did not signify a change in his value system.

44. The term *remembrance* is chosen to signify the Danish *erindring* or *slægtserindring*, which in Hansen's works refers to mythical, suprapersonal memory.

45. The Danish philosopher Vilhelm Grönbech (1873 - 1948), who exerted a considerable influence on the Heretica-circle, had proclaimed the age's need for a new myth. In an article honoring Grönbech's memory, Hansen not only compares him to Nicolai Frederik Severin Grundtvig and Sören Kierkegaard but also voices a reverence for Grönbech and his dream of a cultural synthesis. See "Den tredie Store," *Heretica*, 1 (1948), 232 - 38.

46. See in particular "Gartneren, Dyret og Barnet," *Efterslæt*, pp. 147 - 57.

47. Hansen's insistence on the necessity of a choice may well echo Kierkegaard, who repeatedly emphasized that the single individual must exercise his free will and choose to choose.

48. The question arises as to what extent Hansen consciously infused his texts with ambiguity. Although this question cannot be resolved, it is tempting to suggest not only that a great majority of the conflicting symbols are intended, but also that "the implied author" can often be at variance with Hansen, the writer.

49. Björnvig points out that Hansen sometimes voices a Job-like accusation against Nature and discusses Hansen's preoccupation with Job. See *Kains Alter*, pp. 155 - 57, 177 - 80, 253.

50. This mixture of repulsion and attraction may be understood in terms of Kierkegaard's concept of dread, *Begrebet Angest* (1844).

51. See "De episke Kvinder," *Nationaltidende*, July 11, 1948; reprinted in *Tanker i en Skorsten* (1948).

52. "Jakobs Kvinder," *Efterslæt*, pp. 80 - 88, which is not analyzed in this study, exemplifies this anti-individualistic view.

53. See Grodal, "Sælens lyst og sjælens ubodelige ensomhed," pp. 9 - 10.

54. Grodal, pp. 7 - 9.

55. The mournful identification with Moses is voiced in the poem "Den fredlöse" ("The Fugitive"); the poem was not published in Hansen's lifetime but is quoted by Wivel in *Martin A. Hansen*, I, 230 - 31.

56. One dominant theme in Hansen's work is a suspicion of one's own motivation and, consequently, of all one's acts. The artist, in particular, seems prone to this self-doubt.

57. The term "Janus head" is used by Martin, the narrator in *Lykkelige Kristoffer* (1945).

Chapter Two

1. Kristen, who is younger than Lars, has inherited the family farm.

2. Martin A. Hansen, *Nu Opgiver Han* (1935; rpt. Copenhagen: Gyldendal, 1961), p. 197.

3. Martin A. Hansen, *Kolonien* (1937; rpt. Copenhagen: Gyldendal, 1957), p. 176.

Notes and References

4. Ibid., p. 178.
5. The canonized view is that with these two novels Hansen, respectively, probed into and rejected Marxism. See Frederik Nielsen, *Dansk digtning i dag* (Copenhagen: Fremad, 1957), p. 33; Björnvig, *Kains Alter*, pp. 27 - 29; and Wivel, *Martin A. Hansen*, I, 103.
6. *Kolonien*, p. 179.
7. Sexual dualism was quite common in the literature of Hansen's age (for example, in the works of the novelist H. C. Branner). Although in these two novels by Hansen that dualism is the target of much irony, such a dualism continues to be expressed in Hansen's works.

Chapter Three

1. (Copenhagen: Gyldendal, 1941). Hansen's revisions, to which he alludes in his "Farewell to the Book," in *Jonatans Rejse*, 2nd ed. (Copenhagen: Gyldendal, 1950), p. 250, consisted in the deletion of a number of tales about the smith in a rather thorough rewriting of the work in 1947. All references will be made to the second edition.
2. "Askelad" is the name of many a Nordic fairy tale hero; he is the masculine counterpart to "Cinderella."
3. *Jonatans Rejse*, p. 85. Most critics view the scene at the mill as a positive representation of the values inherent in the old culture. The miller's wife, however, calls the grinding of the corn a daring of God. It is certainly a vain and drunken daring of the elements.
4. Aleksander Aleksander has created a village reminiscent of that of his childhood, but representative of a false, idealized dream of the past. His village is a burden to the lives of modern men, who must barter their freedom to live there, whereas Jonatan's village is a source of strength and a place of refuge for those whose lives are corrupted by the present.
5. After confiding in the smith, the jailer has found himself deserted by the smith who, caught up in the excitement of the moment, has never again tried to find the patiently waiting jailer and has thus betrayed his trust.
6. Jonatan also adopts the fixed ideas of others: the miller's, Margaret's father's, the jailer's, and the police chief's — to name a few.
7. Björnvig, in a discussion of *Lögneren* in *Kains Alter*, p. 223, treats the opposite theme of finding one's own motives suspect, which makes the act of the reflective man seem evil, but the impulse of the spontaneous man seem honest or good.
8. Vilhelm's allegorical tales usually employ the theme of unrequited love and its effect.
9. The smiths of mythology include Hephæstus (Hera's son, cast down to earth), Weland or Völund (the vengeful captive of elfin heritage in the *Elder Edda*), and the Nordic race of dwarfs (shape-changers and forgers of the treasures of the gods). The dwarfs are usually associated with a subterranean life rather than a heavenly one.

10. The doctor is nearly blackmailed into living a better life by the secret of his unconfessed guilt. The murderer by arson is an excellent example of a man whose faith was strengthened by suffering — if he *did* die accidentally and was not a suicide as his neighbors say and as his ghost implies. The Freeborn's suffering is said to have made his apostolic nature evident.

11. The prostitution of art is admirably demonstrated by one of the smith's earlier acquaintances, the poet at the town festival.

12. *Jonatans Rejse*, p. 207. "Forliste" means "shipwrecked," "foundered," or "sunk"; it is translated here as "derelict."

13. In "The Editor's Well-meant Preface," in *Jonatans Rejse*, pp. 7 - 8, reference is made to the classics from which the author has borrowed. Björnvig, in *Kains Alter*, pp. 36, 47, has stressed those as being Cervantes' *Don Quixote*, Shakespeare's *The Tempest*, and Ewald's odes and psalms. One might add Musäus's "The Bottle Imp," and Asbjörnson and Moe's "The Smith They Didn't Dare Let into Heaven."

14. World War II revealed to Hansen man's inescapable contamination with evil even when he tries to serve the good. The "hope" Hansen recognized seems to have lain in the ideal of justice inherited by the Nordic peoples.

Chapter Four

1. Martin A. Hansen (1945; rpt. Copenhagen: Gyldendal, 1953), p. 169.
2. Björnvig, *Kains Alter*, p. 54.
3. In spite of Martin's love of the old, he — unlike Jonatan — has much of the modern man in him.
4. *Lykkelige Kristoffer*, p. 247. Kristoffer finally declares, "Just once I want to live in a full and dignified manner."
5. Ibid., p. 196.
6. The novel was being composed during the last phase of the Occupation when people were risking their lives.
7. *Lykkelige Kristoffer*, p. 142.
8. Ibid., pp. 112 - 13.
9. Ibid., p. 142.
10. Ibid., p. 92.
11. Ibid., p. 75.
12. Ibid., p. 182.
13. Ibid., p. 21.
14. Ibid., p. 182.
15. A parallel is suggested to Paulus Heliæ's so-called *Skiby Krönike*, which was supposedly written during the siege of Copenhagen. That anti-Lutheran chronicle was found in a secret niche in Skiby Church in 1650 and was thought to have been smuggled from Copenhagen and subsequently hidden by one of the old Catholic's disciples.

Notes and References 179

Chapter Five

1. Martin A. Hansen, "Paaskeklokken," *Tornebusken* (1946; rpt. Copenhagen: Gyldendal, 1955), p. 26. The Danish word "linde" means "linden trees"; however, in sound the word resembles "lin," as in "Linormen," the world-encircling serpent that was one of the mortal enemies of the gods of Nordic mythology.

2. "Paaskeklokken," p. 88. Ingrid utters these words as she watches Johan swing her dress like a matador's cape before the bull. Her words are ambiguous enough to imply that she may wish she were able to be used to protect him in place of the dress.

3. Martin A. Hansen, "Midsommerfesten," in *Tornebusken*, pp. 220 - 21. Since suicide is mentioned as an approximation of a "sacred crime," a third definition must be added to those given in the book: the destruction of oneself for oneself and in spite of others. This act, which would deny suffering, would counterbalance Georg's father's acceptance of suffering. All sacred crimes seem to deny the concept of law, which implies a belief in justice.

4. Ibid., p. 217. Georg must understand and carry out his grandfather's wish before the godlike old man dies; afterward, Georg may do as he likes without what he does mattering for him.

5. Ibid., p. 235.

6. Ibid., p. 110.

7. Ibid., p. 113.

8. Ibid., pp. 119 - 21. The scene is an attempt on the part of the "author" in the story to describe the biological spiritually. The dunghill and town festival have their counterparts in descriptions of the city and town festival in *Jonatans Rejse*.

9. "Midsommerfesten," p. 121.

10. It is the "author" of the story who seduces the women into an appreciation of the spirit of the farm.

11. Ibid., pp. 222, 226. The "author" implies that the "reader's" familiarity with him would rend the curtain of illusion. Alma the reader and Alma on Blood Hill are both suddenly faced with the possibility that what they have believed in is only an aesthetic illusion, a lie imposed on them. Their own lives must now be seen as a part of that fiction unless they are willing and able to continue believing on their own.

12. Ibid., p. 227. When "the author" addresses "the reader" as "the woman," he calls himself "the scribbler," just as he had when he refused to listen to the edifying speeches being given at the festival (see p. 137).

13. The text calls the works of Augustin Eugène Scribe (1791 - 1861) "vaudeville," but the present discussion uses the more encompassing term of "comedy."

14. This sarcastic ditty refers to a war over the duchies of Schleswig and Holstein. Denmark lost the war to Prussia and Austria.

15. Martin A. Hansen, "Septembertaagen," in *Tornebusken*, p. 258. "Fear of the good" is equated with the "demonaic" in Kierkegaard's *The Concept of Dread*.
16. "Septembertaagen," pp. 244 - 45.
17. Ibid., p. 268. The idea is subtly brought home by an oath: "... den Satans Krigsliderlighed" ("that damned [or literally 'satanic'] lust for war").
18. Ibid., p. 245. Sören Kierkegaard's *Fear and Trembling (Frygt og Bæven* [1843]), which — through the story of Abraham's willingness to sacrifice Isaac — treats the question of whether an absolute duty to God can suspend ethical law, considers the demonaic to be the person placed outside the universal by nature or historical circumstance.
19. "Septembertaagen," pp. 254 - 55.
20. Ibid., p. 260. This is an allusion to Hans Christian Andersen's nightmarish fairy tale "The Story of a Mother" ("Historien om en Moder" [1848]).
21. "Septembertaagen," p. 273. Bonfires are lit on St. John's Eve to drive away witches.
22. Exod. 3:1 - 10.
23. "Septembertaagen," p. 267. Björnvig, in *Kains Alter*, p. 133, points out that the grown man's tragedy was meant to clarify the child's experience and that it, in turn, attempted to clarify the man's and, finally, that the "death" of the boy's father revealed to him the incomprehensibility of war.
24. "Septembertaagen," pp. 242 - 43.
25. These seasonal and geographic sequences, as well as the first story's sacral significance (see text), were first pointed out by Nielsen, *Dansk Digtning i Dag*, pp. 36 - 38.
26. The poem "Cyclus" ("Kreslöbet") by Nis Petersen (1897 - 1943), a Danish poet, journalist, and novelist, first appeared posthumously in *Digte*, ed. Hans Brix (1949; rpt. Copenhagen: Gyldendal, 1954), p. 311.

Chapter Six

1. Hansen originally called the three sections *legende, erkendelse,* and *myte* (legend, perception, and myth); see Wivel, *Martin A. Hansen*, I, 347.
2. Finn Stefánsson has pointed out that the partridge can be found in four stories: "Agerhönen," "Bogen," "Martsnat," and "Manden fra Jorden"; see "Myte og syntese: Et kompositions- og livstolkningstema i Martin A. Hansens Agerhönen," *Meddelelser fra Dansklærerforeningen*, No. 2 (1973), p. 189.
3. Martin A. Hansen, *Agerhönen* (1947; rpt. Copenhagen: Gyldendal, 1963), p. 48.
4. Ibid., p. 71.
5. The story is based upon a legend from Halland; see Björnvig, *Kains Alter*, pp. 152 - 53.
6. Björnvig, pp. 156 - 57.
7. Some critics find that the text's grim mood is counterbalanced by the little girl's willingness to sacrifice herself for the sake of society. Such a reading seems

Notes and References

to neglect not only the spirit with which society carries out the sacrifice but also the fate that society, in fact, allots the person who served as its executor, Anna. See Stefánsson, "Myte og syntese," p. 180; and Frederik Nielsen, *Fra Martin A. Hansens Værksted* (Haslev: Gyldendal, 1971), pp. 51 - 53.

8. *Agerhönen*, p. 83.
9. Ibid., p. 94.
10. Ibid.
11. Björnvig, *Kains Alter*, pp. 162 - 63; and Wivel, *Martin A. Hansen*, I, 361.
12. *Agerhönen*, p. 152.
13. Hansen's father died in March 1945.
14. See Björnvig, *Kains Alter*, pp. 175 - 82.
15. *Agerhönen*, p. 172.
16. The inspiration to the story is "Den sjuende Far i Huset," a Norwegian folk tale. See Björnvig, *Kains Alter*, p. 187.
17. *Agerhönen*, p. 195.
18. *Orm og Tyr* (Copenhagen: Wivels Forlag, 1952); references are to the reprint (Copenhagen: Gyldendal, 1956); see p. 382.
19. According to Old Norse mythology, the cow Audhumla licked Bure, the ancestor of the Asirs, from salty ice-blocks.

Chapter Seven

1. Hansen wrote the first sketch for "The Ice Breaks" in 1942. The story itself (written in 1945) was first published in the magazine *Hjemmet*, August 19, 1969. It has been reprinted in *Omkring Lögneren*, ed. Ole Wivel, Værkserien (Copenhagen: Hans Reitzel, 1971), pp. 9 - 21. *Lögneren* was first published in serial form, intermittantly, for two and a half months in *Berlingske Aftenavis*, January 21 - March 8, 1950. The work was revised and reprinted in book form later that year. References here are to the reprint (Copenhagen: Gyldendal, 1957).

2. Hansen, *Lögneren*, pp. 7, 17 - 18. Vig views Natanael as being almost like a son — or perhaps a younger version of himself. Natanael is one in whom there "is no guile" (John 1:47).

3. Göran Printz-Pahlson, in *"The Liar:* The Paradox of Fictional Communication in Martin A. Hansen," *Scandinavian Studies*, 36 (1964), 263 - 80, has given the name "John Fraud" to Vig. Vig may also have something in common with Sören Kierkegaard's "Johannes the Seducer" in *Either/Or (Enten/Eller* [1843]).

4. *Lögneren*, p. 149. Vig likens the island's contours to those of a wooden shoe (see p. 118), but on the drawn map, the island resembles more a whale than a shoe.

5. Ibid., pp. 21, 131. In the King James version Eccles. 3:15 reads "and God requireth that which is past."

6. *Lögneren*, p. 135. Björnvig, *Kains Alter*, p. 40, points out that for Dostoyevsky the author's call lay in revealing the human heart as the scene of

battle between God and Satan. Jan Nissen, in "En fortolkning of *Lögneren,*" *Dansk Udsyn,* 39 (1959), 346 - 59 and reprinted in *Omkring Lögneren,* pp. 104 - 18, draws attention to the modern (predestined) man who recognizes his sin, thinks himself to be confronted by an Old Testament God, and finds punishment inescapable; see *Omkring Lögneren,* p. 116.

7. *Lögneren,* pp. 115 - 16, 127. Finn Stein Larsen, in "Leviathans kontur: Om den episke mönsterdannelse i Martin A. Hansens *Lögneren,*" in *"Omkring Lögneren,"* pp. 140 - 42, points out the repetitive pattern in Vig's love life: he is involved in a love triangle, sins against others, suffers guilt for it, and finds himself in a similar situation a few years later.

8. *Lögneren,* pp. 87, 149; Vig declares that Oluf's swim from death will become a legend on the island and that to be remembered in legend is the most to which a man can aspire (see p. 50).

9. Marie, Annemari, and Rigmor are all described in terms of the nature of the island. Marie is like a monolith, Annemari like a migratory bird, and Rigmor like an elfin presence. Vig identifies with all these women in one way or another, but he finds that Rigmor, in her hopelessness, self-destructive detachment, and longing for death, resembles him most.

10. *Lögneren,* pp. 53 - 56. Björnvig, in *Kains Alter,* pp. 224 - 25, 228, views Vig's drunkenly crying in the church as indicative of the purity of his determination to live up to Christian ideals by giving up Annemari.

11. *Lögneren,* pp. 54 - 55. Wivel, in *Martin A. Hansen,* I, 19 - 20, points out Hansen's fascination with tales in which an abandoned god (like Odin) or the king of the elves or the dead, but once powerful, lord of an area becomes its ghostly haunter riding on nocturnal hunts. Through his haunting he "protects" the region, ensures it peace, and binds the memory of the past to the present. (He, the restless outlaw of his own realm, seems almost to be a leader of the mythic "oskorei," the dead who belong neither to heaven nor to hell).

12. *Lögneren,* pp. 72 - 74, 76. Many critics see Vig, who first felt himself to be empty and light and then possessed, as an example of the demoniac through "fear of the good," a state described by Kierkegaard in *The Concept of Dread.* See, for example, Nissen, "En fortolkning," pp. 109 - 10. (Vig's feelings, however, may simply be akin to those expressed in Ecclesiastes.)

13. *Lögneren,* p. 79. See Luke 11: 17 - 18.

14. *Lögneren,* pp. 137, 143. Annemari is said to seek the false modern dream of happiness, but Marie represents law. Most critics see Marie's dedication to the law, her family, and the island as something of an ideal for Vig. Erik M. Christensen, *Ex auditorio: Kunst og Ideer hos Martin A. Hansen* (Fredensborg: Forfatternes Forlag Arena, 1965), pp. 78 - 79, and Marie Klövstad Öye, *Det gotiske og det romanske livstema: En studie i Martin A. Hansen's Lögneren* (Oslo: Universitetsforlaget, 1970), pp. 109 - 13, discuss Marie's paradoxical attitudes as being, on the one hand, in the spirit of the Old Testament with its stress on "nomos," the law, and, on the other hand, in the spirit either of pre-Christian attitudes with a stress on "eros" (Christensen) or of the pre-Gothic cult of the Nordic past with its preoccupation with death (Öye).

Notes and References

15. Vig's actions may explain the riddle that he has posed Natanael: Vig has called himself a man who is simultaneously vain — one who would appear more interesting than he really is — and ambitionless.
16. Egil Skallagrimsson (? -990+) was a renowned Icelandic bard and warrior and is the hero of *Egil Skallagrimsson's Saga* (ca. 1250).
17. *Lögneren*, p. 31.
18. Ibid., pp. 13, 16.

Chapter Eight

1. Martin A. Hansen, *Paradisæblerne og andre Historier* (Copenhagen: Fremad, 1953), p. 91.
2. Martin A. Hansen, *Konkyljen*, ed. Vera Hansen and Ole Wivel (Copenhagen: Gyldendal, 1955), pp. 50 - 81. This central text has received much critical attention; see Björnvig, *Kains Alter*, pp. 407 - 22; Wivel, *Martin A. Hansen*, II, 44 - 52; Finn Stein Larsen, *Prosaens mönstre: Nærlæsninger af danske litterære prosatekster* (Copenhagen: Berlingske Forlag, 1971), pp. 146 - 60; and Henriksen, *Gotisk tid*, pp. 128 - 34.
3. *Konkyljen*, p. 81.
4. Björnvig, *Kains Alter*, p. 424.
5. This motif has often inspired literary artists, most notably, the Swedish Romanticist Per Daniel Amadeus Atterbom, *Lycksalighetens ö* (1824 - 1827). See also Björnvig, *Kains Alter*, pp. 597 - 98.
6. *Konkyljen*, p. 201.
7. Björnvig, *Kains Alter*, pp. 460 - 62.
8. Wivel points out that, in the story's treatment of the returning soldier motif, Hansen relied on his family's memory of his grandfather, his mother's father. He had participated in the Napoleonic Wars (1807 - 1814) and returned as a marked and restless man. See *Martin A. Hansen*, I, 37 - 38.
9. Martin A. Hansen, *Efterslæt*, p. 103. Björnvig suggests interesting similarities to other literary texts, for example, the folk ballad "Ebbe Skammelsön"; see *Kains Alter*, pp. 462 - 65.
10. Björnvig, *Kains Alter*, p. 466.
11. *Efterslæt*, p. 148.
12. Ibid.
13. Ibid., p. 153.
14. Ibid., p. 156.
15. Ibid., p. 157.
16. Ibid.

Chapter Nine

1. *Politiken*, October 10, 1942; reprinted in revised form in *Tanker i en Skorsten* (1948; rpt. Copenhagen: Gyldendal, 1956), pp. 7 - 14. See pp. 12 - 23.

2. Published as "De Gamle Heste," *Politikens Magasin,* June 2, 1956; reprinted in revised form in *Midsommerkrans,* pp. 113 - 21. See p. 116.
3. *Nationaltidende,* May 3, 1946; reprinted in *Tanker i en Skorsten,* pp. 57 - 67. See p. 64.
4. *Midsommerkrans,* p. 141.
5. Published as "Sjællandske Portrætter," in *Aarhuus Stiftstidende,* June 19, 1941; reprinted in revised form in *Tanker i en Skorsten,* pp. 15 - 24.
6. See "Valfart," *Nationaltidende,* November 12, 1944.
7. See in particular "Gamle Venner," in *Midsommerkrans,* pp. 113 - 21; "Sagn i September," in *Efterslæt,* pp. 172 - 79; "En Sjællandsk Hezekiel," in *Tanker i en Skorsten,* pp. 42 - 48; and "Asken," in *Efterslæt,* pp. 122 - 27.
8. "Den mörke Middelalder," *Aarhuus Stiftstidende,* March 2, 1941; reprinted in *Midsommerkrans,* pp. 53 - 61. "Völven og Jomfruen," *Aarhuus Stiftstidende,* February 18, 1943; reprinted in revised form in *Tanker i en Skorsten,* pp. 75 - 82. "Öksen," *Berlingske Aftenavis,* March 10, 1945; reprinted in revised form in *Tanker i en Skorsten,* pp. 93 - 111.
9. *Midsommerkrans,* p. 58.
10. *Det tredie Standpunkt,* No. 2 (November 1947); reprinted in *Verdensromanen,* pp. 53 - 61.
11. *Tanker i en Skorsten,* p. 77.
12. Published as "En Verdensroman," *Berlingske Aftenavis,* September 8, 1948; reprinted in *Verdensromanen,* pp. 30 - 38.
13. Björnvig, *Kains Alter,* p. 517.
14. Published as "Et Digterværk i Sagnhistorien," *Aarhuus Stiftstidende,* October 4, 1942; reprinted in revised form in *Midsommerkrans,* pp. 70 - 77.
15. See "De ukrænkelige Cirkler," in *Tanker i en Skorsten,* pp. 157 - 61; and "Dialog om Drab og Ansvar," in *Verdensromanen,* pp. 135 - 46.
16. *Berlingske Aftenavis,* November 18, 1944; reprinted in *De gyldne Laurbær,* ed. Ole Wivel (Copenhagen: Carit Andersens Forlag, 1963), pp. 7 - 11. See p. 11.
17. See "Hos 'Hine Enkelte,' " in *Tanker i en Skorsten,* pp. 144 - 51.
18. *Nationaltidende,* June 22, 1948; reprinted in revised form in *Tanker i en Skorsten,* pp. 126 - 33.
19. *Tanker i en Skorsten,* p. 129.
20. See "Himmerland og Historierne," in *Midsommerkrans,* pp. 141 - 48.
21. *Politiken,* December 29, 1948; reprinted in *Midsommerkrans,* pp. 119 - 40. See p. 135.
22. *Politiken,* September 19, 1947; reprinted in *Tanker i en Skorsten,* pp. 182 - 211.
23. Several critics have stressed Kierkegaard's impact on Hansen's writings. Björnvig states that "the philosophical spine in Martin A. Hansen's authorship is simply Kierkegaardian"; see *Kains Alter,* p. 532 and also pp. 325 - 30. See also Jan Nissen, "En Fortolkning af *Lögneren,*" in *Omkring Lögneren,* pp. 104 - 18; and Göran Printz-Pahlson, "The Liar: the Paradox," pp. 186 - 206.
24. See Wivel, *Martin A. Hansen,* I, 310.

Notes and References

25. *Tanker i en Skorsten*, p. 209.
26. These essays, all mentioned earlier, are reprinted in *Ved Korsvejen*.
27. *Midsommerkrans*, pp. 182 - 83. These passages offer very concrete evidence for Hansen's cognizance of the fact that his texts could well contain unintentional material; that is, that the author as a person and the author as he speaks from a text may be at variance.
28. *Tanker i en Skorsten*, p. 196.
29. Ibid., p. 187.
30. The last work Hansen was to complete was the preface to a new translation of Herman Melville's *Moby Dick* (translated by Mogens Boisen in 1955). That preface was reprinted in *Ved Korsvejen*, pp. 186 - 204.
31. *Tanker i en Skorsten*, p. 189.
32. *Ved Korsvejen*, p. 177.
33. Wivel, *Martin A. Hansen*, II, 254.
34. *Midsommerkrans*, pp. 141 - 48.
35. *Ved Korsvejen*, p. 119.
36. *Midsommerkrans*, p. 156.
37. *Leviathan* (Copenhagen: Wivels Forlag, 1950); references are to 2nd ed. (Haslev: Gyldendal, 1970); see p. 42.
38. Ibid., p. 173.
39. Ibid., p. 160.
40. Björnvig, *Kains Alter*, p. 298.
41. Ibid., p. 287.

Chapter Ten

1. Martin A. Hansen, *Orm og Tyr*, p. 8. For full reference see chapter 6, note 18.
2. The genesis of *Orm og Tyr* is described in detail by Wivel in *Martin A. Hansen*, II, 203 - 22.
3. Wivel states that with *Orm og Tyr* Hansen would be realizing the dream of his youth: to narrate history with a starting point in his own and his family's recollections and then to expand them into the remembrance of mankind. See *Martin A. Hansen*, II, 215, 253.
4. *Orm og Tyr*, p. 9.
5. Hansen called Odin "poetry's tragic demon." See *Orm og Tyr*, p. 179.
6. *Orm og Tyr*, p. 350.
7. Ibid., p. 368. Marie Klövstad Öye points out the significance of these two figures in *Det gotiske og romanske livstema*, pp. 21 - 24.
8. *Orm og Tyr*, p. 382.

Chapter Eleven

1. Martin A. Hansen, *Dansk Vejr* (Copenhagen: Steen Hasselbalchs Forlag, 1953), p. 72.
2. In a number of essays Hansen recorded his impressions from his travels in

Schleswig; see "Sydslesvig," "Fra Ægirs Dör til Vigleds," and "Fra Ejdersted til Immervad," in *Verdensromanen*, pp. 97 - 102, 103 - 15, and 116 - 27.

3. *Kringen: Billeder fra övre Gudbrandsdal* (Copenhagen: Gyldendal, 1953), pp. 30 - 31.

4. *Dansk Vejr*, p. 23.

5. Ibid., p. 25.

6. Ibid., pp. 82 - 83.

7. Ibid., p. 108.

8. Ibid., p. 109.

9. See "Tömmer paa Sperillen," "Butikken," "Sommeren kommer til Aadalen," and "Linerla" in *Midsommerkrans*, pp. 88 - 95, 96 - 101, 102 - 10, and 111 - 18.

10. *Tanker i en Skorsten*, pp. 61 - 63. Here, as elsewhere, Hansen reacts strongly against Romanticism's pantheism and adoration of the spectacular.

11. Ibid., p. 67.

12. *Kringen*, p. 59.

13. Ibid., pp. 35 - 37.

14. Ibid., p. 56.

15. Ibid.

16. *Rejse paa Island* (1954; rpt. Copenhagen: Carit Andersens Forlag, 1963), p. 286.

Chapter Twelve

1. Alan Friedman, in *The Turn of the Novel: The Transition to Modern Fiction* (New York: Oxford University Press, 1966), suggests that, at the beginning of the twentieth century, the closed ended novel, a novel with a fixed interpretation of the human condition, was replaced with the open ended narrative that did not give any final interpretation to existence.

2. The detrimental effect of a prominent author's easily detectable, but hardly imitable, diction on disciples is one that the sad examples of Hemingway's and Faulkner's imitators illustrate in America.

3. *Lögneren*, p. 31.

Selected Bibliography

BIBLIOGRAPHY

KETTEL, HENRIK. *Martin A. Hansens Forfatterskab: En Bibliografi.* Copenhagen: Gyldendal, 1966. Complete bibliography through the year 1964; cites Hansen's works in Danish and other languages.

PRIMARY SOURCES

1. Works in Danish (Date of first publication, if by same publisher, in parenthesis.)

Nu Opgiver Han (1935). Mindeudgave 1. Copenhagen: Gyldendal, 1961.
Kolonien (1937). Copenhagen: Gyldendal, 1957.
Jonatans Rejse (1941). 2nd ed. rev. 1950; rpt. Copenhagen: Gyldendal, 1954.
Lykkelige Kristoffer (1945). Copenhagen: Gyldendal, 1953.
Tornebusken (1946). Copenhagen: Gyldendal, 1955. Includes "Paaskeklokken," "Midsommerfesten," and "Septembertaagen."
Agerhönen (1947). Copenhagen: Gyldendal, 1963.
Tanker i en Skorsten (1948). Copenhagen: Gyldendal, 1956.
Lögneren. (*Berlingske Aftenavis,* January 21 - April 8, 1950.) Rev. ed. 1950; rpt. Copenhagen: Gyldendal, 1957.
"Eneren og Massen." In *Mennesket i Tiden.* Edited by Erling Nielsen. Copenhagen: Hans Reitzels Forlag, 1950. I, 31 - 83.
Leviathan. Copenhagen: Wivels Forlag, 1950; 2nd ed. Haslev: Gyldendal, 1970.
Orm og Tyr. Copenhagen: Wivels Forlag, 1952; rpt. Copenhagen: Gyldendal, 1956.
Kringen: Billeder fra övre Gudbrandsdal. Copenhagen: Gyldendal, 1953.
Paradisæblerne og andre Historier. Copenhagen: Forlaget Fremad, 1953.
Dansk Vejr. Copenhagen: Steen Hasselbalchs Forlag, 1953.
Rejse paa Island (1954). Copenhagen: Carit Andersens Forlag, 1963.
Konkyljen. Edited by Vera Hansen and Ole Wivel. Copenhagen: Gyldendal, 1955.
Gyldendals Julebog 1955: Martin A. Hansen. Edited by Ole Wivel, with Vera Hansen. Copenhagen: Gyldendal, 1955.

Midsommerkrans. Edited by Vera Hansen and Ole Wivel. Copenhagen: Gyldendal, 1956.
Af Folkets Danmarkshistorie: Seks Kapitler fortalt for Ungdommen (1957). Edited by Vera Hansen and Ole Wivel. Copenhagen: Gyldendal, 1959.
Martin A. Hansen Fortæller. Edited by Hans Röpke and Ole Wivel. Copenhagen: Gyldendal, 1958.
Efterslæt: Sidste Noveller og Skildringer. Edited by Thorkild Björnvig and Ole Wivel. Copenhagen: Gyldendal, 1959.
Ved Korsvejen: Litterære Essays. Edited by Thorkild Björnvig and Ole Wivel. Gyldendals Ugleböger. Copenhagen: Gyldendal, 1965.
Martsnat. Edited by Thorkild Björnvig. Dansklærerforeningen. Copenhagen: Gyldendal, 1965.
Verdensromanen: Historiske Essays. Edited by Thorkild Björnvig and Ole Wivel. Gyldendals Ugleböger. Copenhagen: Gyldendal, 1966.
Martin A. Hansen og Skolen. Edited by Hans Röpke and Ole Wivel. Copenhagen: Gyldendal, 1968.
Isen bryder: Novelleforlægget til Lögneren. Edited by Ole Wivel. Gyldendals Bogklub. Haslev: Gyldendal, 1969. Also in *Hjemmet*, August 19, 1969.

2. Works in English

"The Birds." (From *Agerhönen*, 1947.) Translated by K. R. Keigwin. In *Contemporary Danish Prose: An Anthology.* Edited by Elias Bredsdorff. Copenhagen: Gyldendal, 1958. Pp. 331 - 51.
"The Book." (From *Agerhönen*, 1947.) Translated by Lydia Cranfield. *The Norseman*, 10 (1952), 192 - 97.
"The Countenance." (1949; rev. in *Konkyljen*, 1955.) Translated by Niels Lyhne Jensen and James McFarlane. *The Norseman*, 13 (1955), 328 - 33.
"The Gardener, the Beast, and the Child." (*Heretica*, 3 [1948]; *Efterslæt*, 1959.) Translated by Hallberg Hallmundsson. In *An Anthology of Scandinavian Literature: From the Viking Period to the Twentieth Century.* Edited by Hallberg Hallmundsson. Collier Books. New York: Macmillan, 1965. Pp. 87 - 95.
"Harvest Feast." (1944; rev. in *Agerhönen*, 1947.) Translated by Evelyn Heepe, with Jean Koefoed. In *New World Writing*. Editor unknown. Mentor Selection 8. New York: New American Library of World Literature, 1955. Pp. 110 - 25.
"Letter to a Beginner." (From *Vindrosen*, No. 4 [Oct. 1955]) Translated by P[hilip] M[arshall] Mitchell. *The Literary Review*, 6 (1963), 431 - 40.
The Liar. Translated by John Jepson Egglishaw. Letchworth, Herts: J. M. Dent & Sons, 1954. Reprinted with an introduction. The Library of Scandinavian Literature 5. New York: American-Scandinavian Foundation and Twayne Publishers, 1969.
Lucky Kristoffer. Translated by John Jepson Egglishaw. The Library of

Scandinavian Literature 25. New York: The American-Scandinavian Literature 25. New York: The American-Scandinavian Foundation and Twayne Publishers, 1974.

"March Night." (1945; rev. in *Agerhønen*, 1947.) Translated by Lydia Cranfield. *The Norseman*, 8 (1950), 54 - 60.

"The Morning Hour." (Rev. in *Agerhønen*, 1947.) Translated by Martha Lepawsky. *The Literary Review*, 8 (1964), 31 - 39.

"Paradise Apples." (1949; rev. in *Paradisæblerne og Andre Historier*, 1953.) Translated by Faith Ingwersen. In *Anthology of Danish Literature: Bilingual Edition*. Edited by F[rederik] J[ulius] Billeskov Jansen and P[hilip] M[arshall] Mitchell. Carbondale and Edwardsville, Ill.: Southern Illinois University Press, 1971. Paperback edition in two volumes but with same pagination. See Vol. 2: *Realism to the Present*. Pp. 528 - 47.

"The Paradise Apples." Translated by Marion Marzolf. *The American-Scandinavian Review*, 52 (1964), 72 - 78.

"The Partridge." (1943; rev. in *Agerhønen*, 1947.) Translated by Janet Beverley. *Adam* (London), 16 (1948), 188ff.

"The Partridge." Translated by Erik J. Friis. *The American-Scandinavian Review*, 43 (1955), 383 - 86.

"Sacrifice." (1946; rev. in *Agerhønen*, 1947.) Translated by Evelyn Heepe. In *Swans of the North: Short Stories by Modern Danish Authors*. Edited by Evelyn Heepe. Copenhagen: G. E. C. Gads Forlag, 1953. Pp. 51 - 75.

"The Soldier and the Girl." (*Agerhønen*, 1947.) Translated by Richard Vowles. *Accent: A Quarterly of New Literature*, 27 (1957), 43ff.

"The Soldier and the Girl." Translated by James E. Anderson.*The American-Scandinavian Review*, 60 (1972), 63 - 67.

"Wind, Weather, and Men's Mind." (*Det danske Magasin*, 2 [1954].) Anonymous translation. *Danish Foreign Office Journal*, No. 12 (June 1954), pp. 1 - 3.

SECONDARY SOURCES

BJÖRNVIG, THORKILD. *Martin A. Hansen*. Copenhagen: Wivels Forlag, 1948.

———. *Kains Alter: Martin A. Hansens Digtning og Tænkning*. Copenhagen: Gyldendal, 1964.

———. *Forsvar for Kains Alter: En Kritisk Efterskrift*. Copenhagen: Gyldendal, 1965.

BREDSDORFF, ELIAS. "Introduction." In *The Liar*, by Martin A. Hansen. The Library of Scandinavian Literature 5. New York: The American-Scandinavian Foundation and Twayne Publishers, 1969.

BUKDAHL, JÖRGEN K. "Martin A. Hansen som 'genoptager af de gamles eksistenstænkning': Om Thorkild Björnvigs disputats." *Vindrosen*, 12, No. 3 (1965), pp. 47 - 59.

CHRISTENSEN, ERIK M. *Ex auditorio: Kunst og Ideer hos Martin A. Hansen*. Fredensborg: Forfatternes Forlag Arena, 1965.

GRODAL, TORBEN KRAGH. "Sælens lyst og sjælens ubodelige ensomhed: En analyse af Martin A. Hansens *Løgneren.*" *Poetik,* 5 (1972), 1 - 22.
HEGGELUND, KJELL. *Fiksjon og virkelighet: En studie i tre nordiske jegromaner.* Oslo: Universitetsforlaget, 1966, 43 - 72.
HELLERN, VICTOR. *Martin A. Hansen: Studier i et forfatterskap.* Copenhagen: Gyldendal, 1958.
HENRIKSEN, AAGE. *Gotisk tid: Fire litterære afhandlinger.* Haslev: Gyldendal, 1971.
INGWERSEN, FAITH. "The Truthful Liars: A Comparative Analysis of Knut Hamsun's *Mysterier* and Martin A. Hansen's *Løgneren.*" Ph.D. dissertation, University of Chicago, 1974.
INGWERSEN, NIELS. "Introduction." *Lucky Kristoffer,* by Martin A. Hansen. The Library of Scandinavian Literature 25. New York: The American-Scandinavian Foundation and Twayne Publishers, 1974.
JESSEN, JES TANGE. "Troldfuglen: En tolkning af *Løgneren.*" *Dansk Udsyn,* 43 (1963), 313 - 47. Reprinted in *Omkring Løgneren.* Edited by Ole Wivel (see Wivel entry). Pp. 153 - 86.
LARSEN, FINN STEIN. "Leviathans Kontur: Om den episke mönsterdannelse i Martin A. Hansens *Løgneren.*" In *Omkring Løgneren.* Edited by Ole Wivel (see Wivel entry). Pp. 128 - 51.
————. *Prosaens mönstre: Nærlæsninger af danske litterære prosatekster.* Berlingske Leksikon Bibliotek 53. Copenhagen: Berlingske Forlag, 1971. Pp. 146 - 60.
LINGS, JENS K. KJELGAARD. "Pigro, en sneppehund — og?: Et tema i *Løgneren.*" *Meddelelser fra Dansklærerforeningen,* No. 3 (1967), pp. 344 - 50.
NIELSEN, FREDERIK. "Martin A. Hansen." In *Danske Digtere i det 20. Aahundrede.* Edited by Ernst Frandsen and Niels Kaas Johansen. Copenhagen: G. E. C. Gads Forlag, 1951. II, 691 - 713.
————. *Dansk digtning i dag.* Copenhagen: Fremad, 1957.
————. *Martin A. Hansen: Möder med en digter og hans böger.* Copenhagen: Carit Andersens Forlag, 1961. Expanded and reissued as *Fra Martin A. Hansens Værksted.* Gyldendals Uglebøger. Haslev: Gyldendal, 1971.
————. "Martin A. Hansen." In *Danske Digtere i det 20. Århundrede.* Edited by Frederik Nielsen and Ole Restrup. Copenhagen: G. E. C. Gads Forlag, 1966. III, 243 - 72.
NISSEN, JAN. "En fortolkning af *Løgneren.*" *Dansk Udsyn,* 39 (1959), 346 - 59. Reprinted in *Omkring Løgneren.* Edited by Ole Wivel (see Wivel entry). Pp. 104 - 18.
————. *Studiebog til Løgneren.* Copenhagen: Gjellerup, 1966.
————. "Sneppen og den vilde ungdomskraft: En fortolkning af *Løgneren.*" *Meddelelser fra Dansklærerforeningen,* No. 4 (1966), pp. 159 - 89. Reprinted in *Omkring Løgneren.* Edited by Ole Wivel (see Wivel entry). Pp. 265 - 93.

Selected Bibliography

OLSEN, IB SPANG. *I Kristoffers spor.* Gyldendals Bogklub. Copenhagen: Gyldendal, 1973.
PETERSEN, NIS. "Kreslöbet." In *Digte* (1949). Edited by Hans Brix. Copenhagen: Gyldendal, 1954. P. 311.
PRINTZ-PÅHLSON, GÖRAN. "*The Liar:* The Paradox of Fictional Communication in Martin A. Hansen." *Scandinavian Studies*, 36 (1964), 263 - 80. Reprinted in *Omkring Lögneren.* Edited by Ole Wivel (see Wivel entry). Pp. 186 - 206.
RAMLÖV, PREBEN. "Martin A. Hansen, det sjællandske 'man' og det nordiske retssyn." *Dansk Udsyn,* 45 (1965), 13 - 28.
STEFÁNSSON, FINN. "Myte og syntese: Et kompositions- og livstolkningstema i Martin A. Hansens *Agerhönen.*" *Meddelelser fra Dansklærerforeningen,* No. 2 (1973), pp. 175 - 89.
SÖRENSEN, BIRGITTE DENCKER; ANDERSEN, HERDIS HOFF; MÖLLER, JÖRN; and ÖSTERGARD, KIRSTEN. "En sammenligning af Martin A. Hansens romaner *Lykkelige Kristoffer* og *Lögneren.*" *Meddelelser fra Dansklærerforeningen,* No. 1 (1971), pp. 3 - 32.
SÖRENSEN, JÖRGEN. "En sammenhæng i *Lögneren.*" *Meddelelser fra Dansklærerforeningen,* No. 4 (1971), pp. 329 - 43.
VOWLES, RICHARD B. "Martin A. Hansen and the Uses of the Past." *The American-Scandinavian Review,* 46 (1958), 33 - 40.
WIVEL, OLE, ed. *De gyldne Laurbær.* Copenhagen: Carit Andersens Forlag, 1963. Pp. 7 - 11.
―――. *Kunsten og Krigen.* Copenhagen: Gyldendal, 1965.
―――. *Martin A. Hansen.* 2 vols. Copenhagen: Gyldendal, 1967 - 1969. Vol. 1: *Fra Barndommen til Krigens Aar* (1967); Vol. 2: *Fra Krigens Aar til Döden* (1969).
―――, ed. *Martin A. Hansen: Til minde.* Copenhagen: Gyldendal, 1955.
―――, ed. *Omkring Lögneren.* Værkserien 5. Copenhagen: Hans Reitzels Forlag, 1971.
WOEL, CAI M. *Martin A. Hansen: Liv og Digtning.* Ladager, Lille Skensved: Midstjællands Forlag, 1959.
ÖYE, MARIA KLÖVSTAD. *Det gotiske og romanske livstema: En studie i Martin A. Hansen's Lögneren.* Oslo: Universitetsforlaget, 1970.

Index

Angst, 145 - 46
Art, 26, 56, 146, 171
Artist:
   duty of, 152
   in trap, 34 - 35
   justification, 72
   view of, 20, 23, 26, 67, 73, 150
   vocation vs. human relationships, 133

Becker, Knuth, 16
Björnvig, Thorkild: *Kains Alter,* 11 - 12, 22, 136
Blicher, Steen Steensen, 149
Bronze Age, 156

Cassirer, Ernst, 152
Cervantes, Miguel de, 16; *Don Quixote,* 148
Christianity:
   advent of, 143, 157, 158
   failure of, 151
   and Kierkegaard, 146
   source of symbols, 31
   values in, 160
City, 51, 53 - 54, 56
Collective farm, 41
Communal farming, 16
Communist Manifesto (Marx), 94
Creation myth, 109
Culture, 27, 70, 152
   agrarian, 27, 143
   in "Our Lady's Hunter," 131
   old culture, 132, 134, 135; in essays, 140, 141, 143, 145, 149, 166, 167
   vs. nature, 29, 35, 71, 72, 118, 126 - 27, 137 - 39, 141, 160

Dalecarlia, 59
Danish history, 142 - 43, 154 *See also* Hansen, Martin A., Works: *Serpent and Bull*
Danish landscape painting, 163
Danish literature, 151 *See also* essays by Hansen
Darwinism, 149, 151
Death:
   fear of, 167 - 68
   in "September Fog," 91 - 92
   role in lives of living, 155, 156
   search for meaning in, 19, 24 - 25, 107, 109, 110
   subject of essays, 144 - 45
   symbols of, 97
Denmark:
   agricultural crisis of 1930s, 37
   general strike, 18
   invasion by Germans, 166
   Occupation of, 17, 142
   peace agreement with Sweden, 60
   resistance to Nazis, 19
   See also Danish history; Danish landscape painting; Danish literature; Hansen, Martin A., Works: *Danish Weather*
Don Quixote, 61, 108

Epic, 147 - 49
"ethical pessimism," 22, 110
Evil, 17, 53, 55
   man's struggle against, 57 - 58, 98, 123
   vs. good, 18, 73, 98, 118

Farm life, 15, 16, 37, 73, 132, 134, 141
Fiction:
  form, 73
  levels of, 78
  new uses for, 24
  "form-spirit," 146 - 49, 153
Frederik I (king of Denmark), 60

Gothic arch, 158
Grodal, Torben Kragh, 12
Gudbrand Valley, Norway, 25, 165
Guilt, 20 - 21

Hansen, Martin A.:
  birth, 13; childhood, 13; choice of vocation, 15; coeditor of *Heretica*, 22; confirmed, 14; credo, 152; crises, 12, 20; death, 25; disillusionment, 16; essays, 19, 140 - 50; experiments in form, 21, 22, 73, 146; farm work, 14; first novel published, 15; graduate of Hasley Teachers' College, 14 - 15; historical writing, 25, 142 - 43; hospitalized, 25; impact on other writers, 170; influences on, 15, 146, 149; joined Social Realists, 15, 16; lectured, 25; left Copenhagen for Sealand, 25; *The Liar* commissioned by Danish radio, 23; literary criticism, 145 - 49, 151; major themes, 16, 26 - 36, 58; married, 15; meaning for modern readers, 170 - 71; posthumous publications, 25; prose style, 150; quest for meaning, 128, 150, 169; his reading, 16; recognized as major Danish writer, 22; studies by Bjornvig and Wivel, 11 - 13; teaching in Copenhagen, 15; 10-volume memorial edition, 25; travel to Iceland and Norway, 25, 164- 66; turning point in *Jonatan's Journey*, 16; urged spiritual resistance, 20; view of the individual, 17; his vocation, 12 - 13, 20, 23; work during Nazi occupation, 17 - 19, 21, 144

WORKS: POETRY
  "Man" ("Menneske"), 23

WORKS: PROSE

ESSAYS:
  Aftermath (Efterslaet), 25, 136 - 39, 140
  "Astern" ("Agterude"), 141, 164
  At the Crossroads (Ved Korsvejen), 21, 140
  "The Axe" ("Oksen"), 142
  "Convention and Form-spirit," 147
  "The Dark Ages" ("Den Möke Middelalder"), 17, 142
  "The Decline of the Novel," 148
  "Double Portrait in a Carved Frame" ("Dobbeltportraet"), 142
  "The Eumenides" ("Eumeniderne"), 145, 146, 147
  From the People's History of Denmark (Af Folkets Danmarks-historie), 140
  "Himmerland and the Stories" ("Himmerland og Historierne"), 149
  "July '44" (Juli '44), 18, 19
  "Kindred" ("AEtten"), 145
  "Legends in September," 26
  Leviathan, 23, 140, 150 - 53
  Martin A. Hansen and the School (Martin A. Hansen og Skolen), 15, 140
  "Midsummer Wreath" ("Midsommerkrans"), 14, 25, 140
  "The Nordic Caesar" ("Nordens Caesar"), 143
  "Old Friends" ("Gamle Venner"), 141
  "Pilgrimage" ("Valfart"), 14
  "The Plow" ("Ploven"), 141
  "The Sibyl and the Virgin" ("Völven og Jomfruen"), 142
  "The Storyteller from Vinje" ("Fortaelleren fra Vinje"), 145, 149
  Thoughts in a Chimney (Tanker i en Skorsten), 22, 140, 141, 145, 164
  "The Uffe-Poet" ("Uffe digteren"), 143 - 44
  "Unfinished Postscript" ("Uafsluttet Efterskrift"), 144
  The World Novel (Verdensromanen), 140, 143

NOVELS:
  "Cain's Altar" ("Kains Alter") (outline), 20 - 23

Index

The Colony (Kolonien), 15, 37, 41 - 44
Jonatan's Journey (Jonatans Rejse), 16, 17, 18, 26, 45 - 58, 64, 107, 148
The Liar (Lögneren), 23 - 24, 58, 111 - 29, 150, 171
Lucky Kristoffer (Lykkelige Kristoffer), 17, 18, 26, 58 - 72, 108, 148
Now He Gives Up (Nu Opgiver Han), 15, 27, 37 - 43
Serpent and Bull (Orm og Tyr), 17, 24, 28, 29, 58, 77, 108, 148, 154 - 61, 163

SHORT STORIES:
  Apples of Paradise (Paradisaeblerne) 25, 130 - 32, 134
  "The Birds" ("Fuglene"), 107 - 108
  "The Book" ("Bogen"), 100, 101
  "The Bridegroom's Oak" ("Brudgommens Eg"), 135 - 36, 164
  The Conch (Konkylien), 25, 132 - 36
  "The Countenance" ("Aasynet"), 132
  "Early Morning" ("Morgenstunden"), 100 - 101
  "The Easter Bell" ("Paaskeklokken"), 73 - 78, 128
  "The Fathers" ("Faedrene"), 107
  "The Gardener, the Beast, and the Child" ("Gartneren, Dyret og Barnet"), 136 - 39
  "Haavn," 133 - 34
  "The Harvest Feast," 102, 103
  "The Homecoming" ("Hjemkomsten"), 136 - 37
  "The Ice Breaks," 111
  "The Man from the Earth" ("Manden fra Jordan"), 108 - 109
  "The Messenger" ("Budbringeren"), 134 - 35
  "The Midsummer Festival" ("Midsommerfesten"), 73, 78 - 84, 103, 104, 106, 128; (the author), 88 - 89; (the author and the reader) 84 - 88
  "Night in March" ("Martsnat"), 105 - 106, 109, 110
  "The Ostrich" ("Strudsen"), 130, 131
  "Our Lady's Hunter" (Vor Frues Jaeger"), 131
  "The Owl" ("Uglen"), 99 - 100, 101
  The Partridge (Agerhönen), 21, 99 - 110, 130, 132
  "The Righteous One" (Den Retfaerdige"), 132 - 33
  "Sacrifice" ("Offer"), 101 - 103, 105
  "September Fog" ("Septembertaagen"), 73, 89 - 95, 128
  "The Sin" ("Synden"), 132, 133,
  "The Soldier and the Girl" ("Soldaren og Pigen"), 106 - 107
  The Thornbush (Tornebusken), 21, 22, 44, 58, 73 - 98, 99, 110, 127
  "The Thornbush" ("Tornebusken"), 95 - 99
  "Tirad," 131 - 32
  "The Waiting Room" ("Ventesalen"), 103 - 105

TRAVEL BOOKS:
  Danish Weather (Dansk Vejr), 25, 162, 163 - 64
  Kringen, 25, 162, 163, 164 - 66
  Travel on Iceland (Rejse paa Island), 25, 163, 166 - 68

Havsteen-Mikkelsen, Sven, 25, 154, 166
Hector *(The Iliad)*, 61 - 62
Henriksen, Aage, 12
Heretica, 22 - 23
Historian, 152
Hitler, 16
Hunter symbol, 117, 118, 120, 125 - 26
Huxley, T. H., 151

Individualism, 17, 143, 152
Iron Age, 156 - 57

Jacobsen, J. P., 151
Jensen, Johannes V., 15, 151
  Hansen's essay on, 145, 149
Job, 31, 55, 123, 125, 126
Jonas, 121
Journey motif, 29, 30, 46, 59, 109

Kierkegaard, Soren, 15, 145, 152, 169; *The Concept of Dread (Begrebet Angest)*, 94, 146
Kirk, Hans, 16
Kivi, Alexis: *Seven Brothers*, 148
Kristensen, Erling, 16

Kristian II, 59, 60
Kristian III, 61

Leviathan symbol, 115, 118, 120, 121, 150
Lübeck, 59, 60
Lutheran Reformation, 59, 60

Marx, Karl: *Communist Manifesto*, 94
Marxism, 16, 23, 150
Melville, Herman: *Moby Dick*, 148
Modernism, 22, 23, 148
Monk, 158, 159
Myths, 28 - 29, 30, 165
  limitations of, 34
  therapeutic power of, 31

Naturalism, 147, 148, 151
Nature, 27, 163, 168
  demonic, 144
  duality of, 69 - 71
  imagery, 29
  resurrection in, 116
  vs. culture, 26, 29, 30, 35, 71, 72, 115, 116, 118, 126 - 27, 138, 139, 141, 160, 169 - 70
  and woman, 32
Nazis, 143, 144
Nielsen, Jörgen, 16
Nietzche, 143
Nihilism, 21 - 22, 29 - 30, 31, 71, 128, 137, 141, 143, 144
  in "The Waiting Room," 103 - 105
Norse mythology, 109
Norse sagas, 147, 167
Norsemen, 168

Odin, 156, 157
Old Norse literature, 157
  See also Viking Age
Oral tales, 147 *See also* Storytelling

Past, 22, 30, 135, 143, 145
  moral values of, 18, 21, 23, 28, 134, 144
Peasant, 158 - 59
Pen symbol, 128 - 29
People and Freedom (Folk og Frihed), 19

Petersen, Nis: "Cyclus," 97 - 98
Poet:
  Hansen's view of, 145, 146, 148
  young poets, 146 - 47
Pontoppidan, Henrik, 151
Poulsen, Björn, 22

Rantzau, Johan, 60, 61
Realm of the dead motif, 135
Rebirth theme, 30, 31, 97, 105, 107, 109, 110
Renaissance, 158
Rigsraadet, 60
Romanesque arch, 158

Saga, 119. *See also* Old Norse literature
Sarvig, Ole, 146
Scandinavia:
  culture, 156
  history, 59 - 61
  landscape, 162, 165
  myths, 165
  union of, 59
Science, 57, 65, 151
Sealand, 13, 25, 162
Sexes:
  inequality of, 33
  relationships, 32 - 33, 43 - 44
Sexuality, 33
Social Realism, 15, 37, 151
Spiritual vs. material, 33 - 34
Stevns, 13, 14, 162, 165
  childhood in, 28, 140 - 142, 154 - 55
  in "Legends in September," 26
  "return" to, 20 - 21, 154
  setting of "Tirad," 131
Stockholm Bloodbath, 59
Stone Age, 154, 155
Storytelling, 24, 26, 147, 149
Symbolism, 30 - 31

Thornbush symbol, 93, 94, 97, 128
Tradition, 27, 57, 152
  belief in, 20 - 21, 23, 24, 28, 58, 151

Ulysses, 62

Vasa, Gustav Eriksson, 59, 60
Vesaas, Tarjei, 149
Viking Age, 142 - 43, 156

Index

Wandering hero tales, 16, 18, 61, 62. *See also Jonatan's Journey; Lucky Kristoffer*
War, 61, 145

Wivel, Ole, 12, 13, 15, 20-23, 136, 152, 154
Womann 68. *See also* Sexes